wxPython Recipes

A Problem - Solution Approach

Mike Driscoll

Apress®

wxPython Recipes

Mike Driscoll
Ankeny, New York, USA

ISBN-13 (pbk): 978-1-4842-3236-1
https://doi.org/10.1007/978-1-4842-3237-8

ISBN-13 (electronic): 978-1-4842-3237-8

Library of Congress Control Number: 2017963132

Cover image designed by Freepik

Managing Director: Welmoed Spahr
Editorial Director: Todd Green
Acquisitions Editor: Todd Green
Development Editor: James Markham
Technical Reviewer: Kevin Ollivier and Andrea Gavana
Coordinating Editor: Jill Balzano
Copy Editor: Lori Jacobs
Compositor: SPi Global
Indexer: SPi Global
Artist: SPi Global

Distributed to the book trade worldwide by Springer Science+Business Media New York, 233 Spring Street, 6th Floor, New York, NY 10013. Phone 1-800-SPRINGER, fax (201) 348-4505, e-mail orders-ny@springer-sbm.com, or visit www.springeronline.com. Apress Media, LLC is a California LLC and the sole member (owner) is Springer Science + Business Media Finance Inc (SSBM Finance Inc). SSBM Finance Inc is a **Delaware** corporation.

For information on translations, please e-mail rights@apress.com, or visit http://www.apress.com/rights-permissions.

Apress titles may be purchased in bulk for academic, corporate, or promotional use. eBook versions and licenses are also available for most titles. For more information, reference our Print and eBook Bulk Sales web page at http://www.apress.com/bulk-sales.

Any source code or other supplementary material referenced by the author in this book is available to readers on GitHub via the book's product page, located at www.apress.com/9781484232361. For more detailed information, please visit http://www.apress.com/source-code.

Printed on acid-free paper

This book is dedicated to the wxPython community

Table of Contents

About the Author

Mike Driscoll started coding in Python in 2006, where his first assignments included porting Windows log-in scripts and VBA to Python, which introduced him to wxPython. He's done back-end programming and front-end user interfaces, writes documentation for wxPython, and currently maintains an automated testing framework in Python. He also owns the popular site "Mouse vs Python" at pythonlibrary.org and has written for the Python Software Foundation and DZone and published *Python 101* and *Python 201*.

About the Technical Reviewers

Kevin Ollivier is a software developer who has been working with Python for nearly 20 years. He has been an avid supporter of open source and has contributed to numerous projects, including wxPython. When he's not coding, he's usually either reading, catching up on the latest anime and superhero shows, or gaming. In addition to coding work that he performs for various clients, he is currently working on an educational role-playing game (RPG) called BrightSparc. You can learn more about him and his projects at his company web site: `http://kosoftworks.com`.

Andrea Gavana has been programming Python for almost 15 years, and dabbling with other languages since the late 1990s.

He graduated from university with a Master's Degree in Chemical Engineering, and he is now a Senior Reservoir Engineer working for Maersk Oil in Copenhagen, Denmark.

Andrea enjoys programming at work and for fun, and he has been involved in multiple open source projects, all Python-based.

One of his favorite hobbies is Python coding, but he is also fond of cycling, swimming, and cozy dinners with family and friends.

This is his first book as technical reviewer.

Acknowledgments

I just wanted to take a moment and say thank you to some of the people who have helped me in writing this book.

My technical reviewers, Andrea Gavana and Kevin Ollivier, were very helpful both in the polishing of this book and in my growth as a Python programmer from practically the beginning of my learning of the language.

The wxPython community itself inspired me to write about Python in general and wxPython in particular. They were always encouraging me when I was just starting out learning Python and wxPython and they still are.

I would also like to thank all my blog readers who have reached out to me over the years and asked me to start writing books.

Robin Dunn, the creator of wxPython, has been very helpful to me personally in figuring out wxPython and in the writing of this work. I have asked him repeatedly for help in regard to some of my code examples that worked in one version of wxPython and not in another, or code that worked in one operating system, but didn't behave the same way somewhere else. He has always been patient with me and pointed me in the right direction.

Finally, I would like to thank my family for their support.

And special thanks to you, dear reader, for picking this book up and giving it a chance.

CHAPTER 1

Introduction

Welcome to my wxPython recipes book! As with most cookbooks, this one is made up of a series of recipes. Some recipes will be more involved than others, but most of the time, the recipe will be a nice bite-sized chunk of information that only covers three to five pages or so. There are more than 50 recipes in this book. I have compiled them over the last eight years from people who have asked questions on the wxPython mailing list, StackOverflow, or e-mailed me directly.

Normally I would spend a lot of time in the introduction going over each section of the book, but since this book is a series of recipes, it won't actually be split into sections. Instead, the recipes will be grouped where possible. For example, I have a number of XRC-related recipes, so they will be kept together as a single chapter.

The recipes will include screenshots of the interfaces that you will be creating. There will be additional screenshots included if and when we change the code inside a recipe. A good example of this is in the Frame Styles recipe where we try out various flags that affect how **wx.Frame** is displayed.

Who Should Read This Book

This book is targeted at people who are already familiar with the Python programming language and also have a basic understanding of wxPython. At the very least, it would be helpful if the reader understands event loops and the basics of creating user interfaces (UIs) with another Python UI toolkit, such as **Tkinter** or **PyQt**.

1

© Mike Driscoll 2018
M. Driscoll, *wxPython Recipes*, https://doi.org/10.1007/978-1-4842-3237-8_1

About the Author

You may be wondering who I am and why I might be knowledgeable enough about Python to write about it, so I thought I'd give you a little information about myself. I started programming in Python in Spring 2006 for a job. My first assignment was to port Windows log-in scripts from Kixtart to Python. My second project was to port VBA code (basically a graphical user interface, or GUI, on top of Microsoft Office products) to Python, which is how I first got started in wxPython. I've been using Python ever since, doing a variation of back-end programming and desktop front-end UIs. Currently I am writing and maintaining an automated test framework in Python.

I realized that one way for me to remember how to do certain things in Python was to write about them and that's how my Python blog came about: `www.blog.pythonlibrary.org/`. As I wrote, I would receive feedback from my readers and I ended up expanding the blog to include tips, tutorials, Python news, and Python book reviews. I work regularly with Packt Publishing as a technical reviewer, which means that I get to try to check for errors in the books before they're published. I also have written for the Developer Zone (DZone) and i-programmer web sites as well as the Python Software Foundation. In November 2013, DZone published **The Essential Core Python Cheat Sheet,** which I coauthored. Finally, I have also self-published the following two books:

- **Python 101**, which came out in June 2014.

- **Python 201: Intermediate Python**, which came out in September 2016

Conventions

As with most technical books, this one includes a few conventions that you need to be aware of. New topics and terminology will be in **bold**. You will also see some examples that look like the following:

```
>>> myString = "Welcome to Python!"
```

The >>> is a Python prompt symbol. You will see this in the Python **interpreter** and in **IDLE**. Other code examples will be shown in a similar manner, but without the >>>.

Requirements

You will need a working **Python 2** or **Python 3** installation. Most Linux and Mac machines come with Python already installed; however, they might not have Python in their path. This is rare, but if it happens there are lots of tutorials on the Internet that explain how to add Python to your path for your particular operating system. If you happen to find yourself without Python, you can download a copy from http://python. org/download/. There are up-to-date installation instructions on the web site, so I won't include any installation instructions in this book for Python itself.

The wxPython toolkit is **not** included with Python. We will look at how to install it here. You will want to use the latest version of wxPython, which at the time of writing, is version 4. It also based on the Phoenix branch of wxPython instead of Classic. You don't really need to know the differences between these other than Phoenix supports Python 2 and 3 while Classic does not.

To install wxPython 4, you can just use pip:

pip install wxPython

This works great on Windows and Mac. I have noticed that on some versions of Linux, you may see an error or two about missing dependencies, such as webkit. You will need to install the listed dependency and then try installing wxPython again.

Once you're done installing wxPython, we can check to make sure it works with the following script:

```python
import platform
import wx

class MyFrame(wx.Frame):
    """"""

    def __init__(self):
        """Constructor"""
        wx.Frame.__init__(self, None, size=(500, 200),
                          title='Version Info')
        panel = wx.Panel(self)

        py_version = 'Python version:    ' + platform.python_version()
        wx_version = 'wxPython version: ' + wx.version()
        os_version = 'Operating System: ' + platform.platform()
```

```
        main_sizer = wx.BoxSizer(wx.VERTICAL)
        size = (20, -1)
        main_sizer.Add(
            wx.StaticText(panel, label=py_version), 0, wx.ALL, 5)
        main_sizer.Add(
            wx.StaticText(panel, label=wx_version), 0, wx.ALL, 5)
        main_sizer.Add(
            wx.StaticText(panel, label=os_version), 0, wx.ALL, 5)
        panel.SetSizer(main_sizer)

        self.Show()

if __name__ == '__main__':
    app = wx.App(False)
    frame = MyFrame()
    app.MainLoop()
```

This code should run without error and you will see a simple UI appear on screen. Any additional requirements will be explained later on in the book.

Book Source Code

The book's source code can be found on Github:

https://github.com/driscollis/wxPython_recipes_book_code

Reader Feedback

I welcome feedback about my writings. If you'd like to let me know what you thought of the book, you can send comments to the following address:

comments@pythonlibrary.org

Errata

I try my best not to publish errors in my writings, but it happens from time to time. If you happen to see an error in this book, feel free to let me know by e-mailing me at the following:

errata@pythonlibrary.org

Now let's get started!

CHAPTER 2

Working with Images

Recipe 2-1. How to Take a Screenshot of Your wxPython App

Problem

Have you ever thought that it would be cool to have your wxPython code take a screenshot of itself? Well, Andrea Gavana (one of wxPython's core developers) figured out a cool way to do just that and between what he told us on the wxPython mailing list and what I learned from other sources, you will soon learn how to not only take the screenshot but send it to your printer! Once it's all done, you'll have an application that looks like Figure 2-1.

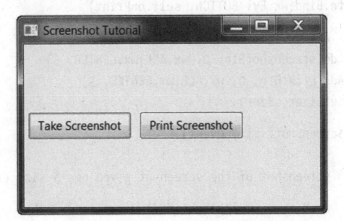

Figure 2-1. *Taking a screenshot*

© Mike Driscoll 2018
M. Driscoll, *wxPython Recipes*, https://doi.org/10.1007/978-1-4842-3237-8_2

Solution

You can tackle this project in several different ways. You could create the code that actually takes the screenshot or you could write an application that calls that code. We will start by creating an application that takes screenshots. Let's take a look.

Listing 2-1. The Code for Taking a Screenshot

```
import sys
import wx
import snapshotPrinter

class MyForm(wx.Frame):

    def __init__(self):
        wx.Frame.__init__(self, None, title="Screenshot Tutorial")

        panel = wx.Panel(self)
        screenshotBtn = wx.Button(panel, label="Take Screenshot")
        screenshotBtn.Bind(wx.EVT_BUTTON, self.onTakeScreenShot)
        printBtn = wx.Button(panel, label="Print Screenshot")
        printBtn.Bind(wx.EVT_BUTTON, self.onPrint)

        sizer = wx.BoxSizer(wx.HORIZONTAL)
        sizer.Add(screenshotBtn, 0, wx.ALL|wx.CENTER, 5)
        sizer.Add(printBtn, 0, wx.ALL|wx.CENTER, 5)
        panel.SetSizer(sizer)

    def onTakeScreenShot(self, event):
        """

        Takes a screenshot of the screen at given pos & size (rect).

        Method based on a script by Andrea Gavana
        """

        print('Taking screenshot...')
        rect = self.GetRect()

        # adjust widths for Linux (figured out by John Torres
        # http://article.gmane.org/gmane.comp.python.wxpython/67327)
```

```python
if sys.platform == 'linux2':
    client_x, client_y = self.ClientToScreen((0, 0))
    border_width = client_x - rect.x
    title_bar_height = client_y - rect.y
    rect.width += (border_width * 2)
    rect.height += title_bar_height + border_width

# Create a DC for the whole screen area
dcScreen = wx.ScreenDC()

# On Windows and Mac, we can just call GetAsBitmap on the
wx.ScreenDC
# and it will give us what we want.
bmp = dcScreen.GetAsBitmap().GetSubBitmap(rect)

if not bmp.IsOk():
    # Create a Bitmap that will hold the screenshot image later on
    # Note that the Bitmap must have a size big enough to hold the
    screenshot
    # -1 means using the current default colour depth
    bmp = wx.EmptyBitmap(rect.width, rect.height)

    #Create a memory DC that will be used for actually taking the
    screenshot
    memDC = wx.MemoryDC()

    # Tell the memory DC to use our Bitmap
    # all drawing action on the memory DC will go to the Bitmap now
    memDC.SelectObject(bmp)

    # Blit (in this case copy) the actual screen on the memory DC
    # and thus the Bitmap
    memDC.Blit( 0, # Copy to this X coordinate
                0, # Copy to this Y coordinate
                rect.width, # Copy this width
                rect.height, # Copy this height
                dcScreen, # Where to copy from
```

```
                            rect.x, # What's the X offset in the original DC?
                            rect.y  # What's the Y offset in the original DC?
                            )

            # Select the Bitmap out of the memory DC by selecting a new
            # uninitialized Bitmap
            memDC.SelectObject(wx.NullBitmap)

        img = bmp.ConvertToImage()
        fileName = "myImage.png"
        img.SaveFile(fileName, wx.BITMAP_TYPE_PNG)
        print('...saving as png!')

    def onPrint(self, event):
        """
        Send screenshot to the printer
        """
        printer = snapshotPrinter.SnapshotPrinter()
        printer.sendToPrinter()

# Run the program
if __name__ == "__main__":
    app = wx.App(False)
    frame = MyForm()
    frame.Show()
    app.MainLoop()
```

How It Works

This piece of code creates a frame with two buttons in it. It's a bit boring, but this is just a simple example after all. The part we care about most is the **onTakeScreenShot** method. As I mentioned earlier, it is based on a script by Andrea Gavana. However, I added a conditional from John Torres that makes this script behave better on Linux since it was originally written for Windows. The comments tell the story of the code, so take your time reading them and when you're done, we can move on to how we can send our result to the printer.

The Snapshot Printer Script

Creating a simple application that can take a screenshot and print it isn't that much more work than just taking a screenshot. You will be able to combine this script with the previous one to make a complete screenshot and printing utility.

The printing utility will end up looking something as shown in Figure 2-2.

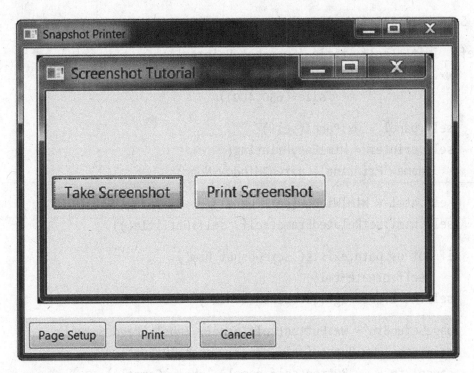

Figure 2-2. *Printing a screenshot*

This initial script actually has the image hard-coded into it, so if you'd like to save the image with a different name, you'll need to add that feature yourself. Let's take a moment to read through the code though, as shown in Listing 2-2:

Listing 2-2. The Application Code That Calls the Screenshot Code

```python
# snapshotPrinter.py

import os
import wx
from wx.html import HtmlEasyPrinting, HtmlWindow

class SnapshotPrinter(wx.Frame):

    def __init__(self, title='Snapshot Printer'):
        wx.Frame.__init__(self, None, title=title,
                          size=(650,400))

        self.panel = wx.Panel(self)
        self.printer = HtmlEasyPrinting(
            name='Printing', parentWindow=None)

        self.html = HtmlWindow(self.panel)
        self.html.SetRelatedFrame(self, self.GetTitle())

        if not os.path.exists('screenshot.htm'):
            self.createHtml()
        self.html.LoadPage('screenshot.htm')

        pageSetupBtn = wx.Button(self.panel, label='Page Setup')
        printBtn = wx.Button(self.panel, label='Print')
        cancelBtn = wx.Button(self.panel, label='Cancel')

        self.Bind(wx.EVT_BUTTON, self.onSetup, pageSetupBtn)
        self.Bind(wx.EVT_BUTTON, self.onPrint, printBtn)
        self.Bind(wx.EVT_BUTTON, self.onCancel, cancelBtn)

        sizer = wx.BoxSizer(wx.VERTICAL)
        btnSizer = wx.BoxSizer(wx.HORIZONTAL)

        sizer.Add(self.html, 1, wx.GROW)
        btnSizer.Add(pageSetupBtn, 0, wx.ALL, 5)
        btnSizer.Add(printBtn, 0, wx.ALL, 5)
```

```python
            btnSizer.Add(cancelBtn, 0, wx.ALL, 5)
        sizer.Add(btnSizer)

        self.panel.SetSizer(sizer)
        self.panel.SetAutoLayout(True)

    def createHtml(self):
        '''
        Creates an html file in the home directory of the application
        that contains the information to display the snapshot
        '''
        print('creating html...')

        html = '''<html>\n<body>\n<center>
        <img src=myImage.png width=516 height=314>
        </center>\n</body>\n</html>'''
        with open('screenshot.htm', 'w') as fobj:
            fobj.write(html)

    def onSetup(self, event):
        self.printer.PageSetup()

    def onPrint(self, event):
        self.sendToPrinter()

    def sendToPrinter(self):
        self.printer.GetPrintData().SetPaperId(wx.PAPER_LETTER)
        self.printer.PrintFile(self.html.GetOpenedPage())

    def onCancel(self, event):
        self.Close()

if __name__ == '__main__':
    app = wx.App(False)
    frame = SnapshotPrinter()
    frame.Show()
    app.MainLoop()
```

This little script uses the **HtmlWindow** widget and the **HtmlEasyPrinting** method to send something to the printer. Basically, you can create some really simple HTML code (see the **createHtml** method) and then use the HtmlWindow to view it. Next you use HtmlEasyPrinting to send it to a printer. It will actually display the printer dialog and let you choose which printer you want to send the document to.

Being able to save a screenshot of your application can be quite valuable for debugging purposes. For example, if you were writing an automated test of your software, you would be able to save from a screenshot when your application crashed or threw a warning and you might be able to diagnose what happened. I hope you have found this recipe useful. I know it's helped me out from time to time.

Recipe 2-2. How to Embed an Image in the Title Bar Problem

There are times when you just want to add something custom to your application's title bar. One fun item to add is an image. Most applications on Windows have the application's logo in the upper left-hand corner of the title bar. When you run a wxPython script it will just use a generic default icon. In this recipe, we will look at three different methods of adding a custom image to our title bar.

The first method is to get an embedded image out of an executable. The second method is to take some image you have and just embed it. The last and final method is to take your image and turn it into a Python file that can be imported. I'm sure you could also mess with the Python Image Library (a.k.a. Pillow) or maybe even use the paint handler too, but I won't cover that in this recipe.

Note   This recipe is Windows only.

Solution

Let's start by learning how to extract an image from an executable. It's actually pretty simple. Here's a super simple example:

```python
Import sys
import wx

class MyForm(wx.Frame):

    def __init__(self):
        wx.Frame.__init__(self, None, title='Image Extractor')

        self.panel = wx.Panel(self)

        loc = wx.IconLocation(sys.executable, 0)
        self.SetIcon(wx.Icon(loc))

if __name__ == '__main__':
    app = wx.App(False)
    frame = MyForm().Show()
    app.MainLoop()
```

How It Works

In this example, I'm grabbing the Python 3.5 icon out of the **python.exe** using the following line:

```python
loc = wx.Icon(r'C:\Python35\python.exe', 0)
```

Then I set the frame's icon using **SetIcon()**. Notice that all I need is **wx.Icon** to extract the icon from the **IconLocation** instance. In wxPython Classic, you would need to replace the call to **wx.Icon** with **wx.IconFromLocation** for this to work.

When you run this code, you should see the screen in Figure 2-3.

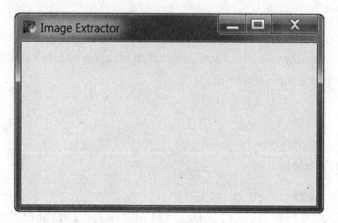

Figure 2-3. *Title bar with custom image from python.exe*

You will note that you can see the Python logo in the corner in this screenshot. Now go and comment out the last two lines in the class's **__init__** method and rerun the code. You should end up seeing something as shown in Figure 2-4.

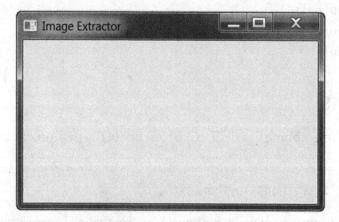

Figure 2-4. *Title bar with generic default image*

That image in the upper left-hand corner is the generic icon that wxPython uses when you don't set the icon yourself.

Using Your Own Image

Using your own image is actually a bit simpler than extracting it from the executable. The primary difference between the following code and the code in the previous example is that I've gotten rid of the calls to **wx.IconLocation** and added a **wx.Icon** object. The wx.Icon object just needs a path to the icon and the **wx.BITMAP_TYPE_ICO** flag.

Let's take a look at how this changes the code.

```
import wx

class MyForm(wx.Frame):

    def __init__(self):
        wx.Frame.__init__(self, None, title='Custom Image')

        self.panel = wx.Panel(self, wx.ID_ANY)


        ico = wx.Icon('py.ico', wx.BITMAP_TYPE_ICO)
        self.SetIcon(ico)

if __name__ == '__main__':
    app = wx.App(False)
    frame = MyForm().Show()
    app.MainLoop()
```

Before you run this code, you will need to find an icon (.ico) file of your own and modify this code to use it. I grabbed a Python icon I had handy on my machine for this example. It's actually the logo of the wxPython framework which you can probably find yourself once you have wxPython installed on your own machine.

When I ran this code, I ended up getting the following application generated (shown in Figure 2-5).

Now we can move on to the final method of adding an image to the title bar!

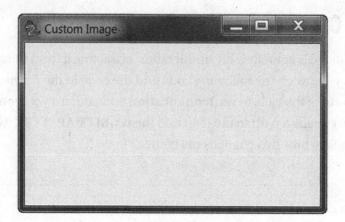

Figure 2-5. *Adding a custom image*

Create the Image in Python Code

The final way I would do this may be the best. In it, I take an icon or image and turn it into a python file using wxPython's **img2py** utility. Why might this be the best? Because by embedding the image file in a Python file, you simplify the process of distributing your application with py2exe. At least, that's been my experience.

On my machine, the **img2py** utility can be found in your Python Scripts folder. I have also found it in Python's **site-packages** under **site-packages\wx-4.0-msw\wx\tools** (Modify this path as appropriate for your version of wxPython).

To make things simpler, I would highly recommend opening a terminal and navigating to the folder that holds your icon file. Then all you need to do is run the following command:

```
img2py python.ico my_icon.py
```

The first argument is the path to the icon file. The last argument that you give is the name of the Python file that you want **img2py** to create (i.e., embed the icon into). Now, copy the Python file you just created over to the folder that contains your wxPython script so it can import it (or you can just copy the code out of the Python file into the text of the application you're creating).

Note   If you are on Windows, there is an img2py.exe in your Python installation's **Scripts** folder. Otherwise you will need to go to your wxPython installation location and navigate to the **tools** folder to run the script directly.

By the way, img2py has a few command line switches you can use. Try running img2py without any arguments to see its man page so you can read up on its options.

I'm going to import our new image module for this example. To get the icon, you call the **GetIcon()** method of the icon file's **PyEmbeddedImage** instance that I imported. Check out the code that follows to see what I'm doing. You might also want to open the Python file I generated to see what that looks like.

```python
import wx
import my_icon

class MyForm(wx.Frame):

    def __init__(self):
        wx.Frame.__init__(self, None, title='Python Image Title')

        self.panel = wx.Panel(self, wx.ID_ANY)

        ico = my_icon.PyEmbeddedImage(my_icon.py)
        self.SetIcon(ico.data.GetIcon())

# Run the program
if __name__ == '__main__':
    app = wx.App(False)
    frame = MyForm().Show()
    app.MainLoop()
```

The application that this code creates should look the same as the one we created earlier except for the title text.

Ideally, this recipe has helped you learn how to use your icon in your application. Remember, you can use these techniques for any image you want to insert into your application—not just for the title bar icon, but for any static image you'd use in your application, such as a taskbar icon or a toolbar icon. Good luck!

Recipe 2-3. How to Put a Background Image on a Panel

Problem

I receive a lot of e-mails from people who are learning Python and wxPython. In one of those e-mails, I received a request to create a graphical user interface (GUI) with Tkinter or wxPython that had an image for the background with buttons on top. After looking at Tkinter, I discovered that its **PhotoImage** widget only supported two formats: **gif** and **pgm** (unless I installed the Pillow package). Because of this, I decided to give wxPython a whirl. Here's what I found out.

A Bad Example

Using some of my Google-Fu, I found a thread on daniweb that seemed like it might work. I'll reproduce a variation of the example here.

```
# create a background image on a wxPython panel
# and show a button on top of the image
import wx

class Panel1(wx.Panel):
    """
    A subclass of wx.Panel
    """

    def __init__(self, parent, id):
        wx.Panel.__init__(self, parent, id)
        try:
            # pick an image file you have in the working
            # folder you can load .jpg  .png  .bmp  or
            # .gif files
            image_file = 'roses.jpg'
            bmp1 = wx.Image(
                image_file,
                wx.BITMAP_TYPE_ANY).ConvertToBitmap()
            # image's upper left corner anchors at panel
            # coordinates (0, 0)
```

```
        self.my_bitmap = wx.StaticBitmap(
            self, -1, bmp1, (0, 0))
        # show some image details
        str1 = "%s  %dx%d" % (image_file, bmp1.GetWidth(),
                            bmp1.GetHeight())
        parent.SetTitle(str1)
    except IOError:
        print("Image file %s not found" % imageFile)
        raise SystemExit

    self.my_button = wx.Button(
        self.my_bitmap, label='Button1',
        pos=(8, 8))

if __name__ == "__main__":
    app = wx.App(False)

    my_frame = wx.Frame(None, -1, "An image on a panel",
        size=(350, 400))
    # create the class instance
    panel = Panel1(my_frame, -1)
    my_frame.Show(True)
    app.MainLoop()
```

My first thought when I saw this was something like the following: "This is probably bad." Why would I think that? Well, the guy who posted this was using a wx.StaticBitmap for the parent of the button. The **StaticBitmap** widget is **not** a container widget like a Panel or Frame is, so I figured this was probably not a good idea. Thus, I asked Robin Dunn on the #wxPython IRC channel what he thought. He said that if I did it as in the aforementioned example, I'd probably have tab traversal issues and such, so he recommended that I use the **EVT_ERASE_BACKGROUND** event to do some custom drawing. Since Robin Dunn is the creator of wxPython, I ended up going this route.

Note   When I ran this code on a Windows 7 box with wxPython Phoenix, it actually had major issues trying to draw the widget and I had some trouble actually killing the process. Use at your own risk!

Solution

A Better Example

Adhering to Robin's advice, I ended up with the following code:

```python
import wx

class MainPanel(wx.Panel):
    """"""

    def __init__(self, parent):
        """Constructor"""
        wx.Panel.__init__(self, parent=parent)
        self.frame = parent

        sizer = wx.BoxSizer(wx.VERTICAL)
        hSizer = wx.BoxSizer(wx.HORIZONTAL)

        for num in range(4):
            label = "Button %s" % num
            btn = wx.Button(self, label=label)
            sizer.Add(btn, 0, wx.ALL, 5)
        hSizer.Add((1,1), 1, wx.EXPAND)
        hSizer.Add(sizer, 0, wx.TOP, 100)
        hSizer.Add((1,1), 0, wx.ALL, 75)
        self.SetSizer(hSizer)
        self.Bind(wx.EVT_ERASE_BACKGROUND, self.OnEraseBackground)

    def OnEraseBackground(self, evt):
        """
        Add a picture to the background
        """
        # yanked from ColourDB.py
        dc = evt.GetDC()
```

```python
        if not dc:
            dc = wx.ClientDC(self)
            rect = self.GetUpdateRegion().GetBox()
            dc.SetClippingRect(rect)
        dc.Clear()
        bmp = wx.Bitmap("big_cat.jpg")
        dc.DrawBitmap(bmp, 0, 0)

class MainFrame(wx.Frame):
    """"""

    def __init__(self):
        """Constructor"""
        wx.Frame.__init__(self, None, size=(600,450))
        panel = MainPanel(self)
        self.Center()

class Main(wx.App):
    """"""

    def __init__(self, redirect=False, filename=None):
        """Constructor"""
        wx.App.__init__(self, redirect, filename)
        dlg = MainFrame()
        dlg.Show()

if __name__ == "__main__":
    app = Main()
    app.MainLoop()
```

Figure 2-6 is an example screenshot using a fun big cat picture I took over the summer for my background image.

Figure 2-6. *Adding a background image*

The main piece of code to care about is the following:

```
def OnEraseBackground(self, evt):
    """
    Add a picture to the background
    """
    # yanked from ColourDB.py
    dc = evt.GetDC()

    if not dc:
        dc = wx.ClientDC(self)
        rect = self.GetUpdateRegion().GetBox()
        dc.SetClippingRect(rect)
    dc.Clear()
    bmp = wx.Bitmap("big_cat.jpg")
    dc.DrawBitmap(bmp, 0, 0)
```

I copied this example from the **ColourDB.py** demo which you can find in the wxPython Demo and edited it a bit to make it work for my application. Basically, you just bind the panel to EVT_ERASE_BACKGROUND and in that handler, you grab the device context (DC), which in this case is the panel (I think). I call it a Clear method mainly because in my real application I used an image with a transparency and it was letting the background bleed through. By clearing it, I got rid of the bleed. Anyway, the conditional checks to see if the DC is None or empty (I'm not quite sure which) and if not, it updates the region (or dirty area–which is any part of the application that was "damaged" by moving another window over it). Then I grab my image and use DrawBitmap to apply it to the background. It's kind of funky and I don't completely understand what's going on, but it does work.

Feel free to try them both out and see which one works the best for you. It's kind of like Robin Dunn's method in that it uses DCs too, but not the same type that I'm using.

At this point, you will have gained the knowledge you need to add a background image to your panel. I still see people asking about how to do this sort of thing from time to time, so I still think it's an important topic to understand. You may use this recipe to create a custom splash screen, for example. Regardless, have fun with this code and play around with it to see what you can do.

CHAPTER 3

Special Effects

Recipe 3-1. Resetting the Background Color

Problem

There are times when you want to change the background color of a Panel widget or some other widget in the wxPython GUI toolkit. Changing the background color is pretty handy for making an error more prominent or just for differentiating states in your application. But what's not so obvious is how you might change the color back. When I first dug into resetting the background color of a Panel, I thought the following would work great:

```
color = wx.SystemSettings.GetColour(wx.SYS_COLOUR_BACKGROUND)
panel.SetBackgroundColour(color)
```

Unfortunately, that won't work in all cases. Instead, Robin Dunn (creator of wxPython) recommended that I use **wx.NullColor** instead . According to Mr. Dunn, the reason is that (wx.NullColor) will tell wx that the widget has no specific color set and so it will use whatever the platform wants to use, which may be controlled by the active theme and may not be a solid color at all. This is a little different from using the system settings color as then wx will act as if a custom color has been set and it doesn't care if it happens to be the same as the system color.

Solution

Let's take that information and write a simple script that demonstrates changing the background color of a Panel object and then resetting it to the normal gray color. We'll also change the background color of a TextCtrl and reset it too just to be thorough.

© Mike Driscoll 2018
M. Driscoll, *wxPython Recipes*, https://doi.org/10.1007/978-1-4842-3237-8_3

```python
import wx

class MyForm(wx.Frame):

    def __init__(self):
        wx.Frame.__init__(self, None, wx.ID_ANY,
                                    "Background Reset Tutorial")

        # Add a panel so it looks the correct on all platforms
        self.panel = wx.Panel(self, wx.ID_ANY)

        self.txt = wx.TextCtrl(self.panel)
        self.txt.SetBackgroundColour("Yellow")

        blueBtn = wx.Button(self.panel,
                            label="Change Background Color")
        blueBtn.Bind(wx.EVT_BUTTON, self.onChangeBackground)
        resetBtn = wx.Button(self.panel, label="Reset")
        resetBtn.Bind(wx.EVT_BUTTON, self.onReset)

        topSizer = wx.BoxSizer(wx.VERTICAL)
        btnSizer = wx.BoxSizer(wx.HORIZONTAL)

        btnSizer.Add(blueBtn, 0, wx.ALL|wx.CENTER, 5)
        btnSizer.Add(resetBtn, 0, wx.ALL|wx.CENTER, 5)

        topSizer.Add(self.txt, 0, wx.ALL, 5)
        topSizer.Add(btnSizer, 0, wx.CENTER)
        self.panel.SetSizer(topSizer)

    def onChangeBackground(self, event):
        """
        Change the background color of the panel
        """
        self.panel.SetBackgroundColour("Blue")
        self.panel.Refresh()

    def onReset(self, event):
        """
        Reset the color of the panel to the default color
        """
```

```
        self.panel.SetBackgroundColour(wx.NullColour)
        self.txt.SetBackgroundColour(wx.NullColour)
        self.panel.Refresh()

if __name__ == "__main__":
    app = wx.App(False)
    frame = MyForm()
    frame.Show()
    app.MainLoop()
```

How It Works

In this code, you will notice that I have set the text control with the initial background color of yellow and I allow the also user to change the panel's background through a button event handler.

The user may also reset the background color of both widgets by pressing the "Reset" button.

Figures 3-1 and 3-2 show the before and after pictures.

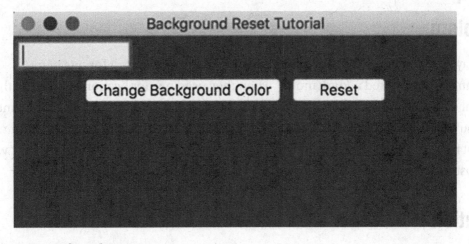

Figure 3-1. *Before the reset*

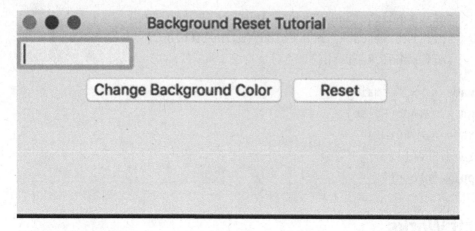

Figure 3-2. *After the reset*

At this point, you now know how to reset the color of wxPython's standard widgets. This can be quite useful in certain cases, but it's probably not something that you'll need all that often. However, it's nice to have this knowledge when you need it.

Recipe 3-2. How to Create a "Dark Mode"
Problem

One day, at a previous job, I was told that we had a feature request for one of my programs. They wanted a "dark mode" when they used my application at night, as the normal colors were kind of glaring. My program is used on laptops for law enforcement, so I could understand their frustration about having a very bright application running in a car at night. I spent some time looking into the matter and I found a solution that works for most widgets.

Solution

Getting the widgets to change color in wxPython is quite easy. The only two methods you need are SetBackgroundColour and SetForegroundColour. The only major problem I ran into when I was doing this was getting my **ListCtrl / ObjectListView** widget to change colors appropriately. You need to loop over each ListItem and change their colors individually. I alternate row colors, so that made things more interesting. The other problem I had was restoring the ListCtrl's background color. Normally you can set a widget's background color to **wx.NullColour** and it will go back to its default color. However, some widgets don't work that way and you have to actually specify a color. It should also be noted that some widgets don't seem to pay any attention to SetBackgroundColour at all. One such widget that that doesn't work as expected is **wx. ToggleButton**.

Now that the introduction to the problem is out of the way, let's look at the solution. Save the following code in a file named "dark_mode.py":

```python
# dark_mode.py
import wx

try:
    from ObjectListView import ObjectListView
except:
    ObjectListView = False

def getWidgets(parent):
    """
    Return a list of all the child widgets
    """
    items = [parent]
    for item in parent.GetChildren():
        items.append(item)
        if hasattr(item, "GetChildren"):
            for child in item.GetChildren():
                items.append(child)
    return items

def darkRowFormatter(listctrl, dark=False):
    """
    Toggles the rows in a ListCtrl or ObjectListView widget.
    """

    listItems = [listctrl.GetItem(i) for i
                 in range(listctrl.GetItemCount())]
    for index, item in enumerate(listItems):
```

```
        if dark:
            if index % 2:
                item.SetBackgroundColour("Dark Grey")
            else:
                item.SetBackgroundColour("Light Grey")
        else:
            if index % 2:
                item.SetBackgroundColour("Light Blue")
            else:
                item.SetBackgroundColour("Yellow")
        listctrl.SetItem(item)

def darkMode(self, normalPanelColor):
    """

    Toggles dark mode
    """

    widgets = getWidgets(self)
    panel = widgets[0]
    if normalPanelColor == panel.GetBackgroundColour():
        dark_mode = True
    else:
        dark_mode = False
    for widget in widgets:
        if dark_mode:
            if isinstance(widget, wx.ListCtrl) or (ObjectListView and
            isinstance(widget, ObjectListView)):
                darkRowFormatter(widget, dark=True)
            widget.SetBackgroundColour("Dark Grey")
            widget.SetForegroundColour("White")
        else:
            if isinstance(widget, wx.ListCtrl) or (ObjectListView and
            isinstance(widget, ObjectListView)):
                darkRowFormatter(widget)
                widget.SetBackgroundColour("White")
                widget.SetForegroundColour("Black")
                continue
```

```
            widget.SetBackgroundColour(wx.NullColour)
            widget.SetForegroundColour("Black")
    self.Refresh()
    return dark_mode
```

How It Works

This code is a little convoluted, but it gets the job done. Let's break it down a bit and see how it works. First, let's try to import **ObjectListView**, a neat third-party widget that wraps wx.ListCtrl and makes it a **lot** easier to use. However, it's not part of wxPython right now, so you need to test for its existence. I just set it to **False** if it doesn't exist.

The GetWidgets function takes a parent parameter, which would usually be a wx.Frame or wx.Panel, and goes through all of its children to create a list of widgets, which it then returns to the calling function. The main function is darkMode. It takes two parameters, too, **self**, which refers to a parent widget, and a default panel color. It calls **GetWidgets** and then uses a conditional statement to decide if dark mode should be enabled or not. Next it loops over the widgets and changes the colors accordingly. When it's done, it will refresh the passed-in parent and return a bool to let you know if dark mode is on or off.

There is one more function called **darkRowFormatter** that is only for setting the colors of the ListItems in a wx.ListCtrl or an ObjectListView widget. Here we use a list comprehension to create a list of wx.ListItems that we then iterate over, changing their colors. To actually apply the color change, we need to call **SetItem** and pass it a **wx. ListItem** object instance.

Trying Out Dark Mode

So now you're probably wondering how to actually use the aforementioned script. This section will answer that question. Here's a simple program with a list control in it and a toggle button too!

```
import wx
import dark_mode

class MyPanel(wx.Panel):
    """"""
```

```python
def __init__(self, parent):
    """Constructor"""
    wx.Panel.__init__(self, parent)
    self.defaultColor = self.GetBackgroundColour()

    rows = [("Ford", "Taurus", "1996", "Blue"),
            ("Nissan", "370Z", "2010", "Green"),
            ("Porche", "911", "2009", "Red")
            ]
    self.list_ctrl = wx.ListCtrl(self, style=wx.LC_REPORT)

    self.list_ctrl.InsertColumn(0, "Make")
    self.list_ctrl.InsertColumn(1, "Model")
    self.list_ctrl.InsertColumn(2, "Year")
    self.list_ctrl.InsertColumn(3, "Color")

    index = 0
    for row in rows:
        self.list_ctrl.InsertStringItem(index, row[0])
        self.list_ctrl.SetStringItem(index, 1, row[1])
        self.list_ctrl.SetStringItem(index, 2, row[2])
        self.list_ctrl.SetStringItem(index, 3, row[3])
        if index % 2:
            self.list_ctrl.SetItemBackgroundColour(index, "white")
        else:
            self.list_ctrl.SetItemBackgroundColour(index, "yellow")
        index += 1

    btn = wx.ToggleButton(self, label="Toggle Dark")
    btn.Bind(wx.EVT_TOGGLEBUTTON, self.onToggleDark)
    normalBtn = wx.Button(self, label="Test")

    sizer = wx.BoxSizer(wx.VERTICAL)
    sizer.Add(self.list_ctrl, 0, wx.ALL|wx.EXPAND, 5)
    sizer.Add(btn, 0, wx.ALL, 5)
    sizer.Add(normalBtn, 0, wx.ALL, 5)
    self.SetSizer(sizer)
```

```
    def onToggleDark(self, event):
        """"""

        dark_mode.darkMode(self, self.defaultColor)

class MyFrame(wx.Frame):
    """"""

    def __init__(self):
        """Constructor"""
        wx.Frame.__init__(self, None,
                          title="MvP ListCtrl Dark Mode Demo",
                          size=(400, 400))
        panel = MyPanel(self)
        self.Show()

if __name__ == "__main__":
    app = wx.App(False)
    frame = MyFrame()
    app.MainLoop()
```

If you run this code, you should see something like Figure 3-3.

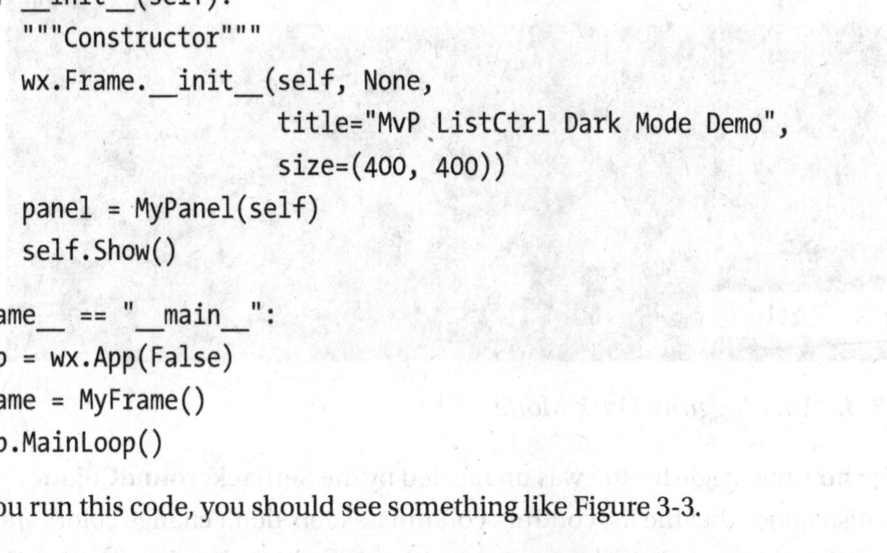

Figure 3-3. *Before toggling Dark Mode*

If you click the **ToggleButton**, you should see something like the screen in Figure 3-4.

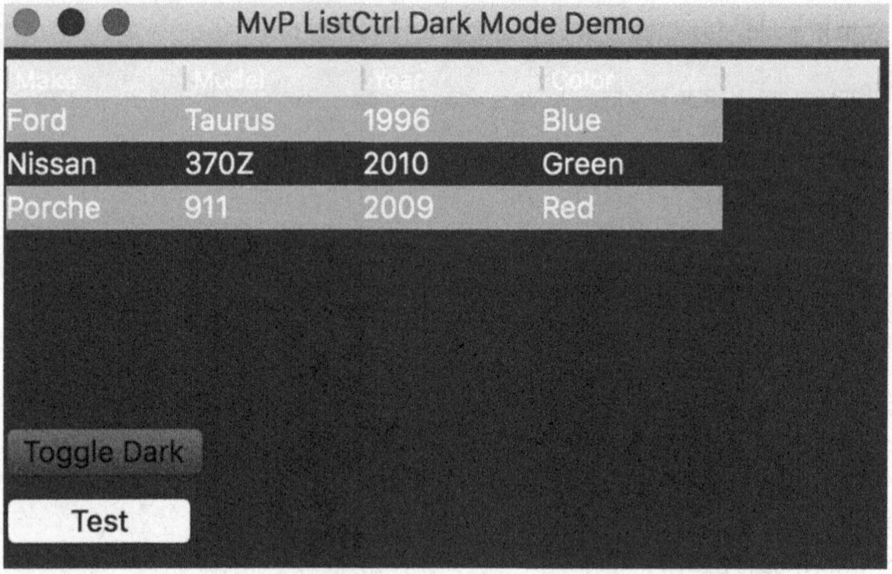

Figure 3-4. *After toggling Dark Mode*

Notice how the toggle button was unaffected by the **SetBackgroundColour** method. Also notice that the list control's column headers don't change colors either. Unfortunately, wxPython doesn't expose access to the column headers, so there's no way to manipulate their color.

Anyway, let's take a moment to see how the dark mode code is used. First we need to import it. In this case, the module is called dark_mode. To actually call it, we need to look at the ToggleButton's event handler.

```
darkMode.darkMode(self, self.defaultColor)
```

As you can see, all we did was call **darkMode.darkMode** with the panel object and a **defaultColor** that we set at the beginning of the wx.Panel's init method. That's all we had to do too. We should probably set it up with a variable to catch the returned value, but for this example we don't really care.

Note   In wxPython 4 (Phoenix), the methods **InsertStringItem** and **SetStringItem** are deprecated. Starting in wxPython 4, you should use **InsertItem** and **SetItem** respectively instead.

Now we're done and you too can create a **dark mode** for your applications. At some point, I'd like to generalize this some more to make into a color changer script where I can pass whatever colors I want to it. What would be really cool is to make it into a mix-in. But that's something for the future. For now, enjoy!

Recipe 3-3. How to Fade-in a Frame/Dialog

Problem

Microsoft Outlook and several other programs have a neat little visual trick wherein they will show a status dialog that fades into view, solidifies, and then fades back out. The wxPython toolkit provides a simple way to accomplish this feat by changing the alpha transparency of any top-level widget. Any widgets that are children of said widget will also inherit its transparency so you won't end up with just the background of your application fading in and out.

Solution

For this example I will use a frame object as the top-level object and a timer to change the alpha transparency by a unit of 5 every second. The timer's event handler will cause the frame to fade into view and then back out again. The range of values is 0–255 with 0 being completely transparent and 255 being completely opaque.

```
import wx

class Fader(wx.Frame):

    def __init__(self):
        wx.Frame.__init__(self, None, title='Fader Example')
        self.amount = 5
        self.delta = 5
        panel = wx.Panel(self, wx.ID_ANY)

        self.SetTransparent(self.amount)

        # Fader Timer
        self.timer = wx.Timer(self, wx.ID_ANY)
```

```
        self.timer.Start(60)
        self.Bind(wx.EVT_TIMER, self.AlphaCycle)

    def AlphaCycle(self, evt):
        """
        Fade the frame in and out
        """
        self.amount += self.delta
        if self.amount >= 255:
            self.delta = -self.delta
            self.amount = 255
        if self.amount <= 0:
            self.amount = 0
            self.delta = 5
        self.SetTransparent(self.amount)

if __name__ == '__main__':
    app = wx.App(False)
    frm = Fader()
    frm.Show()
    app.MainLoop()
```

How It Works

As you can see, all you need to do to change the transparency of the top-level widget is to call the **SetTransparent()** method of that widget and pass it the amount to set. I have actually used this method in some of my past applications when I needed to **fade in** an alert, such as when I needed to let a user know that they had received a new e-mail.

While this recipe isn't something that you'll be using in all your applications, it is quite useful if you need a way to pop up a custom message to the user. There is also the **ToasterBox** widget in **wx.lib.agw**. It's a custom widget that is written in pure Python and has a lot of handy built-in features so you don't have to roll your own as we do in this recipe. You should check it out!

Recipe 3-4. Making Your Text Flash

Problem

Back in the early days of the Internet, there were a lot of web sites that had flashing text and banner ads that were supposed to get your attention. I was even asked to create one in my brief stint as a web developer. Some people want the blinky text in their desktop applications too. So in this recipe we will learn how to do this (see Figure 3-5).

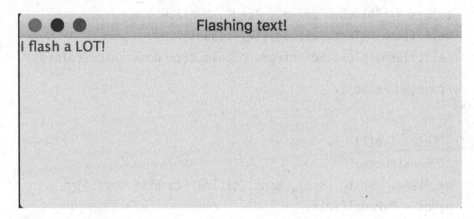

Figure 3-5. *Text that changes colors*

Solution

For our first trick, we will do exactly as requested and just create some text that changes colors "randomly." Let's take a look.

```
import random
import time
import wx

class MyPanel(wx.Panel):
    """"""

    def __init__(self, parent):
        """Constructor"""
        wx.Panel.__init__(self, parent)

        self.font = wx.Font(12, wx.DEFAULT, wx.NORMAL, wx.NORMAL)
        self.label = "I flash a LOT!"
```

```python
        self.flashingText = wx.StaticText(self, label=self.label)
        self.flashingText.SetFont(self.font)

        self.timer = wx.Timer(self)
        self.Bind(wx.EVT_TIMER, self.update, self.timer)
        self.timer.Start(1000)

    def update(self, event):
        """"""
        colors = ["blue", "green", "red", "yellow"]
        self.flashingText.SetLabel(self.label)
        self.flashingText.SetForegroundColour(random.choice(colors))

class MyFrame(wx.Frame):
    """"""

    def __init__(self):
        """Constructor"""
        wx.Frame.__init__(self, None, title="Flashing text!")
        panel = MyPanel(self)
        self.Show()

if __name__ == "__main__":
    app = wx.App(False)
    frame = MyFrame()
    app.MainLoop()
```

How It Works

Basically all you need is a **wx.StaticText** instance and a **wx.Timer**. In this example, the text will "flash" once a second and change to different colors.

Note   The **SetForegroundColour** method doesn't work in all widgets on all platforms as the native widget on some platforms does not implement this method.

Creating Changing Text

Figure 3-6. *Changing text*

Some managers might want to give the application some extra bling by making the text change (see Figure 3-6) as will as blink. Let's update our previous example so it can do that:

```
import random
import time
import wx

class MyPanel(wx.Panel):
    """"""

    def __init__(self, parent):
        """Constructor"""
        wx.Panel.__init__(self, parent)

        self.font = wx.Font(12, wx.DEFAULT, wx.NORMAL, wx.NORMAL)
        self.flashingText = wx.StaticText(self, label="I flash a LOT!")
        self.flashingText.SetFont(self.font)

        self.timer = wx.Timer(self)
        self.Bind(wx.EVT_TIMER, self.update, self.timer)
        self.timer.Start(1000)
```

```python
    def update(self, event):
        """"""
        now = int(time.time())
        mod = now % 2
        print (now)
        print (mod)
        if mod:
            self.flashingText.SetLabel("Current time: %i" % now)
        else:
            self.flashingText.SetLabel("Oops! It's mod zero time!")
        colors = ["blue", "green", "red", "yellow"]
        self.flashingText.SetForegroundColour(random.choice(colors))

class MyFrame(wx.Frame):
    """"""

    def __init__(self):
        """Constructor"""
        wx.Frame.__init__(self, None, title="Flashing text!")
        panel = MyPanel(self)
        self.Show()

if __name__ == "__main__":
    app = wx.App(False)
    frame = MyFrame()
    app.MainLoop()
```

Here we just use Python's modulus operator to determine what text to change to. However, you could just create a list of possible text strings and use Python's **random** module to choose one or just skip random and loop over them in sequence.

Now you have a new trick in your arsenal that you can use with old-school managers or bosses. You may even find the techniques used in this chapter useful for doing something completely different as well. It may not be the most interesting feature, but learning how to use a wx.Timer effectively can be quite useful.

CHAPTER 4

The Publish–Subscribe Pattern

Recipe 4-1. An Intro to Pubsub

Problem

The **Publish-Subscribe** (PubSub) pattern is a common design pattern in computer science that is used to communicate with different parts of your application. The basic idea for this is that you will create one or more listeners that are known as *subscribers*. The subscribers are listening for a specific message type that you can send via your *publisher*.

The wxPython GUI toolkit includes an implementation of the Publish-Subscribe pattern in **wx.lib.pubsub**.

Solution

I always find it helpful to actually write some code and see how all these various pieces work. So let's go ahead and write some simple code to see if we can understand the logic.

```python
import wx
from wx.lib.pubsub import pub

class OtherFrame(wx.Frame):
    """"""

    def __init__(self):
        """Constructor"""
        wx.Frame.__init__(self, None, wx.ID_ANY, "Secondary Frame")
        panel = wx.Panel(self)
```

© Mike Driscoll 2018
M. Driscoll, *wxPython Recipes*, https://doi.org/10.1007/978-1-4842-3237-8_4

```python
        msg = "Enter a Message to send to the main frame"
        instructions = wx.StaticText(panel, label=msg)
        self.msgTxt = wx.TextCtrl(panel, value="")
        closeBtn = wx.Button(panel, label="Send and Close")
        closeBtn.Bind(wx.EVT_BUTTON, self.onSendAndClose)

        sizer = wx.BoxSizer(wx.VERTICAL)
        flags = wx.ALL|wx.CENTER
        sizer.Add(instructions, 0, flags, 5)
        sizer.Add(self.msgTxt, 0, flags, 5)
        sizer.Add(closeBtn, 0, flags, 5)
        panel.SetSizer(sizer)

    def onSendAndClose(self, event):
        """

        Send a message and close frame
        """
        msg = self.msgTxt.GetValue()
        pub.sendMessage("panelListener", message=msg)
        pub.sendMessage("panelListener", message="test2", arg2="2nd argument!")
        self.Close()

class MyPanel(wx.Panel):
    """"""

    def __init__(self, parent):
        """Constructor"""
        wx.Panel.__init__(self, parent)
        pub.subscribe(self.myListener, "panelListener")

        btn = wx.Button(self, label="Open Frame")
        btn.Bind(wx.EVT_BUTTON, self.onOpenFrame)

    def myListener(self, message, arg2=None):
        """

        Listener function
        """
```

```
            print("Received the following message: " + message)
            if arg2:
                print("Received another arguments: " + str(arg2))

        def onOpenFrame(self, event):
            """
            Opens secondary frame
            """
            frame = OtherFrame()
            frame.Show()

class MyFrame(wx.Frame):
    """"""

        def __init__(self):
            """Constructor"""
            wx.Frame.__init__(self, None, title="New PubSub API Tutorial")
            panel = MyPanel(self)
            self.Show()

if __name__ == "__main__":
    app = wx.App(False)
    frame = MyFrame()
    app.MainLoop()
```

How It Works

As we have already discussed, the import is different. Let's see what else has changed. In the panel class, we create a listener as follows:

```
pub.subscribe(self.myListener, "panelListener")
```

The **myListener** method can accept one or more arguments. In this case, we set it up to always require one argument (message) and an optional argument (arg2). Next we turn to the **OtherFrame** class where we need to take a look at the **onSendAndClose** method. In this method, we find that it sends out two messages.

```
msg = self.msgTxt.GetValue()
pub.sendMessage("panelListener", message=msg)
pub.sendMessage("panelListener", message="test2", arg2="2nd argument!")
self.Close()
```

The first one just sends the required information whereas the second one sends both. You will note that the new application programming interface (API) requires the use of explicit keyword arguments. If you change the first **sendMessage** command **to pub.sendMessage("panelListener", msg)**, you will receive a TypeError exception.

Now you know the basics of how to use PubSub in your wxPython application. I want to note that PubSub is not thread-safe, so be sure to keep that in mind. If you use PubSub in a thread, you will need to use a thread-safe method such as **wx.CallAfter** or **wx.PostEvent** to post a message to your listeners without having to worry about strange errors occurring in your code. I use PubSub a lot in my programs and have found it quite useful.

Recipe 4-2. Using PyDispatcher Instead of PubSub

Problem

In the previous recipe, we learned how to use wxPython's built-in version of PubSub to send messages within the application. Now we will learn about an alternative to PubSub called **PyDispatcher**. It follows the same idea of Publish–Subscribe that the PubSub module does. Let's take a look!

Solution

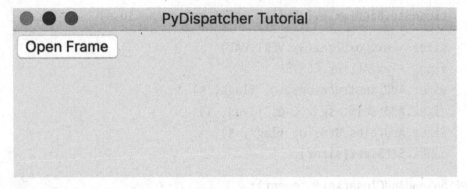

Figure 4-1. *PyDispatcher example application*

First of all, you will need to go get PyDispatcher and install it on your system. If you have pip installed, you can do the following:

```
pip install PyDispatcher
```

Otherwise, go to the project's sourceforge page and download it from there. One of the benefits of using PubSub in wxPython is that it's already included with the standard wxPython distribution. However, if you want to use PubSub *outside* wxPython, you would have to download its stand-alone code base and install it too. There are many developers who do not like to download more dependencies than they need to.

Anyway, now that we have PyDispatcher, let's port the code from PubSub and see what we end up with!

```python
import wx
from pydispatch import dispatcher

class OtherFrame(wx.Frame):
    """"""

    def __init__(self):
        """Constructor"""
        wx.Frame.__init__(self, None, wx.ID_ANY, "Secondary Frame")
        panel = wx.Panel(self)

        msg = "Enter a Message to send to the main frame"
        instructions = wx.StaticText(panel, label=msg)
```

```python
        self.msgTxt = wx.TextCtrl(panel, value="")
        closeBtn = wx.Button(panel, label="Send and Close")
        closeBtn.Bind(wx.EVT_BUTTON, self.onSendAndClose)

        sizer = wx.BoxSizer(wx.VERTICAL)
        flags = wx.ALL|wx.CENTER
        sizer.Add(instructions, 0, flags, 5)
        sizer.Add(self.msgTxt, 0, flags, 5)
        sizer.Add(closeBtn, 0, flags, 5)
        panel.SetSizer(sizer)

    def onSendAndClose(self, event):
        """

        Send a message and close frame
        """

        msg = self.msgTxt.GetValue()
        dispatcher.send("panelListener", message=msg)
        dispatcher.send("panelListener", message="test2", arg2="2nd argument!")
        self.Close()

class MyPanel(wx.Panel):
    """"""

    def __init__(self, parent):
        """Constructor"""
        wx.Panel.__init__(self, parent)

        dispatcher.connect(self.myListener, signal="panelListener",
                           sender=dispatcher.Any)

        btn = wx.Button(self, label="Open Frame")
        btn.Bind(wx.EVT_BUTTON, self.onOpenFrame)

    def myListener(self, message, arg2=None):
        """

        Listener function
        """
```

```
        print("Received the following message: " + message)
        if arg2:
            print("Received another arguments: " + str(arg2))

    def onOpenFrame(self, event):
        """
        Opens secondary frame
        """
        frame = OtherFrame()
        frame.Show()

class MyFrame(wx.Frame):
    """"""

    def __init__(self):
        """Constructor"""
        wx.Frame.__init__(self, None, title="PyDispatcher Tutorial")
        panel = MyPanel(self)
        self.Show()

if __name__ == "__main__":
    app = wx.App(False)
    frame = MyFrame()
    app.MainLoop()
```

How It Works

Let's break this down a bit. First we import **dispatcher** from the **pydispatch** package.
Then we edit the OtherFrame's **onSendAndClose** method so it will send messages to our
panel listener. Following is the first piece we need to change:

```
def onSendAndClose(self, event):
    """
    Send a message and close frame
    """
    msg = self.msgTxt.GetValue()
    dispatcher.send("panelListener", message=msg)
    dispatcher.send("panelListener", message="test2", arg2="2nd argument!")
    self.Close()
```

Next we need to change the **MyPanel** class to setup our new listener:

```
dispatcher.connect(self.myListener, signal="panelListener",
                   sender=dispatcher.Any)
```

This code tells **pydispatcher** to listen for any sender that has a signal of **panelListener**. If it has that signal, then it will call the panel's **myListener** method. That was a pretty simple change.

As I mentioned at the beginning, the PyDispatcher package follows the same idea as the PubSub package but just does it in a slightly different manner under the hood. I personally like PubSub because a version of it is included with wxPython so I don't need any extra dependencies. However, you should take a look at both of their APIs to determine which one makes the most sense to you when you go to program. Sometimes having a nicer API is worth the cost of another dependency.

CHAPTER 5

Wizard Recipes

Recipe 5-1. Creating a Simple Wizard

Problem

Sometimes you will find that you have a need for your users to walk through setting up your application or installing a plug-in. The standard interface to do these sorts of things is called a **wizard**!

Note   The code in this recipe was adapted from the wxPython Demo application

---

© Mike Driscoll 2018
M. Driscoll, *wxPython Recipes*, https://doi.org/10.1007/978-1-4842-3237-8_5

Solution

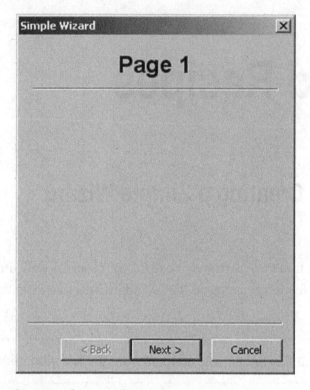

Figure 5-1. *A simple wizard example*

When you need to use a wizard in wxPython, you'll want to import it in a special way. Instead of just importing **wx**, you will have to do the following:

import from wx.adv import Wizard, WizardPage

Side note: In wxPython 3 and earlier, the **Wizard** class was found in **wx.wizard. Wizard** instead of **wx.adv.Wizard**. We will see an example of this in the second recipe in this chapter.

There are two primary types of wizard pages: **WizardPageSimple** and **PyWizardPage**. The former is the easiest, so we'll use that in our simple example.

Here's the code.

```python
import wx
from wx.adv import Wizard, WizardPageSimple

class TitledPage(WizardPageSimple):
    """
```

```python
    def __init__(self, parent, title):
        """Constructor"""
        WizardPageSimple.__init__(self, parent)

        sizer = wx.BoxSizer(wx.VERTICAL)
        self.SetSizer(sizer)

        title = wx.StaticText(self, -1, title)
        title.SetFont(wx.Font(18, wx.SWISS, wx.NORMAL, wx.BOLD))
        sizer.Add(title, 0, wx.ALIGN_CENTRE|wx.ALL, 5)
        sizer.Add(wx.StaticLine(self, -1), 0, wx.EXPAND|wx.ALL, 5)

def main():
    """"""

    wizard = Wizard(None, -1, "Simple Wizard")
    page1 = TitledPage(wizard, "Page 1")
    page2 = TitledPage(wizard, "Page 2")
    page3 = TitledPage(wizard, "Page 3")
    page4 = TitledPage(wizard, "Page 4")

    WizardPageSimple.Chain(page1, page2)
    WizardPageSimple.Chain(page2, page3)
    WizardPageSimple.Chain(page3, page4)
    wizard.FitToPage(page1)

    wizard.RunWizard(page1)

    wizard.Destroy()

if __name__ == "__main__":
    app = wx.App(False)
    main()
    app.MainLoop()
```

How It Works

That's a fair bit of code. Let's take it apart and see if we can figure it out. First off, we import **wx** and the Wizard classes. Next, we create a **TitledPage** class that subclasses **WizardPageSimple**. This class will be the basis for all the pages in our wizard. It basically just defines a page that has a centered title in 18 point font with a line underneath.

In the **main** function we find the real meat. Here we create the wizard using the following syntax: **wx.wizard.Wizard(None, -1, "Simple Wizard")**. This gives the wizard a parent of **None**, an id, and a title. Then we create four pages which are instances of the **TitledPage** class that we mentioned earlier. Finally, we use **wx.wizard. WizardPageSimple.Chain** to chain the pages together. This allows us to use a couple of automatically generated buttons to page forward and backward through the pages. The last couple of lines of code will run the wizard and, when the user is done, destroy the wizard. Pretty simple, right? Now let's move on to the more advanced example.

Using PyWizardPage

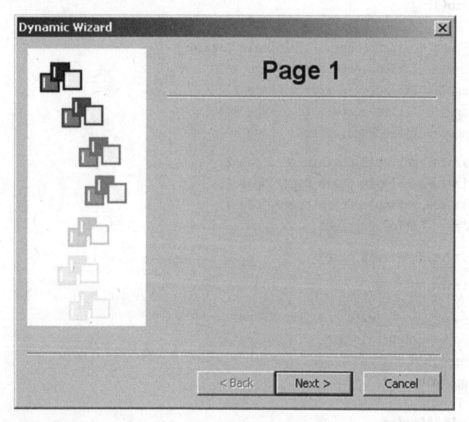

Figure 5-2. *A more advanced wizard*

In this section, we will create a subclass of **PyWizardPage**. We will also have a WizardPageSimple subclass so that we can mix and match the two to create a series of different pages. Let's just jump to the code so you can see it for yourself!

```python
import images
import wx
from wx.adv import Wizard, WizardPageSimple, PyWizardPage

class TitledPage(WizardPageSimple):
    """"""

    def __init__(self, parent, title):
        """Constructor"""
        WizardPageSimple.__init__(self, parent)

        sizer = wx.BoxSizer(wx.VERTICAL)
        self.sizer = sizer
        self.SetSizer(sizer)

        title = wx.StaticText(self, -1, title)
        title.SetFont(wx.Font(18, wx.SWISS, wx.NORMAL, wx.BOLD))
        sizer.Add(title, 0, wx.ALIGN_CENTRE|wx.ALL, 5)
        sizer.Add(wx.StaticLine(self, -1), 0, wx.EXPAND|wx.ALL, 5)

class UseAltBitmapPage(PyWizardPage):

    def __init__(self, parent, title):
        PyWizardPage.__init__(self, parent)
        self.next = self.prev = None
        self.sizer = wx.BoxSizer(wx.VERTICAL)

        title = wx.StaticText(self, label=title)
        title.SetFont(wx.Font(18, wx.SWISS, wx.NORMAL, wx.BOLD))
        self.sizer.Add(title)

        self.sizer.Add(wx.StaticText(self, -1,
                                "This page uses a different bitmap"),
                    0, wx.ALL, 5)
        self.sizer.Layout()

    def SetNext(self, next):
        self.next = next
```

```python
    def SetPrev(self, prev):
        self.prev = prev

    def GetNext(self):
        return self.next

    def GetPrev(self):
        return self.prev

    def GetBitmap(self):
        # You usually wouldn't need to override this method
        # since you can set a non-default bitmap in the
        # wxWizardPageSimple constructor, but if you need to
        # dynamically change the bitmap based on the
        # contents of the wizard, or need to also change the
        # next/prev order then it can be done by overriding
        # GetBitmap.
        return images.WizTest2.GetBitmap()

def main():
    """"""
    wizard = Wizard(None, -1, "Dynamic Wizard",
                        images.WizTest1.GetBitmap())
    page1 = TitledPage(wizard, "Page 1")
    page2 = TitledPage(wizard, "Page 2")
    page3 = TitledPage(wizard, "Page 3")
    page4 = UseAltBitmapPage(wizard, "Page 4")
    page5 = TitledPage(wizard, "Page 5")

    wizard.FitToPage(page1)
    page5.sizer.Add(wx.StaticText(page5, -1, "\nThis is the last page."))

    # Set the initial order of the pages
    page1.SetNext(page2)
    page2.SetPrev(page1)
    page2.SetNext(page3)
    page3.SetPrev(page2)
    page3.SetNext(page4)
```

```
        page4.SetPrev(page3)
        page4.SetNext(page5)
        page5.SetPrev(page4)

        wizard.GetPageAreaSizer().Add(page1)
        wizard.RunWizard(page1)
        wizard.Destroy()

if __name__ == "__main__":
    app = wx.App(False)
    main()
    app.MainLoop()
```

This code starts out in much the same way that the previous code did. In this
example, we also import an **images** module that contains a couple **PyEmbeddedImage**
objects that we will use to demonstrate how to add bitmaps to our wizard page.
Anyway, the first class is exactly the same as the previous one. Next we create a
UseAltBitmapPage class that is a subclass of the **PyWizardPage**. We have to override a
few methods to make it work correctly, but they're pretty self-explanatory. This page will
just be used to change the bitmap image of one page.

In the **main** function, we create a wizard in a slightly different way than we did
previously.

```
wizard = wiz.Wizard(None, -1, "Dynamic Wizard",
        images.WizTest1.GetBitmap())
```

As you can see, this method allows us to add a bitmap that will appear along the left-
hand side of the wizard pages. Anyway, after that, we create five pages with four of them
being instances of the **TitledPage** and one being an instance of a **UseAltBitmapPage**.
We fit the wizard to page one and then we see something odd.

```
page5.sizer.Add(wx.StaticText(page5, -1, "\nThis is the last page."))
```

What does that do? Well, it's a silly way to append a widget to a page. To let the user
know that they've reached the last page, we add a **StaticText** instance to it that explicitly
tells them that they have reached the end. The next few lines set up the order of the
pages using **SetNext** and **SetPrev**. While these methods give you more granular control
over the order of the pages, they're not as convenient as the **WizardPageSimple.Chain**
method. The last few lines of code are the same as in the previous example.

Now you know how to create the two types of wizards that are included with wxPython. You also have learned a fun hack to change the labels of the buttons in the wizard. Let me know if you think I forgot something and I'll update the post or write a follow-up.

Recipe 5-2. How to Disable a Wizard's Next Button Problem

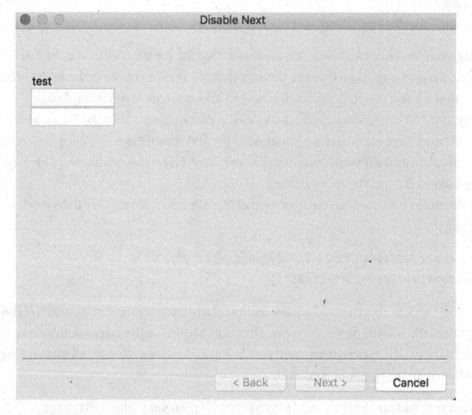

Figure 5-3. *Disabling the next button in the wizard*

Wizards are wonderful when they work. They can also be very aggravating. A lot of wizards will disable their Next button until you have completed a configuration or finished filling out a form. We will be looking at how to do just that in this recipe.

Solution

The idea that the original person had when they posted the question was that they wanted the user to fill out two text controls before being able to continue. That means that we need to disable the Next button until both text widgets have something in them. I came up with an idea where I use a wx.Timer to check the text controls once a second to see if they have data in them. If they do, then the timer's event handler will enable the Next button. Let's take a look at the wizard page class first. The following example is for wxPython Classic:

```python
# wxPython Classic Edition

import wx
import wx.wizard

class WizardPage(wx.wizard.PyWizardPage):

    def __init__(self, parent, title):
        wx.wizard.PyWizardPage.__init__(self, parent)
        self.next = None
        self.prev = None
        self.initializeUI(title)

    def initializeUI(self, title):
        # create grid layout manager
        self.sizer = wx.GridBagSizer()
        self.SetSizerAndFit(self.sizer)

    def addWidget(self, widget, pos, span):
        self.sizer.Add(widget, pos, span, wx.EXPAND)

    # getters and setters
    def SetPrev(self, prev):
        self.prev = prev

    def SetNext(self, next):
        self.next = next
```

```
    def GetPrev(self):
        return self.prev

    def GetNext(self):
        return self.next
```

How It Works

This is a pretty standard subclass of PyWizardPage. It just initializes the Previous and Next buttons in preparation for actually adding a page. Let's move on and see how we can actually use this class.

Add the following code to the same file that you put the previous code into:

```
class MyWizard(wx.wizard.Wizard):
    """"""

    def __init__(self):
        """Constructor"""
        wx.wizard.Wizard.__init__(self, None,
                                  title="Disable Next")
        self.SetPageSize((500, 350))

        mypage1 = self.create_page1()

        forward_btn = self.FindWindowById(wx.ID_FORWARD)
        forward_btn.Disable()

        self.timer = wx.Timer(self)
        self.Bind(wx.EVT_TIMER, self.onUpdate, self.timer)
        self.timer.Start(1)

        self.RunWizard(mypage1)

    def create_page1(self):
        page1 = WizardPage(self, "Page 1")
        d = wx.StaticText(page1, label="test")
        page1.addWidget(d, (2, 1), (1,5))
```

```python
    self.text1 = wx.TextCtrl(page1)
    page1.addWidget(self.text1, (3,1), (1,5))

    self.text2 = wx.TextCtrl(page1)
    page1.addWidget(self.text2, (4,1), (1,5))

    page2 = WizardPage(self, "Page 2")
    page2.SetName("page2")
    self.text3 = wx.TextCtrl(page2)
    self.Bind(wx.wizard.EVT_WIZARD_PAGE_CHANGED, self.onPageChanged)
    page3 = WizardPage(self, "Page 3")

    # Set links
    page2.SetPrev(page1)
    page1.SetNext(page2)
    page3.SetPrev(page2)
    page2.SetNext(page3)

    return page1

def onPageChanged(self, event):
    """"""

    page = event.GetPage()

    if page.GetName() == "page2":
        self.text3.SetValue(self.text2.GetValue())

def onUpdate(self, event):
    """

    Enables the Next button if both text controls have values
    """

    value_one = self.text1.GetValue()
    value_two = self.text2.GetValue()
    if value_one and value_two:
        forward_btn = self.FindWindowById(wx.ID_FORWARD)
        forward_btn.Enable()
        self.timer.Stop()
```

```
def main():
    """"""

    wizard = MyWizard()

if __name__ == "__main__":
    app = wx.App(False)
    main()
    app.MainLoop()
```

Let's break this down a bit. The first class we'll look at is **MyWizard**, which is where all the action is anyway. MyWizard is a subclass of wxPython's Wizard class. In the __ init__, we create a page and we find the Next button so we can disable it. Then we create and start our timer object while binding it to the **onUpdate** method. Finally, we run the wizard. When we create a wizard page, we instantiate the **WizardPage** class. That class is actually pretty self-explanatory. Anyway, we end up creating several widgets that we place on the wizard page. The only other interesting bit is in the **onUpdate** method. Here we check to see if the user has entered data into both of the text controls.

If they have, then we find the Next button, enable it, and stop the timer. There is a potential bug here. What happens if the user goes and removes some content *after* they have filled them both out? The Next button doesn't disable itself again. Here's an updated version of the **onUpdate** method that fixes that issue.

```
def onUpdate(self, event):
    """
    Enables the Next button if both text controls have values
    """

    value_one = self.text1.GetValue()
    value_two = self.text2.GetValue()
    forward_btn = self.FindWindowById(wx.ID_FORWARD)
    if value_one and value_two:
        forward_btn.Enable()
    else:
        if forward_btn.IsEnabled():
            forward_btn.Disable()
```

Here we never stop the timer. Instead, the timer is constantly checking the values of the text controls and if it finds that one of them doesn't have data *and* the next button is enabled, the handler will disable the button.

Getting It to Work with wxPython 4/Phoenix

Now that you understand how the code works, let's modify the code so it will work in the latest version of wxPython. In wxPython 4, the wx.wizard module was moved to wx.adv. So we need to edit the code accordingly, as follows:

```python
import wx
from wx.adv import Wizard, WizardPage

class MyWizardPage(WizardPage):

    def __init__(self, parent, title):
        WizardPage.__init__(self, parent)
        self.next = None
        self.prev = None
        self.initializeUI(title)

    def initializeUI(self, title):
        # create grid layout manager
        self.sizer = wx.GridBagSizer()
        self.SetSizer(self.sizer)

    def addWidget(self, widget, pos, span):
        self.sizer.Add(widget, pos, span, wx.EXPAND)

    # getters and setters
    def SetPrev(self, prev):
        self.prev = prev

    def SetNext(self, next):
        self.next = next

    def GetPrev(self):
        return self.prev

    def GetNext(self):
        return self.next

class MyWizard(Wizard):
    """"""
```

```python
    def __init__(self):
        """Constructor"""
        Wizard.__init__(self, None,
                                title="Disable Next")
        self.SetPageSize((500, 350))

        mypage1 = self.create_page1()

        forward_btn = self.FindWindowById(wx.ID_FORWARD)
        forward_btn.Disable()

        self.timer = wx.Timer(self)
        self.Bind(wx.EVT_TIMER, self.onUpdate, self.timer)
        self.timer.Start(1)

        self.RunWizard(mypage1)

    def create_page1(self):
        page1 = MyWizardPage(self, "Page 1")
        d = wx.StaticText(page1, label="test")
        page1.addWidget(d, (2, 1), (1,5))

        self.text1 = wx.TextCtrl(page1)
        page1.addWidget(self.text1, (3,1), (1,5))

        self.text2 = wx.TextCtrl(page1)
        page1.addWidget(self.text2, (4,1), (1,5))

        page2 = MyWizardPage(self, "Page 2")
        page2.SetName("page2")
        self.text3 = wx.TextCtrl(page2)
        self.Bind(wx.adv.EVT_WIZARD_PAGE_CHANGED, self.onPageChanged)

        page3 = MyWizardPage(self, "Page 3")

        # Set links
        page2.SetPrev(page1)
        page1.SetNext(page2)
        page3.SetPrev(page2)
        page2.SetNext(page3)
```

```
    return page1

def onPageChanged(self, event):
    """"""
    page = event.GetPage()

    if page.GetName() == "page2":
        self.text3.SetValue(self.text2.GetValue())

def onUpdate(self, event):
    """
    Enables the Next button if both text controls have values
    """
    value_one = self.text1.GetValue()
    value_two = self.text2.GetValue()
    if value_one and value_two:
        forward_btn = self.FindWindowById(wx.ID_FORWARD)
        forward_btn.Enable()
        self.timer.Stop()

def main():
    """"""
    wizard = MyWizard()

if __name__ == "__main__":
    app = wx.App(False)
    main()
    app.MainLoop()
```

You will note that now we import the **Wizard** and **WizardPage** classes directly. The other change is to the event binding. We went from **wx.wizard.EVT_WIZARD_PAGE_CHANGED** to **wx.adv.EVT_WIZARD_PAGE_CHANGED**. Otherwise the code is the same.

Recipe 5-3. How to Create a Generic Wizard

Problem

Sometimes you will find that you want to create a wizard with functionality that isn't easy to shoehorn into wxPython's Wizard implementation. When that situation arises, you can actually just create your own wizard using some of wxPython's other widgets.

Solution

If you look at how wxPython's Wizard is designed, you will quickly realize that it is just a series of panels with some buttons on the bottom that are used as navigation. This sounds like all you would need to do is write a panel class that will contain the navigation buttons and have wizard panels (or pages) nested inside it. Let's try writing our own simple wizard using this idea. We will start with the nested wizard page:

```python
import wx


class WizardPage(wx.Panel):
    """A Simple wizard page"""

    def __init__(self, parent, title=None):
        """Constructor"""
        wx.Panel.__init__(self, parent)

        sizer = wx.BoxSizer(wx.VERTICAL)
        self.SetSizer(sizer)

        if title:
            title = wx.StaticText(self, -1, title)
            title.SetFont(wx.Font(18, wx.SWISS, wx.NORMAL, wx.BOLD))
            sizer.Add(title, 0, wx.ALIGN_CENTRE|wx.ALL, 5)
            sizer.Add(wx.StaticLine(self, -1), 0, wx.EXPAND|wx.ALL, 5)
```

How It Works

All this code does is create a simple panel with a label on it if the **title** parameter is set to something other than None. Now let's add the master panel to the same file that you put the above code into.

```python
class WizardPanel(wx.Panel):
    """"""

    def __init__(self, parent):
        """Constructor"""
        wx.Panel.__init__(self, parent=parent)
        self.pages = []
        self.page_num = 0

        self.mainSizer = wx.BoxSizer(wx.VERTICAL)
        self.panelSizer = wx.BoxSizer(wx.VERTICAL)
        btnSizer = wx.BoxSizer(wx.HORIZONTAL)

        # add prev/next buttons
        self.prevBtn = wx.Button(self, label="Previous")
        self.prevBtn.Bind(wx.EVT_BUTTON, self.onPrev)
        btnSizer.Add(self.prevBtn, 0, wx.ALL|wx.ALIGN_RIGHT, 5)

        self.nextBtn = wx.Button(self, label="Next")
        self.nextBtn.Bind(wx.EVT_BUTTON, self.onNext)
        btnSizer.Add(self.nextBtn, 0, wx.ALL|wx.ALIGN_RIGHT, 5)

        # finish layout
        self.mainSizer.Add(self.panelSizer, 1, wx.EXPAND)
        self.mainSizer.Add(btnSizer, 0, wx.ALIGN_RIGHT)
        self.SetSizer(self.mainSizer)

    def addPage(self, title=None):
        """"""

        panel = WizardPage(self, title)
        self.panelSizer.Add(panel, 2, wx.EXPAND)
        self.pages.append(panel)
        if len(self.pages) > 1:
```

```python
            # hide all panels after the first one
            panel.Hide()
            self.Layout()

    def onNext(self, event):
        """"""

        pageCount = len(self.pages)
        if pageCount-1 != self.page_num:
            self.pages[self.page_num].Hide()
            self.page_num += 1
            self.pages[self.page_num].Show()
            self.panelSizer.Layout()
        else:
            print("End of pages!")

        if self.nextBtn.GetLabel() == "Finish":
            # close the app
            self.GetParent().Close()

        if pageCount == self.page_num+1:
            # change label
            self.nextBtn.SetLabel("Finish")

    def onPrev(self, event):
        """"""

        pageCount = len(self.pages)
        if self.page_num-1 != -1:
            self.pages[self.page_num].Hide()
            self.page_num -= 1
            self.pages[self.page_num].Show()
            self.panelSizer.Layout()
        else:
            print("You're already on the first page!")

class MainFrame(wx.Frame):
    """"""
```

```python
    def __init__(self):
        """Constructor"""
        wx.Frame.__init__(self, None, title="Generic Wizard", size=(800,600))

        self.panel = WizardPanel(self)
        self.panel.addPage("Page 1")
        self.panel.addPage("Page 2")
        self.panel.addPage("Page 3")

        self.Show()

if __name__ == "__main__":
    app = wx.App(False)
    frame = MainFrame()
    app.MainLoop()
```

This part of the code is where the main action is. It will create the buttons we use for navigation and it will allow you to add wizard pages. There is a lot more that could be added to this code though. For example, we should probably add the ability to disable the Next or Previous buttons in certain circumstances, such as when the user is required to fill something out before continuing. It would also be nice to have some other Page classes that contain other widgets besides a title label.

I will leave those changes up to you. As it is, this will give you a good start on creating your very own custom wizard. You can add all the bells and whistles that you think are appropriate for whatever project you are working on. Have fun!

CHAPTER 6

Creating Simple Widgets

Recipe 6-1. Creating an About Box

Problem

When I create an application, I usually want to include an "About" box to let the user know more about the application and me, and to give shout-outs to anyone who may have helped in the creation of my program. One cool feature wxPython provides is a custom AboutBox widget. I think it looks a little odd, so I created my own **About box** using the **HtmlWindow** widget. However, I'll show how to do it both ways in this recipe.

Solution

First, we'll create a simple application that will allow you to see how to open the dialog via either a button or a menu item. It will have three buttons, one to open the wx.AboutBox, one to open my Html version of the About box, and a close button.

How It Works

Creating the AboutBox is pretty straightforward. Let's take a look at a simple snippet of code.

```python
def onAboutDlg(self, event):
    info = wx.AboutDialogInfo()
    info.Name = "My About Box"
    info.Version = "0.0.1 Beta"
    info.Copyright = "(C) 2016 Python Geeks Everywhere"
    info.Description = wordwrap(
```

© Mike Driscoll 2018
M. Driscoll, *wxPython Recipes*, https://doi.org/10.1007/978-1-4842-3237-8_6

```
        "This is an example application that shows how to create"
        "different kinds of About Boxes using wxPython!",
        350, wx.ClientDC(self.panel))
info.WebSite = ("http://www.pythonlibrary.org", "My Home Page")
info.Developers = ["Mike Driscoll"]
info.License = wordwrap("Completely and totally open source!", 500,
                        wx.ClientDC(self.panel))
# Show the wx.AboutBox
wx.AboutBox(info)
```

To begin, you instantiate an instance of **wx.AboutDlgInfo**. This gives you a way to set the various pieces of information you want to display in your AboutBox, such as application name, version, copyright, and so on. When you have that all filled in, you create the wx.AboutBox and pass it that information. Notice that this does not require you to explicitly "show" it; that's done automatically.

When done, you should see something like the image in Figure 6-1.

Now we can move on and learn how to create an about dialog using HTML.

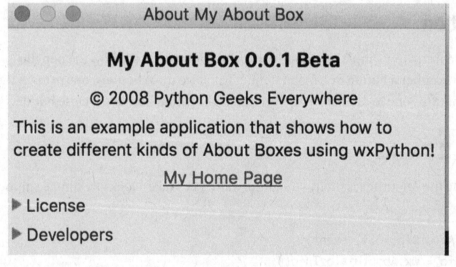

Figure 6-1. *An example of wx.AboutDlgInfo*

Using HtmlWindow for an About Box

Creating the HTML version is a little bit more complex. I prefer splitting the code up into two classes. The two top-level widgets I recommend using to base your About Box on would be wx.Frame or wx.Dialog. In this example I'll use a wx.Frame widget. The second class is only to catch mouse clicks on URLs, if you have some. Let's take a look at the code:

```python
class AboutDlg(wx.Frame):

    def __init__(self, parent):

        wx.Frame.__init__(self, parent, wx.ID_ANY, title="About",
        size=(400,400))

        html = wxHTML(self)

        html.SetPage(
        ''

            "<h2>About the About Tutorial</h2>"

            "<p>This about box is for demo purposes only. It was created in
            June 2006"

            "by Mike Driscoll.</p>"

            "<p><b>Software used in making this demo:</h3></p>"

            '<p><b><a href="http://www.python.org">Python 2.4</a></b></p>'

            '<p><b><a href="http://www.wxpython.org">wxPython 2.8</a></b></p>'
            )

class wxHTML(wx.html.HtmlWindow):

    def OnLinkClicked(self, link):
        webbrowser.open(link.GetHref())
```

The reason I like this so much is that it allows me to specify font sizes, use html tables, insert photos, and more very easily, plus it's completely cross-platform. One definite disadvantage is that this widget doesn't allow advanced html, such as css or javascript. Anyway, when you get done, it should turn into something that looks similar to the screenshot in Figure 6-2.

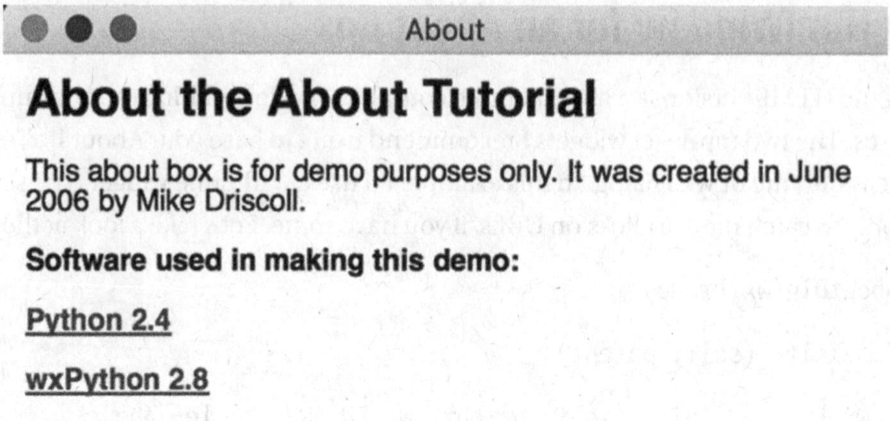

About the About Tutorial

This about box is for demo purposes only. It was created in June 2006 by Mike Driscoll.

Software used in making this demo:

Python 2.4

wxPython 2.8

Figure 6-2. *An about box created using the HTMLWindow widget*

Here's the full source for my demo program, which I used to activate my two About Boxes.

```
Import webbrowser
import wx
import wx.html
from wx.lib.wordwrap import wordwrap

class MyForm(wx.Frame):

    def __init__(self):
        wx.Frame.__init__(self, None, wx.ID_ANY, title='The About Box')

        # Add a panel so it looks correct on all platforms
        self.panel = wx.Panel(self, wx.ID_ANY)

        # Create buttons
        aboutBtn = wx.Button(self.panel, wx.ID_ANY, "Open wx.AboutBox")
        self.Bind(wx.EVT_BUTTON, self.onAboutDlg, aboutBtn)
        aboutHtmlBtn = wx.Button(self.panel, wx.ID_ANY, "Open
        HtmlAboutBox")
        self.Bind(wx.EVT_BUTTON, self.onAboutHtmlDlg, aboutHtmlBtn)

        closeBtn = wx.Button(self.panel, wx.ID_ANY, "Close")
```

```
    self.Bind(wx.EVT_BUTTON, self.onClose, closeBtn)

    # Create Sizers
    topSizer = wx.BoxSizer(wx.VERTICAL)

    # Add widgets to sizers
    topSizer.Add(aboutBtn, 0, wx.ALL|wx.CENTER, 5)
    topSizer.Add(aboutHtmlBtn, 0, wx.ALL|wx.CENTER, 5)
    topSizer.Add(closeBtn, 0, wx.ALL|wx.CENTER, 5)

    # Create the menu
    self.createMenu()
    self.statusBar = self.CreateStatusBar()

    self.panel.SetSizer(topSizer)
    self.SetSizeHints(250,300,500,400)
    self.Fit()
    self.Refresh()

def createMenu(self):
    """ Create the application's menu """
    menubar = wx.MenuBar()

    # Create the file menu
    fileMenu = wx.Menu()

    # Append the close item
    # Append takes an id, the text label, and a string
    # to display in the statusbar when the item is selected
    close_menu_item = fileMenu.Append(wx.NewId(),
                            "&Close",
                            "Closes the application")
    # Bind an event to the menu item
    self.Bind(wx.EVT_MENU, self.onClose, close_menu_item)
    # Add the fileMenu to the menu bar
    menubar.Append(fileMenu, "&File")

    # Create the help menu
    helpMenu = wx.Menu()
```

```python
        about_menu_item = helpMenu.Append(wx.NewId(),
                                          "&About",
                                          "Opens the About Box")
        self.Bind(wx.EVT_MENU, self.onAboutDlg, about_menu_item)
        menubar.Append(helpMenu, "&Help")

        # Add the menu bar to the frame
        self.SetMenuBar(menubar)

    def onAboutHtmlDlg(self, event):
        aboutDlg = AboutDlg(None)
        aboutDlg.Show()

    def onAboutDlg(self, event):
        info = wx.AboutDialogInfo()
        info.Name = "My About Box"
        info.Version = "0.0.1 Beta"
        info.Copyright = "(C) 2008 Python Geeks Everywhere"
        info.Description = wordwrap(
            "This is an example application that shows how to create "
            "different kinds of About Boxes using wxPython!",
            350, wx.ClientDC(self.panel))
        info.WebSite = ("http://www.pythonlibrary.org", "My Home Page")
        info.Developers = ["Mike Driscoll"]
        info.License = wordwrap("Completely and totally open source!", 500,
                                wx.ClientDC(self.panel))
        # Show the wx.AboutBox
        wx.AboutBox(info)

    def onClose(self, event):
        self.Close()

class AboutDlg(wx.Frame):

    def __init__(self, parent):

        wx.Frame.__init__(self, parent, wx.ID_ANY, title="About",
        size=(400,400))
```

```
        html = wxHTML(self)

        html.SetPage(
            "

            "<h2>About the About Tutorial</h2>"

            "<p>This about box is for demo purposes only. It was created in
            June 2006 "

            "by Mike Driscoll.</p>"

            "<p><b>Software used in making this demo:</h3></p>"

            '<p><b><a href="http://www.python.org">Python 2.7 / 3.5</a>
            </b></p>'

            '<p><b><a href="http://www.wxpython.org">wxPython 3.0.2.0 /
            Phoenix</a></b></p>'
        )

class wxHTML(wx.html.HtmlWindow):

    def __init__(self, *args, **kwargs):
        wx.html.HtmlWindow.__init__(self, *args, **kwargs)
        self.Bind(wx.html.EVT_HTML_LINK_CLICKED, self.OnLinkClicked)

    def OnLinkClicked(self, link):
        webbrowser.open(link.GetLinkInfo().GetHref())

# Run the program
if __name__ == '__main__':
    app = wx.App(False)
    frame = MyForm().Show()
    app.MainLoop()
```

The main things to take note of here is how I handle the setup of the menu bar and the related menu bar events. If you're not familiar with hooking those up, then you'll probably find this helpful. I'll be going over this process in more detail in a later post, but suffice it to say that you need to create ar wx.MenuBar object and some wx.Menu objects. The wx.Menu objects are used for the headings of the menu (i.e. "File," "About," etc).

The wx.Menu objects are then appended to the menu bar. Finally you do a `self.SetMenuBar()` command to attach the menu bar to your application's wx.Frame.

Updating the Code for wxPython 4/Phoenix

In wxPython Phoenix, you will need to change the code a bit. The first thing you will need to do is add the following import to the beginning of the file: **import wx.adv**. You see, in Phoenix, the **wx.AboutBox** is now in **wx.adv.AboutBox** and the **wx. AboutDialogInfo** is now **wx.adv.AboutDialogInfo**. What this means is that you will need to update the **onAboutDlg** method to the following for Phoenix:

```python
def onAboutDlg(self, event):
    info = wx.adv.AboutDialogInfo()
    info.Name = "My About Box"
    info.Version = "0.0.1 Beta"
    info.Copyright = "(C) 2008 Python Geeks Everywhere"
    info.Description = wordwrap(
        "This is an example application that shows how to create "
        "different kinds of About Boxes using wxPython!",
        350, wx.ClientDC(self.panel))
    info.WebSite = ("http://www.pythonlibrary.org", "My Home Page")
    info.Developers = ["Mike Driscoll"]
    info.License = wordwrap("Completely and totally open source!", 500,
                            wx.ClientDC(self.panel))
    # Show the wx.AboutBox
    wx.adv.AboutBox(info)
```

The code should now work in Python 3 with wxPython 4!

Now you have the knowledge to create your own About Box. These widgets are quite useful for communicating to the end-user information about your program such as what version they are using. Some developers use the About Box for displaying information about their company or the product. They also use them to allow the user to manually check for updates. You can use yours as you see fit as they are completely customizable.

Recipe 6-2. Creating Graphs with PyPlot

Problem

Some people learn through doing it; others are better with visual stimuli. At least, that's what we're told. So in the spirit of what we've been taught, we're going to take a look at the visual half of the equation and see how we can make graphs with wxPython. You may not know this, but wxPython includes a widget just for this purpose. Its name is PyPlot. PyPlot is great at doing simple plots and it's super fast too! If you need to do weird or complicated plotting, then you'll want to use matplotlib instead. Fortunately, wxPython and matplotlib play well with each other, but we won't be looking at matplotlib in this recipe.

Note   The examples in this chapter do not work in wxPython 3.0.2.0 Classic as there is a known bug (`http://trac.wxwidgets.org/ticket/16767`).

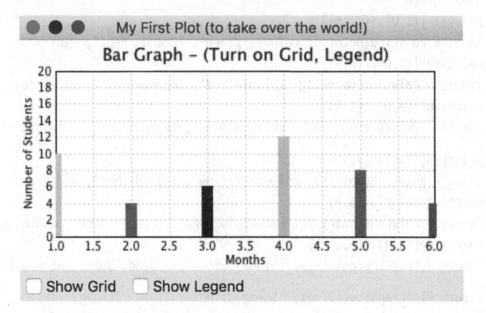

Figure 6-3. *PyPlot's bar graph*

Solution

If you look at the **plot.py** file in the wxPython distribution you'll discover that PyPlot requires Numeric, numarray, or numpy (in reverse order), so make sure you have one of those installed to be able to use this widget. You can use pip to install numpy, which makes things really simple. Open up cmd.exe on Windows or a terminal on your Mac or Linux machine and run the following command:

pip install numpy

   Now that you have NumPy installed, we can take some code from the wxPython demo and create a bar graph!

```
import wx
from wx.lib.plot import PolyLine, PlotCanvas, PlotGraphics

def drawBarGraph():
    # Bar graph
    points1=[(1,0), (1,10)]
    line1 = PolyLine(points1, colour='green', legend='Feb.', width=10)
    points1g=[(2,0), (2,4)]
    line1g = PolyLine(points1g, colour='red', legend='Mar.', width=10)
    points1b=[(3,0), (3,6)]
    line1b = PolyLine(points1b, colour='blue', legend='Apr.', width=10)

    points2=[(4,0), (4,12)]
    line2 = PolyLine(points2, colour='Yellow', legend='May', width=10)
    points2g=[(5,0), (5,8)]
    line2g = PolyLine(points2g, colour='orange', legend='June', width=10)
    points2b=[(6,0), (6,4)]
    line2b = PolyLine(points2b, colour='brown', legend='July', width=10)

    return PlotGraphics([line1, line1g, line1b, line2, line2g, line2b],
                        "Bar Graph - (Turn on Grid, Legend)", "Months",
                        "Number of Students")

class MyGraph(wx.Frame):
```

```python
    def __init__(self):
        wx.Frame.__init__(self, None, wx.ID_ANY,
                          'My First Plot (to take over the world!)')

        # Add a panel so it looks the correct on all platforms
        panel = wx.Panel(self, wx.ID_ANY)

        # create some sizers
        mainSizer = wx.BoxSizer(wx.VERTICAL)
        checkSizer = wx.BoxSizer(wx.HORIZONTAL)

        # create the widgets
        self.canvas = PlotCanvas(panel)
        self.canvas.Draw(drawBarGraph())
        toggleGrid = wx.CheckBox(panel, label="Show Grid")
        toggleGrid.Bind(wx.EVT_CHECKBOX, self.onToggleGrid)
        toggleLegend = wx.CheckBox(panel, label="Show Legend")
        toggleLegend.Bind(wx.EVT_CHECKBOX, self.onToggleLegend)

        # layout the widgets
        mainSizer.Add(self.canvas, 1, wx.EXPAND)
        checkSizer.Add(toggleGrid, 0, wx.ALL, 5)
        checkSizer.Add(toggleLegend, 0, wx.ALL, 5)
        mainSizer.Add(checkSizer)
        panel.SetSizer(mainSizer)

    def onToggleGrid(self, event):
        """"""
        self.canvas.SetEnableGrid(event.IsChecked())

    def onToggleLegend(self, event):
        """"""
        self.canvas.SetEnableLegend(event.IsChecked())

if __name__ == '__main__':
    app = wx.App(False)
    frame = MyGraph()
    frame.Show()
    app.MainLoop()
```

How It Works

The **drawBarGraph** function is pulled directly from the plot.py file that was mentioned earlier. For this example, the function name was changed from "_draw6Objects" to "drawBarGraph" to make the code easier to follow. Let's take a look at it. The points are the points on the graph: [(x1, y1), (x2, y2)]. They tell PyPlot where to plot via the **PolyLine** method. As you can see, PolyLine takes a list of tuples of graph points, and optionally, a color, legend, width, and style (not shown). We create a series of PolyLines and then add them to a **PlotGraphics** instance. The PlotGraphics first method is a list of PolyLines (or other PolyXXX objects), title, xLabel, and yLabel. We return the PlotGraphics object back to the caller which is in our wxPython class.

Now we turn our attention to that class, which has the bland name of **MyGraph**. The first few lines are pretty familiar if you've used wxPython before, so let's skip those and jump right down to the widget creation section. Here we see how to create a **PlotCanvas** with just a plain wx.Panel as its parent. To draw the bar graph, we call our canvas object's Draw method, passing in the **PlotGraphics** object that was returned from the **drawBarGraph** function. Feel free to reread that as many times as needed to understand what's going on before continuing.

Are you ready? Then let's continue! After we draw the bar graph, we create a couple of check boxes to allow us to toggle the graph's grid and legend. Then we lay out the widgets on the frame. The check box's methods are pretty self-explanatory, so you can figure those out on your own. Hint: **IsChecked**() returns a Boolean.

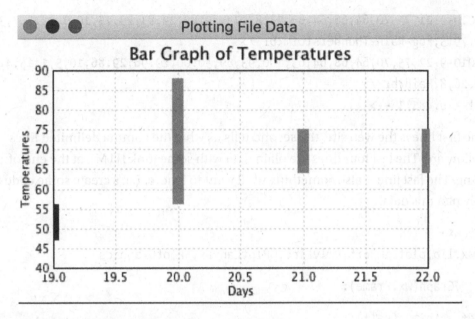

Figure 6-4. *Bar graph created using saved data*

Graphing Using Saved Data

Normally you'll want to read the data from a saved file, database, or a web service rather than using hard-coded data. Here we'll look at using some saved data to create a graph. Following is the data we'll be using (you'll probably want to download the archives from the book's source code on Github):

```
# http://www.wunderground.com/history/airport/KMIW/2010/9/22/WeeklyHistory.
html?format=1
    CDT,Max TemperatureF,Mean TemperatureF,Min TemperatureF,Max Dew
    PointF,MeanDew PointF,Min DewpointF,Max Humidity, Mean Humidity, Min
    Humidity, Max Sea Level PressureIn, Mean Sea Level PressureIn, Min
    Sea Level PressureIn, Max VisibilityMiles, Mean VisibilityMiles, Min
    VisibilityMiles, Max Wind SpeedMPH, Mean Wind SpeedMPH, Max Gust
    SpeedMPH,PrecipitationIn, CloudCover, Events<br />
    2010-9-19,56,52,47,55,49,44,100,97,93,30.21,30.17,30.11,10,5,2,14,9,20,
    0.34,8,Rain-Thunderstorm<br />
    2010-9-20,88,72,56,71,62,55,100,73,46,30.10,29.94,29.77,10,6,0,25,12,
    32,T,4,Fog-Rain<br />
```

```
2010-9-21,75,70,64,66,64,63,93,83,73,29.89,29.83,29.75,10,7,0,22,7,30,
1.79,5,Fog-Rain-Thunderstorm<br />
2010-9-22,75,70,64,68,64,63,100,93,69,30.00,29.96,29.86,10,5,1,15,4,,
0.26,8,Rain<br />
<!-- 0.481:1 -->
```

The first line is the web site, the second tells us what the comma delimited lines
that follow are. The last four lines are plain data with some junk HTML at the end of
each ling. The last line is also something we'll want to ignore. Let's create some code to
actually plot this data!

```python
import wx
from wx.lib.plot import PolyLine, PlotCanvas, PlotGraphics

class MyGraph(wx.Frame):

    def __init__(self):
        wx.Frame.__init__(self, None, wx.ID_ANY,
                            'Plotting File Data')

        # Add a panel so it looks the correct on all platforms
        panel = wx.Panel(self, wx.ID_ANY)
        self.canvas = PlotCanvas(panel)
        self.canvas.Draw(self.createPlotGraphics())

        sizer = wx.BoxSizer(wx.VERTICAL)
        sizer.Add(self.canvas, 1, wx.EXPAND)
        panel.SetSizer(sizer)

    def readFile(self):
        """
        Reads the hard-coded file
        """
        # normally you would want to pass a file path in, NOT hard code it!
        with open("data.txt") as fobj:
            # skip the first two lines of text in the file
            data = fobj.readlines()[2:-1]

        temps = []
```

```
        for line in data:
            parts = line.split(",")
            date = parts[0].split("-")
            day = date[2]
            points = [(day, parts[3]), (day, parts[1])]
            temps.append(points)
        return temps

    def createPlotGraphics(self):
        """
        Create the plot's graphics
        """
        temps = self.readFile()
        lines = []
        for temp in temps:
            tempInt = int(temp[1][1])
            if tempInt < 60:
                color = "blue"
            elif tempInt >=60 and tempInt <= 75:
                color = "orange"
            else:
                color = "red"
            lines.append(PolyLine(temp, colour=color, width=10))

        return PlotGraphics(lines, "Bar Graph of Temperatures",
                            "Days", "Temperatures")

if __name__ == '__main__':
    app = wx.App(False)
    frame = MyGraph()
    frame.Show()
    app.MainLoop()
```

Just like in our previous example, we import a few things and create a **wx.Frame** with a panel and a **PlotCanvas**. We have a simple **readFile** method and a **createPlotGraphics** method too. These two methods are what we will focus on.

The **readFile** method is called by the **createPlotGraphics** method. All it does is read a file. For this example, we have the "path" to the file hard-coded. What you would normally want to do is use some kind of file browser to load the file, but we're going the super-simple route. When we read the lines from the file, we skip over the first two by using the following syntax:

data = f.readlines()[2:-1]

What that does is read in all the lines in the file via the **readlines()** method. The readlines method returns a list object, so we use list slicing (the [2:-1] part) to exclude the first two lines in the file and read to the end, minus one line. By doing it this way, we skip the junk at the beginning and the end. Isn't Python cool? Next we create a simple "for loop" to pull out the data we want, which is just the day and the low and the high temperatures. The rest we just throw away.

In the **createPlotGraphics** method, we take the list of temps returned from the readFile method and loop over those, creating a new list of PolyLines. We use the some "if statements" to decide what color to make each bar in the bar graph. Finally, we put all the PolyLines into a PlotGraphics instance and return that to the called in the __init__ method. That's all there is to it!

Point Plot with Thousands of Points

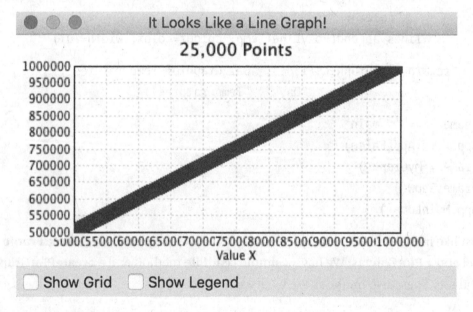

Figure 6-5. *A point plot*

Now we're going to look at how to create a point plot with 25,000 points! This one is also from the demo. Following is the code:

```python
import numpy as _Numeric
import wx
from wx.lib.plot import PlotCanvas, PlotGraphics, PolyLine, PolyMarker

def drawLinePlot():
    # 25,000 point line
    data1 = _Numeric.arange(5e5,1e6,10)
    data1.shape = (25000, 2)
    line1 = PolyLine(data1, legend='Wide Line', colour='green', width=5)

    # A few more points...
    markers2 = PolyMarker(data1, legend='Square', colour='blue',
                          marker='square')
    return PlotGraphics([line1, markers2], "25,000 Points", "Value X", "")

class MyGraph(wx.Frame):

    def __init__(self):
        wx.Frame.__init__(self, None, wx.ID_ANY,
                          'It Looks Like a Line Graph!')

        # Add a panel so it looks the correct on all platforms
        panel = wx.Panel(self, wx.ID_ANY)

        # create some sizers
        mainSizer = wx.BoxSizer(wx.VERTICAL)
        checkSizer = wx.BoxSizer(wx.HORIZONTAL)

        # create the widgets
        self.canvas = PlotCanvas(panel)
        self.canvas.Draw(drawLinePlot())
        toggleGrid = wx.CheckBox(panel, label="Show Grid")
        toggleGrid.Bind(wx.EVT_CHECKBOX, self.onToggleGrid)
        toggleLegend = wx.CheckBox(panel, label="Show Legend")
        toggleLegend.Bind(wx.EVT_CHECKBOX, self.onToggleLegend)
```

```
        # layout the widgets
        mainSizer.Add(self.canvas, 1, wx.EXPAND)
        checkSizer.Add(toggleGrid, 0, wx.ALL, 5)
        checkSizer.Add(toggleLegend, 0, wx.ALL, 5)
        mainSizer.Add(checkSizer)
        panel.SetSizer(mainSizer)

    def onToggleGrid(self, event):
        """"""
        self.canvas.SetEnableGrid(event.IsChecked())

    def onToggleLegend(self, event):
        """"""
        self.canvas.SetEnableLegend(event.IsChecked())

if __name__ == '__main__':
    app = wx.App(False)
    frame = MyGraph()
    frame.Show()
    app.MainLoop()
```

We reuse most of the wxPython code that we saw in our original example and just call a different function here. The **drawLinePlot** function is pretty simple. For this example, we use **numpy** to create the 25,000 plot points and then create a **PolyLine** with them. If you zoom in, you will see that some of the points are square instead of round. That's what the **PolyMarker** class is for. It sets the style of the "marker." Now we're ready to look at our next example! (see Figure 6-6).

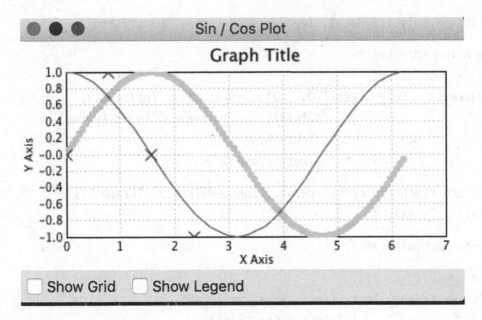

Figure 6-6. *A sine/cosine plot*

Creating a Sine/Cosine Graph

This example shows you how to take a Sine and a Cosine and graph them. It kind of looks like a horizontal double-helix. Anyway, here's the code.

```
import numpy as _Numeric
import wx
from wx.lib.plot import PlotCanvas, PlotGraphics, PolyLine, PolyMarker

def drawSinCosWaves():
    # 100 points sin function, plotted as green circles
    data1 = 2.*_Numeric.pi*_Numeric.arange(200)/200.
    data1.shape = (100, 2)
    data1[:,1] = _Numeric.sin(data1[:,0])
    markers1 = PolyMarker(data1, legend='Green Markers', colour='green',
    marker='circle',size=1)

    # 50 points cos function, plotted as red line
    data1 = 2.*_Numeric.pi*_Numeric.arange(100)/100.
    data1.shape = (50,2)
    data1[:,1] = _Numeric.cos(data1[:,0])
```

```python
    lines = PolyLine(data1, legend= 'Red Line', colour='red')

    # A few more points...
    pi = _Numeric.pi
    markers2 = PolyMarker([(0., 0.), (pi/4., 1.), (pi/2, 0.),
                        (3.*pi/4., -1)], legend='Cross Legend',
                        colour='blue',
                        marker='cross')

    return PlotGraphics([markers1, lines, markers2],"Graph Title", "X
    Axis", "Y Axis")

class MyGraph(wx.Frame):

    def __init__(self):
        wx.Frame.__init__(self, None, wx.ID_ANY,
                        'Sin / Cos Plot')

        # Add a panel so it looks the correct on all platforms
        panel = wx.Panel(self, wx.ID_ANY)

        # create some sizers
        mainSizer = wx.BoxSizer(wx.VERTICAL)
        checkSizer = wx.BoxSizer(wx.HORIZONTAL)

        # create the widgets
        self.canvas = PlotCanvas(panel)
        self.canvas.Draw(drawSinCosWaves())
        toggleGrid = wx.CheckBox(panel, label="Show Grid")
        toggleGrid.Bind(wx.EVT_CHECKBOX, self.onToggleGrid)
        toggleLegend = wx.CheckBox(panel, label="Show Legend")
        toggleLegend.Bind(wx.EVT_CHECKBOX, self.onToggleLegend)

        # layout the widgets
        mainSizer.Add(self.canvas, 1, wx.EXPAND)
        checkSizer.Add(toggleGrid, 0, wx.ALL, 5)
        checkSizer.Add(toggleLegend, 0, wx.ALL, 5)
        mainSizer.Add(checkSizer)
        panel.SetSizer(mainSizer)
```

```python
    def onToggleGrid(self, event):
        """"""""
        self.canvas.SetEnableGrid(event.IsChecked())

    def onToggleLegend(self, event):
        """"""""
        self.canvas.SetEnableLegend(event.IsChecked())

if __name__ == '__main__':
    app = wx.App(False)
    frame = MyGraph()
    frame.Show()
    app.MainLoop()
```

This example is for the math geeks out there. I haven't done trigonometry or geometry in quite a while, so I won't explain the equations here. You can look up that sort of thing with your favorite search engine. This example uses one **PolyLine** and two **PolyMarkers** to create the graph. It's mostly like the other examples though, so there's really not much to say.

By now you should be more than ready to undertake doing graphs on your own with wxPython. If you get stuck, there are several other examples in the plot.py file and the wxPython mailing list members are quite friendly and will probably help you if you ask nicely. Let me know if you create anything cool!

Recipe 6-3. Creating a Simple Notebook

Problem

The **wx.Notebook** widget allows us to create a tabbed user interface. Most examples that you see online tend to be fairly complex, so it's always good to start with something that's super simple. Let's start by looking at something that's really easy to follow and then we'll take that example and refactor it a bit to make it easier to extend in the future.

Solution

Our simple notebook widget will consist of two tabs that have a pseudo-random background color (see Figure 6-7).

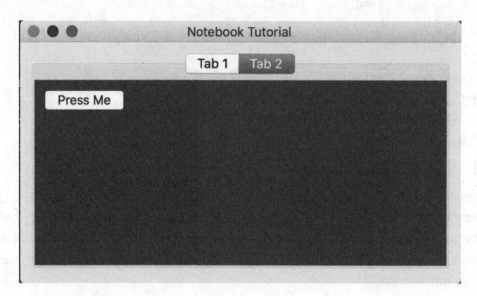

Figure 6-7. *A simple notebook*

Let's take a look.

```
import random
import wx

class TabPanel(wx.Panel):

    def __init__(self, parent):
        """"""
        wx.Panel.__init__(self, parent=parent)

        colors = ["red", "blue", "gray", "yellow", "green"]
        self.SetBackgroundColour(random.choice(colors))

        btn = wx.Button(self, label="Press Me")
        sizer = wx.BoxSizer(wx.VERTICAL)
        sizer.Add(btn, 0, wx.ALL, 10)
        self.SetSizer(sizer)
```

```python
class DemoFrame(wx.Frame):
    """
    Frame that holds all other widgets
    """

    def __init__(self):
        """Constructor"""
        wx.Frame.__init__(self, None, wx.ID_ANY,
                          "Notebook Tutorial",
                          size=(600,400)
                          )
        panel = wx.Panel(self)

        notebook = wx.Notebook(panel)
        tabOne = TabPanel(notebook)
        notebook.AddPage(tabOne, "Tab 1")

        tabTwo = TabPanel(notebook)
        notebook.AddPage(tabTwo, "Tab 2")

        sizer = wx.BoxSizer(wx.VERTICAL)
        sizer.Add(notebook, 1, wx.ALL|wx.EXPAND, 5)
        panel.SetSizer(sizer)
        self.Layout()

        self.Show()

if __name__ == "__main__":
    app = wx.App(False)
    frame = DemoFrame()
    app.MainLoop()
```

How It Works

That code is pretty short and sweet. Let's take a moment and unpack this example. In the **DemoFrame** class, we have a main panel which is the only child widget of the Frame. Inside that, we have the Notebook control. Each page of the Notebook is an instance of our TabPanel class, which should have a "random" background color and one button that doesn't do anything. We add the Notebook to a sizer and set it to expand with a proportion of 1. This means that it will fill the panel, and since the panel fills the frame, the notebook will fill the frame too. To be honest, that's really all there is to it.

Another topic of note is that the Notebook events, such as **EVT_NOTEBOOK_PAGE_CHANGED**, may need to have an "event.Skip()" call in their event handler to make them function properly. The event hierarchy in wxPython is a little hard to grasp, but think of it as air bubbles in a pond. If you bind a widget to a particular event and don't call Skip(), then your event is handled ONLY in that particular handler. This is like having the bubble popped part way from the bottom of the pond. However, occasionally you'll need the event to be handled higher up, as in the widget's parent or grandparent. If so, call Skip() and your event "bubble" will rise to the next handler. The wxPython wiki has more on this as does the "wxPython in Action" book by Robin Dunn.

That covers the simple Notebook example, so let's spend a few moments refactoring it a bit!

The Refactored Notebook

You might be wondering why we want to refactor code that's already simple and easy to follow.

The main reason is that we want to make sure our code can handle changing requirements that will likely come later on in the project. We also want to be able to write the code in such a way that we can extend it easily, such as when a new feature is requested. One of the simplest ways of refactoring the code is to make it more modular. To do that, we can subclass the major widgets. Let's take a look.

```python
import random
import wx

class TabPanel(wx.Panel):
    """
    The panel class to derive the tabs of the Notebook from
    """

    def __init__(self, parent):
        """"""

        wx.Panel.__init__(self, parent=parent)
```

```
        colors = ["red", "blue", "gray", "yellow", "green"]
        self.SetBackgroundColour(random.choice(colors))

        btn = wx.Button(self, label="Press Me")
        sizer = wx.BoxSizer(wx.VERTICAL)
        sizer.Add(btn, 0, wx.ALL, 10)
        self.SetSizer(sizer)

class DemoNotebook(wx.Notebook):
    """

    Our Notebook class
    """

    def __init__(self, parent):
        wx.Notebook.__init__(self, parent)

        tabOne = TabPanel(self)
        self.AddPage(tabOne, "Tab 1")

        tabTwo = TabPanel(self)
        self.AddPage(tabTwo, "Tab 2")

class DemoPanel(wx.Panel):
    """

    The main panel used by the frame
    """

    def __init__(self, parent):
        """"""""

        wx.Panel.__init__(self, parent=parent)

        notebook = DemoNotebook(self)

        sizer = wx.BoxSizer(wx.VERTICAL)
        sizer.Add(notebook, 1, wx.ALL|wx.EXPAND, 5)
        self.SetSizer(sizer)

class DemoFrame(wx.Frame):
    """

    Frame that holds all other widgets
```

95

```
    """

    def __init__(self):
        """Constructor"""
        wx.Frame.__init__(self, None, wx.ID_ANY,
                            "Notebook Tutorial",
                            size=(600,400)
                            )
        panel = DemoPanel(self)

        self.Layout()

        self.Show()

if __name__ == "__main__":
    app = wx.App(False)
    frame = DemoFrame()
    app.MainLoop()
```

Here we take the **wx.Panel** that we had before and put it into its own subclass,
DemoPanel. We do the same thing with our **wx.Notebook** widget when we put it into
our **DemoNotebook** class. Take note of the fact that when we do this, we can change
our references from the instance names (panel or notebook) to simply **self**. This change
greatly reduced the **DemoFrame** class.

Now that everything is in a different class, we can move the various classes into separate
modules and import them as needed. This makes the code easier to share across projects
and easier to manage in that we no longer need to store everything in one module. Go
ahead and take a few moments and try putting some of these new classes into separate
modules that you can import. You will quickly see how easy it is to use and how useful
this concept can be.

CHAPTER 7

Using Config Files

Recipe 7-1. Generating a Dialog from a Config File

Problem

After writing an article about the wonderful **ConfigObj** package on my blog, one of my readers asked if there was a way to use a config file to generate a dialog. I took this idea and decided to give it a try. For this recipe, you will need to install ConfigObj in addition to wxPython. If you don't already have ConfigObj, all you need to do is use pip to install it:

pip install configobj

Now that you have ConfigObj installed, we can continue. The first thing we need to do is to create some sort of configuration file that we can use to generate our dialog. Put the following into a file called **config.ini**:

```
[Labels]
server = Update Server:
username = Username:
password = Password:
update interval = Update Interval:
agency = Agency Filter:
filters = ""

[Values]
server = http://www.someCoolWebsite/hackery.php
username = ""
password = ""
update interval = 2
```

© Mike Driscoll 2018
M. Driscoll, *wxPython Recipes*, https://doi.org/10.1007/978-1-4842-3237-8_7

```
agency_choices = Include all agencies except, Include all agencies except,
Exclude all agencies except
filters = ""
```

This configuration file has two sections: **Labels** and **Values**. The *Labels* section has the labels we will use to create **wx.StaticText** controls with. The *Values* section has some sample values we can use for the corresponding text control widgets and one combo box. Note that the **agency_choices** field is a list. The first item in the list will be the default option in the combo box and the other two items are the real contents of the widget.

Solution

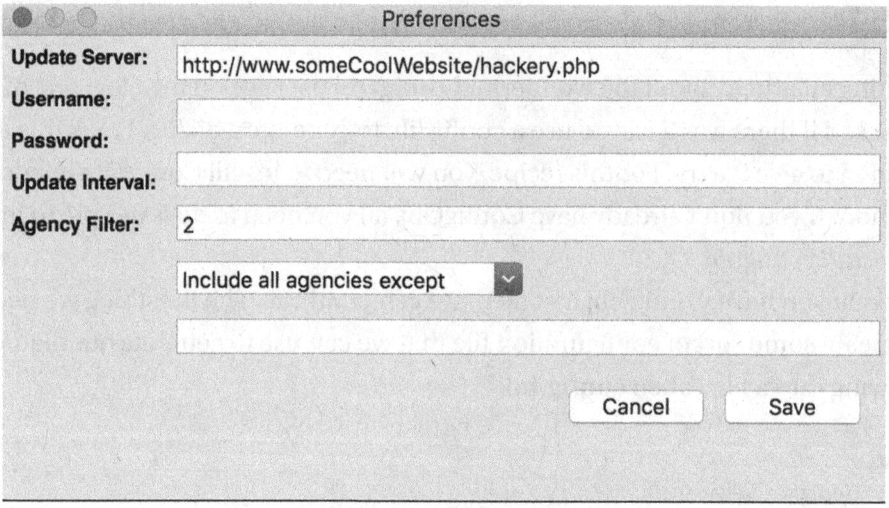

Figure 7-1. A dialog generated from a configuration file

Now that we know what we're going to base our user interface on, we can write our code. When the code is finished you'll end up with a dialog that looks like that in Figure 7-1. Let's dive into the code itself now.

```
import configobj
import wx

class PreferencesDialog(wx.Dialog):
    """

    Creates and displays a preferences dialog that allows the user to
```

change some settings.
"""

```python
def __init__(self):
    """
    Initialize the dialog
    """
    wx.Dialog.__init__(self, None, title='Preferences',
                       size=(550,300))
    self.createWidgets()

def createWidgets(self):
    """
    Create and layout the widgets in the dialog
    """
    lblSizer = wx.BoxSizer(wx.VERTICAL)
    valueSizer = wx.BoxSizer(wx.VERTICAL)
    btnSizer = wx.StdDialogButtonSizer()
    colSizer = wx.BoxSizer(wx.HORIZONTAL)
    mainSizer = wx.BoxSizer(wx.VERTICAL)

    iniFile = "config.ini"
    self.config = configobj.ConfigObj(iniFile)

    labels = self.config["Labels"]
    values = self.config["Values"]
    self.widgetNames = values
    font = wx.Font(12, wx.SWISS, wx.NORMAL, wx.BOLD)

    for key in labels:
        value = labels[key]
        lbl = wx.StaticText(self, label=value)
        lbl.SetFont(font)
        lblSizer.Add(lbl, 0, wx.ALL, 5)

    for key in values:
        print(key)
        value = values[key]
```

```
            if isinstance(value, list):
                default = value[0]
                choices = value[1:]
                cbo = wx.ComboBox(self, value=value[0],
                                  size=wx.DefaultSize, choices=choices,
                                  style=wx.CB_DROPDOWN|wx.CB_READONLY,
                                  name=key)
                valueSizer.Add(cbo, 0, wx.ALL, 5)
            else:
                txt = wx.TextCtrl(self, value=value, name=key)
                valueSizer.Add(txt, 0, wx.ALL|wx.EXPAND, 5)

        saveBtn = wx.Button(self, wx.ID_OK, label="Save")
        saveBtn.Bind(wx.EVT_BUTTON, self.onSave)
        btnSizer.AddButton(saveBtn)

        cancelBtn = wx.Button(self, wx.ID_CANCEL)
        btnSizer.AddButton(cancelBtn)
        btnSizer.Realize()

        colSizer.Add(lblSizer)
        colSizer.Add(valueSizer, 1, wx.EXPAND)
        mainSizer.Add(colSizer, 0, wx.EXPAND)
        mainSizer.Add(btnSizer, 0, wx.ALL | wx.ALIGN_RIGHT, 5)
        self.SetSizer(mainSizer)

    def onSave(self, event):
        """

        Saves values to disk
        """

        for name in self.widgetNames:
            widget = wx.FindWindowByName(name)
            if isinstance(widget, wx.ComboBox):
                selection = widget.GetValue()
                choices = widget.GetItems()
                choices.insert(0, selection)
                self.widgetNames[name] = choices
```

```
            else:
                value = widget.GetValue()
                self.widgetNames[name] = value
        self.config.write()
        self.EndModal(0)

class MyApp(wx.App):
    """"""

    def OnInit(self):
        """Constructor"""
        dlg = PreferencesDialog()
        dlg.ShowModal()
        dlg.Destroy()

        return True

if __name__ == "__main__":
    app = MyApp(False)
    app.MainLoop()
```

How It Works

To start, we subclass a **wx.Dialog** and use its **createWidgets** method. This method will read our config file and use the data therein to create the display. Once the config is read, we loop over the keys in the Labels section and create static text controls as needed. Next, we loop over the values in the other section and use a conditional to check the type of widget. In this case, we only care about **wx.TextCtrl** and **wx.Combobox**. This is where ConfigObj helps since it actually can typecast some of the entries in our configuration file. If you use a **configspec**, you can get even more granular and that may be the way you'll want to go to extend this tutorial. Note that for the text controls and combo box, I set the name field. This is important for saving the data, which we'll be seeing in just a moment.

Anyway, in both loops, we use vertical **BoxSizers** to hold our widgets. You may want to swap this for a GridBagSizer or FlexGridSizer for your specialized interface. I personally really like BoxSizers. I also used a StdDialogButtonSizer for the buttons. If you use the correct standard ids for the buttons, this sizer will place them in the right order in a cross-platform way. It's quite handy, although it doesn't take many arguments.

The next method that we care about is **onSave**. Here is where we save whatever the user has entered.

Earlier in the program, I grabbed the widget names from the configuration and we loop over those now. We call **wx.FindWindowByName** to find the widget by name. Then we use **isinstance** again to check what kind of widget we have. Once that's done, we grab the value that the widget holds using GetValue and assign that value to the correct field in our configuration. When the loop finishes, we write the data to disk. The last step is to call **EndModal(0)** to close the dialog and, in turn, the application.

Now you know the basics of generating a dialog from a configuration file. I think using some kind of dictionary with widget-type names (probably in strings) might be an easy way to make this script work with other widgets. You will also note that I have no validation in this example at all! This is something for you to do to extend this piece of code. Use your imagination and let me know what you come up with.

Recipe 7-2. Saving Data to a Config File

Problem

There are lots of ways for you to persist your data in your application. When you are writing a user interface, there are many times that you will want to save the user's preferences. You could use a simple database, like SQLite, or you could use a configuration file. For this example, we will opt for the configuration file. Python has a handy library built into it called **configparser,** which you can use for creating and manipulating config files. However, I prefer using **ConfigObj**, which is a package that you'll have to download and install.

Solution

ConfigObj is a bit easier to use than **configparser** and provides validation too. ConfigObj can also return Python types from the config file, while configparser just returns strings. If you don't have ConfigObj installed then you can do so with pip.

pip install configobj

Once that's installed, we can go ahead and create a simple controller for creating and accessing our configuration file with ConfigObj.

Creating a Controller

It is common when designing a user interface to follow the model-view-controller paradigm. The controller usually houses the code that actully does something, like reading and writing data from a config file. The model is usually a description of a database or even the widgets themselves, which wxPython supports via XRC. The view is the code that draws the interface for the user, so in this case, it will be the majority of the wxPython code. We don't need to concern ourselves with a model this time, so we'll start off with the controller.

```python
# controller.py
import configobj
import os
import sys

appPath = os.path.abspath(os.path.dirname(os.path.join(sys.argv[0])))
inifile = os.path.join(appPath, "example.ini")

def create_config():
    """

    Create the configuration file
    """

    config = configobj.ConfigObj()
    config.filename = inifile
    config['update server'] = "http://www.someCoolWebsite/hackery.php"
    config['username'] = ""
    config['password'] = ""
    config['update interval'] = 2
    config['agency filter'] = 'include'
    config['filters'] = ""
    config.write()

def get_config():
    """

    Open the config file and return a configobj
    """

    if not os.path.exists(inifile):
        create_config()
    return configobj.ConfigObj(inifile)
```

How It Works

This piece of code is pretty straightforward. In the **create_config** function, it creates an **example.ini** file in the same directory as the one that this script is run from. The config file gets six fields but no sections. In the **get_config** function, the code checks for the existence of the configuration file and creates it if it does not exist. Regardless, the function returns a ConfigObj object to the caller. We'll put this script into **controller.py**.

Creating the View

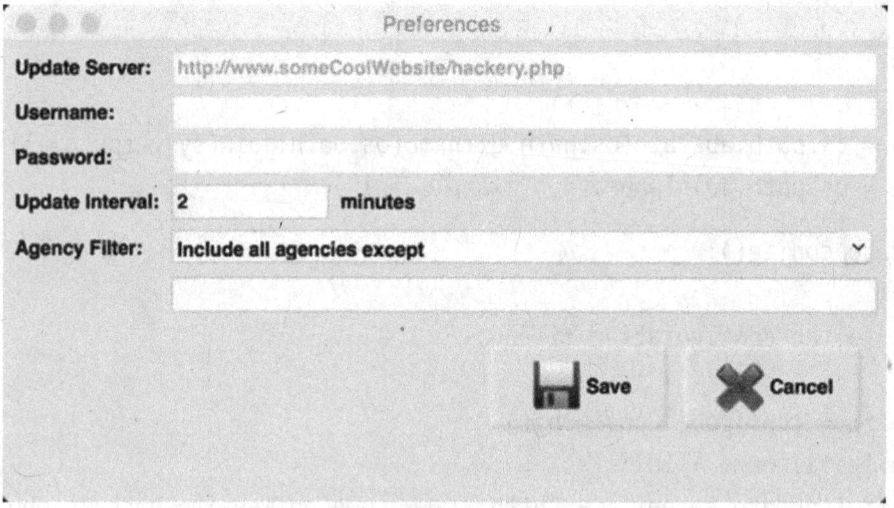

Figure 7-2. Saving a configuration file with wxPython

All we need to do for our view is to subclass the wx.Dialog class to create a preferences dialog. This piece of code is a bit long, so let's go over it in pieces instead.

```
import controller
import os
import sys
import wx
from wx.lib.buttons import GenBitmapTextButton

appPath = os.path.abspath(os.path.dirname(os.path.join(sys.argv[0])))

class CloseBtn(GenBitmapTextButton):
    """
```

```
    Creates a reusable close button with a bitmap
    """

    def __init__(self, parent, label="Close"):
        """Constructor"""
        font = wx.Font(16, wx.SWISS, wx.NORMAL, wx.BOLD)
        img = wx.Bitmap(r"%s/images/cancel.png" % appPath)
        GenBitmapTextButton.__init__(self, parent, wx.ID_CLOSE, img,
                                     label=label, size=(110, 50))
        self.SetFont(font)
```

This first chunk just creates a simple button to close the application. We abstracted it out to make sharing this code simpler. You could even put this code into its own module that could be imported by multiple applications, for example. Now let's take a look at the main dialog code.

```
class PreferencesDialog(wx.Dialog):
    """

    Creates and displays a preferences dialog that allows the user to
    change some settings.
    """

    def __init__(self):
        """

        Initialize the dialog
        """
        wx.Dialog.__init__(self, None, wx.ID_ANY, 'Preferences', size=(550,400))
        appPath = controller.appPath

        # Create widgets
        font = wx.Font(12, wx.SWISS, wx.NORMAL, wx.BOLD)
        serverLbl = wx.StaticText(self, label="Update Server:")
        self.serverTxt = wx.TextCtrl(self)
        self.serverTxt.Disable()

        usernameLbl = wx.StaticText(self, label="Username:")
        self.usernameTxt = wx.TextCtrl(self)
        self.usernameTxt.Disable()
```

```python
        passwordLbl = wx.StaticText(self, label="Password:")
        self.passwordTxt = wx.TextCtrl(self,
                                        style=wx.TE_PASSWORD)
        self.passwordTxt.Disable()

        updateLbl = wx.StaticText(self, label="Update Interval:")
        self.updateTxt = wx.TextCtrl(self)
        minutesLbl = wx.StaticText(self, label="minutes")

        agencyLbl = wx.StaticText(self, label="Agency Filter:")
        choices = ["Include all agencies except",
                    "Exclude all agencies except"]
        self.agencyCbo = wx.ComboBox(
            self, value="Include all agencies except",
            choices=choices,
            style=wx.CB_DROPDOWN|wx.CB_READONLY)
        self.agencyCbo.SetFont(font)
        self.filterTxt = wx.TextCtrl(self, wx.ID_ANY, "")

        img = wx.Bitmap(r"%s/images/filesave.png" % appPath)
        saveBtn = GenBitmapTextButton(
            self, wx.ID_ANY, img, "Save", size=(110, 50))
        saveBtn.Bind(wx.EVT_BUTTON, self.savePreferences)
        cancelBtn = CloseBtn(self, label="Cancel")
        cancelBtn.Bind(wx.EVT_BUTTON, self.onCancel)

        # Set the widgets font
        widgets = [serverLbl, usernameLbl, passwordLbl,
                    updateLbl, agencyLbl, minutesLbl,
                    self.serverTxt, self.usernameTxt,
                    self.passwordTxt, self.updateTxt,
                    self.agencyCbo, self.filterTxt, saveBtn,
                    cancelBtn]
        for widget in widgets:
            widget.SetFont(font)
```

```
# layout widgets
mainSizer = wx.BoxSizer(wx.VERTICAL)
updateSizer = wx.BoxSizer(wx.HORIZONTAL)
btnSizer = wx.BoxSizer(wx.HORIZONTAL)
prefSizer = wx.FlexGridSizer(cols=2, hgap=5, vgap=5)
prefSizer.AddGrowableCol(1)

prefSizer.Add(serverLbl, 0, wx.ALIGN_LEFT | wx.ALIGN_CENTER_
VERTICAL)
prefSizer.Add(self.serverTxt, 0, wx.EXPAND)
prefSizer.Add(usernameLbl, 0, wx.ALIGN_LEFT | wx.ALIGN_CENTER_
VERTICAL)
prefSizer.Add(self.usernameTxt, 0, wx.EXPAND)
prefSizer.Add(passwordLbl, 0, wx.ALIGN_LEFT | wx.ALIGN_CENTER_
VERTICAL)
prefSizer.Add(self.passwordTxt, 0, wx.EXPAND)
prefSizer.Add(updateLbl, 0, wx.ALIGN_LEFT | wx.ALIGN_CENTER_
VERTICAL)
updateSizer.Add(self.updateTxt, 0, wx.RIGHT, 5)
updateSizer.Add(minutesLbl, 0, wx.ALIGN_LEFT | wx.ALIGN_CENTER_
VERTICAL)
prefSizer.Add(updateSizer)
prefSizer.Add(agencyLbl, 0, wx.ALIGN_LEFT | wx.ALIGN_CENTER_
VERTICAL)
prefSizer.Add(self.agencyCbo, 0, wx.EXPAND)
prefSizer.Add((20,20))
prefSizer.Add(self.filterTxt, 0, wx.EXPAND)

mainSizer.Add(prefSizer, 0, wx.EXPAND|wx.ALL, 5)
btnSizer.Add(saveBtn, 0, wx.ALL, 5)
btnSizer.Add(cancelBtn, 0, wx.ALL, 5)
mainSizer.Add(btnSizer, 0, wx.ALL | wx.ALIGN_RIGHT, 10)
self.SetSizer(mainSizer)

# load preferences
self.loadPreferences()
```

All this code does is initialize and lay out all the widgets that we'll need to create our application. It also sets up event handlers and sets the same font characteristics across all the widgets. The final chunk we will look at is the event handlers section.

```python
def loadPreferences(self):
    """

    Load the preferences and fill the text controls
    """

    config = controller.get_config()
    updateServer = config['update server']
    username = config['username']
    password = config['password']
    interval = config['update interval']
    agencyFilter = config['agency filter']
    filters = config['filters']

    self.serverTxt.SetValue(updateServer)
    self.usernameTxt.SetValue(username)
    self.passwordTxt.SetValue(password)
    self.updateTxt.SetValue(interval)
    self.agencyCbo.SetValue(agencyFilter)
    self.filterTxt.SetValue(filters)

def onCancel(self, event):
    """

    Closes the dialog
    """

    self.EndModal(0)

def savePreferences(self, event):
    """

    Save the preferences
    """

    config = controller.get_config()

    config['update interval'] = self.updateTxt.GetValue()
    config['agency filter'] = str(self.agencyCbo.GetValue())
    data = self.filterTxt.GetValue()
```

```
    if "," in data:
        filters = [i.strip() for i in data.split(',')]
    elif " " in data:
        filters = [i.strip() for i in data.split(' ')]
    else:
        filters = [data]
    text = ""
    for f in filters:
        text += " " + f
    text = text.strip()
    config['filters'] = text
    config.write()

    dlg = wx.MessageDialog(
        self, "Preferences Saved!", 'Information',
        wx.OK|wx.ICON_INFORMATION)
    dlg.ShowModal()
    dlg.EndModal(0)

if __name__ == "__main__":
    app = wx.App(False)
    dlg = PreferencesDialog()
    dlg.ShowModal()
    dlg.Destroy()
```

The previous code allows us to load a configuration from a file using ConfigObj. You can see how that works by reading the code in the **loadPreferences** method. The other major piece is how the code saves the preferences when the user changes them. For that, we need to look at the **savePreferences** method. This is a pretty straightforward method in that all it does is grab the various values from the widgets using wx's specific getter functions. There's also a conditional that does some minor checking on the filter field. The main reason for that is that in my original program, I use a space as the delimiter and the program needed to convert commas and such to spaces. This code is still a work in progress though as it does not cover all the cases that a user could enter. Feel free to expand it to cover more edge cases.

Anyway, once we have the values inside the ConfigObj's dict-like interface, we write the ConfigObj instance's data to file. Then the program displays a simple dialog to let the user know that's saved.

You will also note that to close our Dialog correctly, we called **EndModal** in our **onCancel** method.

Now, let's say that our program's specifications change such that we need to add or remove a preference. All that is required to do so is to add or delete it in the configuration file. ConfigObj will pick up the changes and we just need to remember to add or remove the appropriate widgets in our graphical user interface (GUI). One of the best things about ConfigObj is that it won't reset the data in your file; it will just add the changes as appropriate. Give it a try and find out just how easy it is!

At this point, you should be able to create your own preferences dialog and use ConfigObj to populate it. I find ConfigObj to be more "Pythonic" when it comes to reading and writing configuration files. I think you will too. If you'd like a challenge, you should try opening some preference dialogs in some popular applications, such as Microsoft Word, and then try emulating them using wxPython. It's a great learning exercise as you'll have to learn how to use new widgets and get more creative with your configuration file too.

CHAPTER 8

Working with Events

Recipe 8-1. Binding Multiple Widgets to the Same Handler

Problem

From time to time, you will find that you need to have multiple buttons call the same event handler. Usually this happens when you have more than one button that does very similar things. Other times, you'll want to bind a Close button and a Close menu item to the same event handler so you don't have multiple functions that do the same thing. This followd the **Don't Repeat Yourself (DRY) Principle**.

© Mike Driscoll 2018
M. Driscoll, *wxPython Recipes*, https://doi.org/10.1007/978-1-4842-3237-8_8

Solution

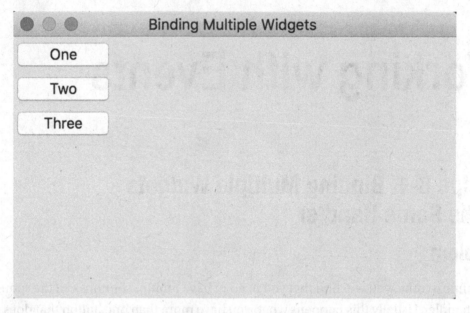

Figure 8-1. *Binding multiple widgets to the same handler*

To begin, we will write some code that contains multiple buttons. We will go through an example that shows two different ways to get the button object so you can manipulate your program as needed. Following is the code you've been waiting for:

```
import wx

class MyForm(wx.Frame):

    def __init__(self):
        wx.Frame.__init__(
            self, None, title="Binding Multiple Widgets")
        panel = wx.Panel(self, wx.ID_ANY)

        sizer = wx.BoxSizer(wx.VERTICAL)
        buttonOne = wx.Button(panel, label="One", name="one")
        buttonTwo = wx.Button(panel, label="Two", name="two")
        buttonThree = wx.Button(panel, label="Three", name="three")
        buttons = [buttonOne, buttonTwo, buttonThree]
```

```
    for button in buttons:
        self.buildButtons(button, sizer)

    panel.SetSizer(sizer)

def buildButtons(self, btn, sizer):
    """"""
    btn.Bind(wx.EVT_BUTTON, self.onButton)
    sizer.Add(btn, 0, wx.ALL, 5)

def onButton(self, event):
    """
    This method is fired when its corresponding button is pressed
    """
    button = event.GetEventObject()
    print("The button you pressed was labeled: " + button.GetLabel())
    print("The button's name is " + button.GetName())

    button_id = event.GetId()
    button_by_id = self.FindWindowById(button_id)
    print("The button you pressed was labeled: " + button_by_
    id.GetLabel())
    print("The button's name is " + button_by_id.GetName())

if __name__ == "__main__":
    app = wx.App(False)
    frame = MyForm()
    frame.Show()
    app.MainLoop()
```

How It Works

To start, we create three button objects. Then to make things slightly less messy, we put them into a list and iterate over the list to add the buttons to a sizer and bind them to an event handler. This is a good way to cut down on spaghetti code (i.e., copied and pasted code) and makes it a little cleaner and easier to debug. Some people go ahead and create some elaborate helper methods, like **buildButtons,** that can handle other widgets and are more flexible.

The part we really care about though is the event handler itself. The easiest way to get the widget in the event handler is by calling the event object's **GetEventObject()** method. That will return the widget and then you can do whatever you like. Some people will change the widget's value or label; others will use the widget's ID or unique name and set up some conditional structures to do something if this button is pressed and to do something else if a different button is pressed. The functionality is up to you.

The second way to get the widget is a two-step process where we need to extract the ID from the event using its **GetID()** method. Then we pass that result to our frame object's **FindWindowById()** method and we once again have the widget in question.

Now you know the "secret" of binding multiple widgets to the same event handler. All you really need to know is that if you write two functions that do the same thing or you copy and paste a function and only make minimal changes, then you should refactor your code to prevent issues down the road.

Recipe 8-2. How to Fire Multiple Event Handlers

Problem

There are a few occasions where you will want to fire a series of event handlers. While this is not something that you'll use in most of your programs, it's a nice feature to have. Fortunately, wxPython makes it very easy to accomplish.

Solution

Firing multiple event handlers is actually quite trivial. As usual, it is useful to take a look at a simple example that demonstrates how to do this.

```python
import wx


class MyPanel(wx.Panel):
    """"""

    def __init__(self, parent):
        """Constructor"""
        wx.Panel.__init__(self, parent)
        btn = wx.Button(self, label="Press Me")
```

```
        btn.Bind(wx.EVT_BUTTON, self.HandlerOne)
        btn.Bind(wx.EVT_BUTTON, self.HandlerTwo)

    def HandlerOne(self, event):
        """"""
        print("handler one fired!")
        event.Skip()

    def HandlerTwo(self, event):
        """"""
        print("handler two fired!")
        event.Skip()

class MyFrame(wx.Frame):
    """"""

    def __init__(self):
        """Constructor"""
        wx.Frame.__init__(self, None, title="Test")
        panel = MyPanel(self)
        self.Show()

if __name__ == "__main__":
    app = wx.App(False)
    frame = MyFrame()
    app.MainLoop()
```

How It Works

As you can see, all you had to do was call the widget's **Bind()** method twice and pass it the same event but different handlers. The next key piece is that you have to use **event. Skip()**. **Skip** will cause wxPython to look for other handlers that may need to handle the event. Events travel up the hierarchy to the parents until either they're handled or nothing happens. The book, **wxPython in Action** by Robin Dunn, explains this concept really well.

You can also bind a widget to different events at the same time. This is more common with something like a wx.TextCtrl or a Grid widget where you might need to bind to focus and text events.

While this recipe is on the short side, it demonstrates one of the many powerful features of the wxPython GUI graphical user interface) toolkit. That feature is the ability to bind a widget to multiple event handlers. You might find this useful if you need to save some information to a database while also calling a long-running process, for example. Take a few moments and I'm sure you can think of your own scenarios where this concept might prove useful.

Recipe 8-3. Get the Event Name Instead of an Integer
Problem

A few years ago I saw a post on the StackOverflow web site that I thought was interesting. It asked how to get the event name from the event object, such as EVT_BUTTON, rather than the event's ID number. So I did some investigation into the subject and there is nothing built in to wxPython that does this task. Robin Dunn, creator of wxPython, recommended that I create a dictionary of the events and their IDs to accomplish this feat. So in this tutorial, we'll take a look at how to go about that.

Solution

I tried to figure this out myself, but then I decided to make sure that someone else hadn't already done it. After a brief Google search, I found a forum thread where Robin Dunn described how to do it. Following is the basic gist:

```
import wx

eventDict = {}
for name in dir(wx):
    if name.startswith('EVT_'):
        evt = getattr(wx, name)
        if isinstance(evt, wx.PyEventBinder):
            eventDict[evt.typeId] = name
```

That only gets the general events though. There are special events in some of the sublibraries in wx, such as in **wx.grid**. You will have to account for that sort of thing.

While I haven't come up with a general solution yet I can show you how to add those grid events. Let's take a look!

```python
import wx
import wx.grid

class MyForm(wx.Frame):

    def __init__(self):
        wx.Frame.__init__(self, None, title="Tutorial")

        self.eventDict = {}
        evt_names = [x for x in dir(wx) if x.startswith("EVT_")]
        for name in evt_names:
            evt = getattr(wx, name)
            if isinstance(evt, wx.PyEventBinder):
                self.eventDict[evt.typeId] = name

        grid_evt_names = [x for x in dir(wx.grid) if x.startswith("EVT_")]
        for name in grid_evt_names:
            evt = getattr(wx.grid, name)
            if isinstance(evt, wx.PyEventBinder):
                self.eventDict[evt.typeId] = name

        panel = wx.Panel(self, wx.ID_ANY)
        btn = wx.Button(panel, wx.ID_ANY, "Get POS")

        btn.Bind(wx.EVT_BUTTON, self.onEvent)
        panel.Bind(wx.EVT_LEFT_DCLICK, self.onEvent)
        panel.Bind(wx.EVT_RIGHT_DOWN, self.onEvent)

    def onEvent(self, event):
        """

        Print out what event was fired
        """

        evt_id = event.GetEventType()
        print(self.eventDict[evt_id])
```

```
if __name__ == "__main__":
    app = wx.App(redirect=True)
    frame = MyForm().Show()
    app.MainLoop()
```

How It Works

As you can see, we changed the loop slightly. We took the loop in the first example and combined it with the first IF statement to create a list comprehension. This returns a list of event name strings. Then we loop over that using the other conditionals to add to the dictionary. We do it twice, once for the regular events and then again for the wx.grid events. Then we bind a few events to test our event dictionary. If you run this program, you will see that if you execute any of the bound events, it will print those event names to stdout. Since we set the **wx.App** object to redirect stdout, wxPython will open a special window to display what gets printed out as in Figure 8-2.

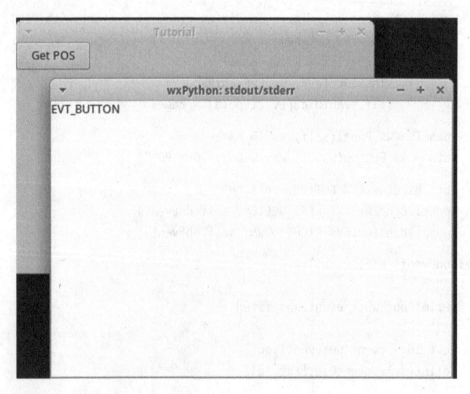

Figure 8-2. *Getting the event name*

Now you know how to get the event name of the event instead of just the integer. This can be helpful when debugging as sometimes you want to bind multiple events to one handler and you need to check and see which event was fired.

Recipe 8-4. Catching Key and Char Events
Problem

In this recipe, I'll detail how to catch specific key presses and why this can be useful. There really isn't much to catching key presses, but it can be a little confusing when one widget behaves slightly differently from another. The really complicated stuff comes in when you need to capture the character events (i.e., wx.EVT_CHAR).

Note   The examples in this recipe do not work on Mac OSX El Capitan.

First I'll cover the key events, **wx.EVT_KEY_DOWN** and **wx.EVT_KEY_UP** and then I'll go over the intricacies of **wx.EVT_CHAR**.

Solution

Catching key events is very easy to do in wxPython. All you need to do is look up what key code you want to catch in wxPython's documentation or catch all keys and note the key codes of the buttons as you press them. Let's take a look.

```python
import wx

class MyForm(wx.Frame):

    def __init__(self):
        wx.Frame.__init__(self, None, title="Key Press Tutorial")

        panel = wx.Panel(self, wx.ID_ANY)
        btn = wx.Button(panel, label="OK")

        btn.Bind(wx.EVT_KEY_DOWN, self.onKeyPress)

    def onKeyPress(self, event):
```

```
        keycode = event.GetKeyCode()
        print(keycode)
        if keycode == wx.WXK_SPACE:
            print("you pressed the spacebar!")
        event.Skip()
if __name__ == "__main__":
    app = wx.App(True)
    frame = MyForm()
    frame.Show()
    app.MainLoop()
```

How It Works

You will notice that the only widgets of consequence in this piece of code are a panel and a button.

I bind the button to the event, **EVT_KEY_DOWN,** and in the handler I check if the user has pressed the spacebar. The event only fires if the button has focus. You'll notice that I also call **event.Skip** at the end. If you don't call Skip, then the key will get "eaten" and there won't be a corresponding char event. This won't matter on a button, but you might care in a text control as char events are the proper way of catching upper and lower case, accents, umlauts, and the like.

I've used a similar method to catch arrow key presses in a spreadsheet-type application of mine. I wanted to be able to detect these keys so that if I was editing a cell, an arrow key press would make the selection change to a different cell. That is not the default behavior. In a grid, each cell has its own editor and pressing the arrow keys just moves the cursor around within the cell.

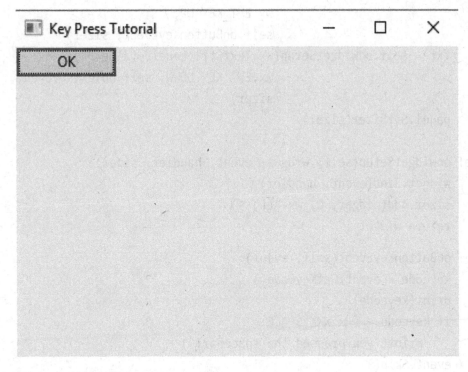

Figure 8-3. *Catching key presses*

When you run the previous code and press the spacebar, you will see something similar to the following screenshot (Figure 8-3):

Just for fun, I created a similar example to the one above where I bound to the key-up and the key-down events, but with two different widgets. Check it out in the following code:

```
import wx

class MyForm(wx.Frame):

    def __init__(self):
        wx.Frame.__init__(self, None, title="Key Press Tutorial 2")

        panel = wx.Panel(self, wx.ID_ANY)
        sizer = wx.BoxSizer(wx.VERTICAL)

        btn = self.onWidgetSetup(wx.Button(panel, label="OK"),
```

```
                            wx.EVT_KEY_UP,
                            self.onButtonKeyEvent, sizer)
        txt = self.onWidgetSetup(wx.TextCtrl(panel, value=""),
                            wx.EVT_KEY_DOWN, self.onTextKeyEvent,
                            sizer)

        panel.SetSizer(sizer)

    def onWidgetSetup(self, widget, event, handler, sizer):
        widget.Bind(event, handler)
        sizer.Add(widget, 0, wx.ALL, 5)
        return widget

    def onButtonKeyEvent(self, event):
        keycode = event.GetKeyCode()
        print(keycode)
        if keycode == wx.WXK_SPACE:
            print("you pressed the spacebar!")
        event.Skip()

    def onTextKeyEvent(self, event):
        keycode = event.GetKeyCode()
        print(keycode)
        if keycode == wx.WXK_DELETE:
            print("you pressed the delete key!")
        event.Skip()

if __name__ == "__main__":
    app = wx.App(True)
    frame = MyForm()
    frame.Show()
    app.MainLoop()
```

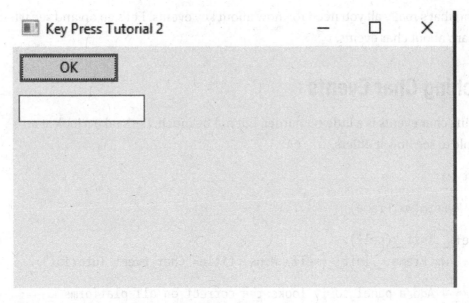

Figure 8-4. *Catching additional key presses*

If you run the previous code, try clicking the button and then pressing the spacebar. Then change the focus to the text control and hit your delete key. If you do that, you should see something like the following screenshot (Figure 8-4):

Try pressing other keys and you will see the key codes printed out for each key.

Admittedly, this code is mostly for illustration. The main thing to know is that you really don't use EVT_KEY_UP unless you need to keep track of multi-key combinations, like CTRL+K+Y or something (on a semirelated note, see the **wx.AcceleratorTable**). While I'm not doing this in my example, it is important to note that if you are checking for the CTRL key, then it's best to use **event.CmdDown()** rather than **event. ControlDown**—the reason being that **CmdDown** is the equivalent of **ControlDown** on Windows and Linux, but on a Mac it simulates the Command key. Thus, CmdDown is the best cross-platform way of checking if the CTRL key has been pressed.

And that's really all you need to know about key events. Let's go on and see what we can learn about char events.

Catching Char Events

Catching char events is a little bit harder, but not by much. Let's take a look at an example to see how it differs.

```python
import wx

class MyForm(wx.Frame):

    def __init__(self):
        wx.Frame.__init__(self, None, title="Char Event Tutorial")

        # Add a panel so it looks the correct on all platforms
        panel = wx.Panel(self, wx.ID_ANY)
        btn = wx.TextCtrl(panel, value="")

        btn.Bind(wx.EVT_CHAR, self.onCharEvent)

    def onCharEvent(self, event):
        keycode = event.GetKeyCode()
        controlDown = event.CmdDown()
        altDown = event.AltDown()
        shiftDown = event.ShiftDown()

        print(keycode)
        if keycode == wx.WXK_SPACE:
            print("you pressed the spacebar!")
        elif controlDown and altDown:
            print(keycode)
        event.Skip()

if __name__ == "__main__":
    app = wx.App(True)
    frame = MyForm()
    frame.Show()
    app.MainLoop()
```

I think the main thing that is different is that you want to check for accents or international characters. Thus, you'll have complex conditionals that check if certain keys are pressed and in what order. Robin Dunn (creator of wxPython) said that **wxSTC** checks for both key and char events. If you plan on supporting users outside the United States, you'll probably want to learn how this all works.

Robin Dunn went on to say that *"if you want to get the key events in order to handle 'commands' within the application, then using the raw values in a EVT_KEY_DOWN handler is appropriate. However if the intent is to handle the entry of 'text' then the application should use the cooked values in an EVT_CHAR event handler in order to get the proper handling for non US keyboards and input method editors.* (Note: key up and key down events are considered 'raw' whereas char events have been 'cooked' for you.) As Robin Dunn explained it to me, *on non-US keyboards then part of cooking the key events into char events is mapping the physical keys to the national keyboard map, to produce characters with accents, umlauts, and such."*

When you're actually playing around with this demo, you will see that it prints out the key codes as you press them. If you want to see special key combination codes, try pressing CTRL or SHIFT plus another key. You should be able to catch ALT here as well, but I noticed that this does not work on my Windows 7 machine or my Macbook.

At this point you should be capable of writing your own desktop application that can capture key and char events. You might also want to use Google to look up wxPython's **AcceleratorTable**. This class allows the developer to capture key combinations that the user strikes while running your program. Check it out when you get a chance.

Recipe 8-5. Learning About Focus Events

Problem

There are really only two focus events that I've ever seen used: wx.EVT_SET_FOCUS and wx.EVT_KILL_FOCUS. The event EVT_SET_FOCUS is fired when a widget receives focus, such as when you click a blank panel or put your cursor inside a TextCtrl widget. When you tab or click a widget that has focus, then the EVT_KILL_FOCUS is fired.

One of the few "gotchas" that I've seen mentioned on the wxPython mailing list is that the wx.Panel only accepts focus when it does not have a child widget that can accept focus. The best way to explain this is with a series of examples.

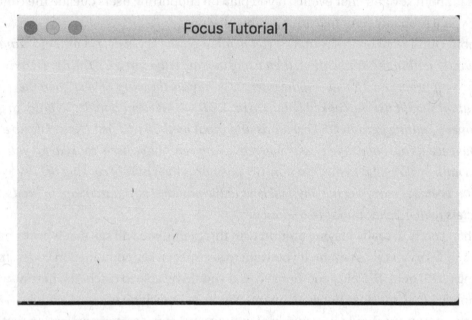

Figure 8-5. *Getting the panel to focus*

Solution

Let's try writing some code that will attempt to catch the focus event on a wx.Panel object.

```
import wx

class MyForm(wx.Frame):

    def __init__(self):
        wx.Frame.__init__(self, None, title="Focus Tutorial 1")

        panel = wx.Panel(self)
        panel.Bind(wx.EVT_SET_FOCUS, self.onFocus)

    def onFocus(self, event):
        print("panel received focus!")

# Run the program
```

```
if __name__ == "__main__":
    app = wx.App(False)
    frame = MyForm().Show()
    app.MainLoop()
```

How It Works

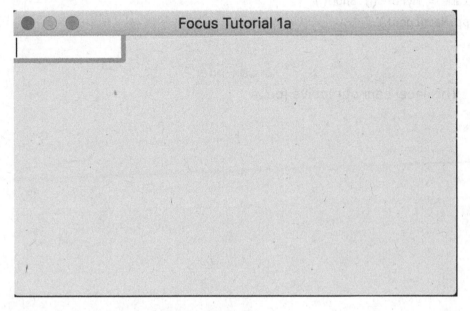

Figure 8-6. *Getting the text control to focus*

Now this code will display a blank panel with nothing on it. You'll notice that stdout immediately gets *panel received focus!* printed to it if you run this on Windows or Mac. You will see the same message on Linux if you happen to click the Panel. Now if we add a TextCtrl or a Button, they will receive focus and the OnFocus event handler will not get fired. Try running the code that follows to see this in action:

```
import wx

class MyForm(wx.Frame):

    def __init__(self):
        wx.Frame.__init__(self, None, title="Focus Tutorial 1a")

        panel = wx.Panel(self)
```

```
        panel.Bind(wx.EVT_SET_FOCUS, self.onFocus)
        txt = wx.TextCtrl(panel, wx.ID_ANY, "")

    def onFocus(self, event):
        print("panel received focus!")

if __name__ == "__main__":
    app = wx.App(False)
    frame = MyForm().Show()
    app.MainLoop()
```

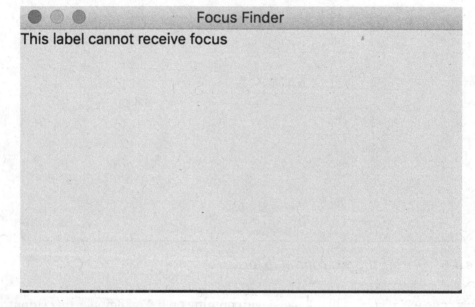

Figure 8-7. *Getting the text control to focus*

Just for fun, try putting a StaticText control in there instead of a TextCtrl. Which widget do you expect will get the focus? Depending on which platform you run the following code on, you may end up finding that nothing is in focus. This happened to me on Linux. On Windows 7, the panel was in focus. Back when I had Windows XP, it was the Frame that got the focus. Anyway, let's take a look at the code.

```python
import wx

class MyForm(wx.Frame):

    def __init__(self):
        wx.Frame.__init__(self, None, title="Focus Finder")

        panel = wx.Panel(self, wx.ID_ANY)
        panel.Bind(wx.EVT_SET_FOCUS, self.onFocus)
        txt = wx.StaticText(
            panel, label="This label cannot receive focus")

        self.timer = wx.Timer(self)
        self.Bind(wx.EVT_TIMER, self.onTimer)
        self.timer.Start(1000)

    def onFocus(self, event):
        print("panel received focus!")

    def onTimer(self, evt):
        print('Focused window:', wx.Window.FindFocus())

if __name__ == "__main__":
    app = wx.App(False)
    frame = MyForm().Show()
    app.MainLoop()
```

The main takeaway here is that **wx.Window.FindFocus()** is a very useful function and quite helpful when trying to figure out why the focus isn't where you expect it to be. Of course, some people would rather know when the mouse enters the frame and that information can be had with **EVT_ENTER_WINDOW** (which I won't be covering here).

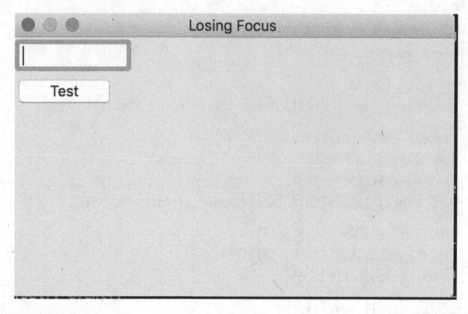

Figure 8-8. *Losing focus*

Losing Focus

Now let's take a quick look at **wx.EVT_KILL_FOCUS**. I've created a simple example with just two controls. Try to guess what will happen if you tab between them.

```
import wx

class MyForm(wx.Frame):

    def __init__(self):
        wx.Frame.__init__(self, None, title="Losing Focus")

        # Add a panel so it looks the correct on all platforms
        panel = wx.Panel(self, wx.ID_ANY)

        txt = wx.TextCtrl(panel, value="")
        txt.Bind(wx.EVT_SET_FOCUS, self.onFocus)
        txt.Bind(wx.EVT_KILL_FOCUS, self.onKillFocus)
        btn = wx.Button(panel, wx.ID_ANY, "Test")
```

```python
        sizer = wx.BoxSizer(wx.VERTICAL)
        sizer.Add(txt, 0, wx.ALL, 5)
        sizer.Add(btn, 0, wx.ALL, 5)
        panel.SetSizer(sizer)

    def onFocus(self, event):
        print("widget received focus!")

    def onKillFocus(self, event):
        print("widget lost focus!")

if __name__ == "__main__":
    app = wx.App(False)
    frame = MyForm().Show()
    app.MainLoop()
```

As you've probably surmised, as you tab between them, the **TextCtrl** is either firing a kill focus or a set focus event. How do you know which widget is firing those events? Look at my Bind methods. Only the text control is bound to focus events. As an exercise, try binding the button to those handlers too and print out which widget is firing what.

The last focus event I'm going to mention **is wx.EVT_CHILD_FOCUS**, something I've never used. This event is used to determine when a child widget has received focus and to figure out which child it is. According to Robin Dunn, **wx.lib.scrolledpanel** uses this event. One of my readers told me of about a handy use-case for wx.EVT_CHILD_FOCUS: "you can use it on the frame to simply clear the Statusbar when you click any other child widget. This way you don't have an old 'Error' message or some such text in the statusbar when you click a different child widget."

At this point, you should know enough about how focusing works in wxPython that you can use it yourself. You learned how to acquire focus in various circumstances. We also created an application that can tell when it is in focus and when it is not. Finally we learned about losing focus, which is also quite handy in certain circumstances.

CHAPTER 9

Drag and Drop

Recipe 9-1. How to Use Drag and Drop

Problem

Most computer users of this day and age use drag and drop (DnD) instinctively. You probably used it to transfer some files from one folder to another this week! The wxPython GUI (graphical user interface) toolkit provides DnD functionality baked in. In this recipe, we'll see just how easy it is to implement!

Solution

wxPython provides several different kinds of drag and drop. You can have one of the following types:

- wx.FileDropTarget

- wx.TextDropTarget

- wx.PyDropTarget

The first two are pretty self-explanatory. The last one, **wx.PyDropTarget**, is just a loose wrapper around wx.DropTarget itself. It adds a couple of extra convenience methods that the plain wx.DropTarget doesn't have. We'll start with a wx.FileDropTarget example.

© Mike Driscoll 2018
M. Driscoll, *wxPython Recipes*, https://doi.org/10.1007/978-1-4842-3237-8_9

Creating a FileDropTarget

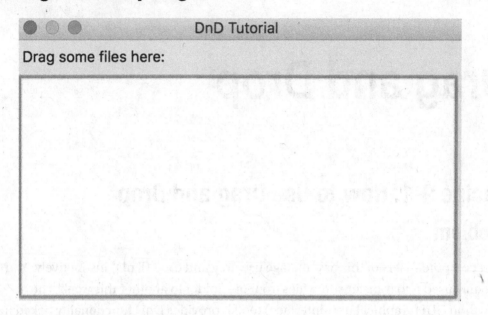

Figure 9-1. *A FileDropTarget example*

The wxPython toolkit makes the creation of a drop target pretty simple. You do have to override a method to make it work right, but other than that, it's pretty straightforward. Let's take a moment to look over this example code and then I'll spend some time explaining it.

```python
import wx

class MyFileDropTarget(wx.FileDropTarget):
    """"""

    def __init__(self, window):
        """Constructor"""
        wx.FileDropTarget.__init__(self)
        self.window = window

    def OnDropFiles(self, x, y, filenames):
        """
        When files are dropped, write where they were dropped and then
        the file paths themselves
        """
```

```python
        self.window.SetInsertionPointEnd()
        self.window.updateText("\n%d file(s) dropped at %d,%d:\n" %
                               (len(filenames), x, y))
        for filepath in filenames:
            self.window.updateText(filepath + '\n')

        return True

class DnDPanel(wx.Panel):
    """"""

    def __init__(self, parent):
        """Constructor"""
        wx.Panel.__init__(self, parent=parent)

        file_drop_target = MyFileDropTarget(self)
        lbl = wx.StaticText(self, label="Drag some files here:")
        self.fileTextCtrl = wx.TextCtrl(self,
            style=wx.TE_MULTILINE|wx.HSCROLL|wx.TE_READONLY)
        self.fileTextCtrl.SetDropTarget(file_drop_target)

        sizer = wx.BoxSizer(wx.VERTICAL)
        sizer.Add(lbl, 0, wx.ALL, 5)
        sizer.Add(self.fileTextCtrl, 1, wx.EXPAND|wx.ALL, 5)
        self.SetSizer(sizer)

    def SetInsertionPointEnd(self):
        """
        Put insertion point at end of text control to prevent overwriting
        """
        self.fileTextCtrl.SetInsertionPointEnd()

    def updateText(self, text):
        """
        Write text to the text control
        """
        self.fileTextCtrl.WriteText(text)
```

```
class DnDFrame(wx.Frame):
    """"""

    def __init__(self):
        """Constructor"""
        wx.Frame.__init__(self, parent=None, title="DnD Tutorial")
        panel = DnDPanel(self)
        self.Show()

if __name__ == "__main__":
    app = wx.App(False)
    frame = DnDFrame()
    app.MainLoop()
```

How It Works

That wasn't too bad, was it? The first thing to do is to subclass **wx.FileDropTarget**, which we do with our **MyFileDropTarget** class. Inside that we have one overridden method, **OnDropFiles**. It accepts the x/y position of the mouse and the file paths that are dropped, and then it writes those out to the text control. To hook up the drop target to the text control, you'll want to look in the **DnDPanel** class where we call the text control's **SetDropTarget** method and set it to an instance of our drop target class. We have two more methods in our panel class that the drop target class calls to update the text control: **SetInsertionPointEnd** and **updateText**. Note that since we are passing the panel object as the drop target, we can call these methods whatever we want to. If the **TextCtrl** had been the drop target, we'd have to do it differently, which we will see in our next example!

Creating a TextDropTarget

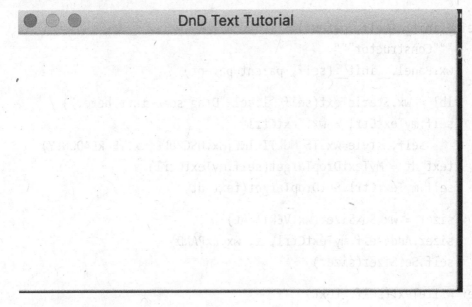

Figure 9-2. A TextDropTarget example

The **wx.TextDropTarget** is used when you want to be able to DnD some selected text into a text control. Probably one of the most common examples is dragging a URL on a web page up to the address bar or some text up into the search box in Firefox. Let's spend some time learning how to create one of these kinds of drop targets in wxPython!

```python
import wx

class MyTextDropTarget(wx.TextDropTarget):

    def __init__(self, textctrl):
        wx.TextDropTarget.__init__(self)
        self.textctrl = textctrl

    def OnDropText(self, x, y, text):
        self.textctrl.WriteText("(%d, %d)\n%s\n" % (x, y, text))
        return True

    def OnDragOver(self, x, y, d):
        return wx.DragCopy
```

```python
class DnDPanel(wx.Panel):
    """"""

    def __init__(self, parent):
        """Constructor"""
        wx.Panel.__init__(self, parent=parent)

        lbl = wx.StaticText(self, label="Drag some text here:")
        self.myTextCtrl = wx.TextCtrl(
            self, style=wx.TE_MULTILINE|wx.HSCROLL|wx.TE_READONLY)
        text_dt = MyTextDropTarget(self.myTextCtrl)
        self.myTextCtrl.SetDropTarget(text_dt)

        sizer = wx.BoxSizer(wx.VERTICAL)
        sizer.Add(self.myTextCtrl, 1, wx.EXPAND)
        self.SetSizer(sizer)

    def WriteText(self, text):
        self.text.WriteText(text)

class DnDFrame(wx.Frame):
    """"""

    def __init__(self):
        """Constructor"""
        wx.Frame.__init__(
            self, parent=None, title="DnD Text Tutorial")
        panel = DnDPanel(self)
        self.Show()

if __name__ == "__main__":
    app = wx.App(False)
    frame = DnDFrame()
    app.MainLoop()
```

Once again we have to subclass our drop target class. In this case, I call it
MyTextDropTarget. In that class, we have to override **OnDropText** and **OnDragOver**.
I was unable to find satisfactory documentation on the latter, but I'm guessing it just
returns a copy of the data dragged. The **OnDropText** method writes text out to the text

control. Note that since we've bound the drop target directly to the text control (see the panel class) we *have* to use a method named **WriteText** to update the text control. If you change it, you'll receive an error message.

Custom DnD with PyDropTarget

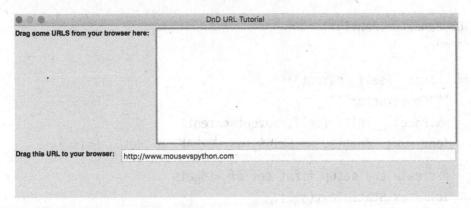

Figure 9-3. *A PyDropTarget Example*

In case you haven't guessed yet, these examples have been slightly modified versions of the DnD demos from the official wxPython demo. We'll be using some code based on their URLDragAnd-Drop demo to explain PyDropTarget. The fun bit about this demo is that you not only get to create a widget that can accept dragged text but you also can drag some text from another widget back to your browser! Let's take a look.

```
import wx

class MyURLDropTarget(wx.PyDropTarget):

    def __init__(self, window):
        wx.PyDropTarget.__init__(self)
        self.window = window

        self.data = wx.URLDataObject();
        self.SetDataObject(self.data)

    def OnDragOver(self, x, y, d):
        return wx.DragLink

    def OnData(self, x, y, d):
```

```python
        if not self.GetData():
            return wx.DragNone

        url = self.data.GetURL()
        self.window.AppendText(url + "\n")

        return d

class DnDPanel(wx.Panel):
    """"""

    def __init__(self, parent):
        """Constructor"""
        wx.Panel.__init__(self, parent=parent)
        font = wx.Font(12, wx.SWISS, wx.NORMAL, wx.BOLD, False)

        # create and setup first set of widgets
        lbl = wx.StaticText(self,
            label="Drag some URLS from your browser here:")
        lbl.SetFont(font)
        self.dropText = wx.TextCtrl(
            self, size=(200,200),
            style=wx.TE_MULTILINE|wx.HSCROLL|wx.TE_READONLY)
        dt = MyURLDropTarget(self.dropText)
        self.dropText.SetDropTarget(dt)
        firstSizer = self.addWidgetsToSizer([lbl, self.dropText])

        # create and setup second set of widgets
        lbl = wx.StaticText(self, label="Drag this URL to your browser:")
        lbl.SetFont(font)
        self.draggableURLText = wx.TextCtrl(self,
            value="http://www.mousevspython.com")
        self.draggableURLText.Bind(wx.EVT_MOTION, self.OnStartDrag)
        secondSizer = self.addWidgetsToSizer([lbl, self.draggableURLText])

        # Add sizers to main sizer
        mainSizer = wx.BoxSizer(wx.VERTICAL)
        mainSizer.Add(firstSizer, 0, wx.EXPAND)
        mainSizer.Add(secondSizer, 0, wx.EXPAND)
        self.SetSizer(mainSizer)
```

```python
    def addWidgetsToSizer(self, widgets):
        """
        Returns a sizer full of widgets
        """
        sizer = wx.BoxSizer(wx.HORIZONTAL)
        for widget in widgets:
            if isinstance(widget, wx.TextCtrl):
                sizer.Add(widget, 1, wx.EXPAND|wx.ALL, 5)
            else:
                sizer.Add(widget, 0, wx.ALL, 5)
        return sizer

    def OnStartDrag(self, evt):
        """"""
        if evt.Dragging():
            url = self.draggableURLText.GetValue()
            data = wx.URLDataObject()
            data.SetURL(url)

            dropSource = wx.DropSource(self.draggableURLText)
            dropSource.SetData(data)
            result = dropSource.DoDragDrop()

class DnDFrame(wx.Frame):
    """"""

    def __init__(self):
        """Constructor"""
        wx.Frame.__init__(self, parent=None,
                          title="DnD URL Tutorial", size=(800,600))
        panel = DnDPanel(self)
        self.Show()

if __name__ == "__main__":
    app = wx.App(False)
    frame = DnDFrame()
    app.MainLoop()
```

The first class is our drop target class. Here we create a **wx.URLDataObject** that stores our URL information. Then in the **OnData** method we extract the URL and append it to the bound text control. In our panel class, we hook up the drop target in the same way that we did in the other two examples, so we'll skip that and go on to the new stuff. The second text control is where we need to pay attention. Here we bind the text control to mouse movement via **EVT_MOTION**. In the mouse movement event handler (**OnStartDrag**), we check to make sure that the user is dragging. If so, then we grab the value from the text box and add it to a newly created **URLDataObject**. Next we create an instance of a **DropSource** and pass it our second text control since it *is* the source. We set the source's data to the **URLDataObject**. Finally we call **DoDragDrop** on our drop source (the text control) which will respond by moving, copying, canceling, or failing. If you dragged the URL to your browser's address bar, it will copy. Otherwise it probably won't work. Now let's take what we've learned and create something original!

Note   Some web browsers may not work with this code. For example, I was able to make it work fine with Google Chrome on Linux but not with Mozilla Firefox.

Creating a Custom Drag-and-Drop App

Name	Date created	Date modified	Size
cat_o.jpg	08/16/2016 08:35 PM	08/16/2016 08:34 PM	229.97 KB
config.ini	08/22/2016 08:35 PM	08/22/2016 08:35 PM	369
darkMode.py	08/22/2016 08:31 PM	08/22/2016 08:31 PM	1.94 KB
darkMode.pyc	08/22/2016 08:31 PM	08/22/2016 08:31 PM	2.11 KB
generic.py	08/22/2016 08:45 PM	08/22/2016 08:45 PM	2.80 KB
get_titles.py	08/17/2016 08:44 PM	08/17/2016 08:44 PM	245

OLV DnD Tutorial

Figure 9-4. A custom drag-and-drop application

I thought it would be fun to take the file drop target demo and make it into something with an ObjectListView widget (a ListCtrl wrapper) that can tell us some information about the files we're dropping into it. We'll be showing the following information: file name, creation date, modified date, and file size. Here's the code.

```python
import os
import stat
import time
import wx

from ObjectListView import ObjectListView, ColumnDefn

class MyFileDropTarget(wx.FileDropTarget):
    """"""

    def __init__(self, window):
        """Constructor"""
        wx.FileDropTarget.__init__(self)
        self.window = window

    def OnDropFiles(self, x, y, filenames):
        """
        When files are dropped, update the display
        """
        self.window.updateDisplay(filenames)
                return True

class FileInfo(object):
    """"""

    def __init__(self, path, date_created, date_modified, size):
        """Constructor"""
        self.name = os.path.basename(path)
        self.path = path
        self.date_created = date_created
        self.date_modified = date_modified
        self.size = size

class MainPanel(wx.Panel):
    """"""

    def __init__(self, parent):
        """Constructor"""
        wx.Panel.__init__(self, parent=parent)
        self.file_list = []
```

```python
        file_drop_target = MyFileDropTarget(self)
        self.olv = ObjectListView(
            self, style=wx.LC_REPORT|wx.SUNKEN_BORDER)
        self.olv.SetDropTarget(file_drop_target)
        self.setFiles()

        sizer = wx.BoxSizer(wx.VERTICAL)
        sizer.Add(self.olv, 1, wx.EXPAND)
        self.SetSizer(sizer)

    def updateDisplay(self, file_list):
        """"""

        for path in file_list:
            file_stats = os.stat(path)
            creation_time = time.strftime(
                "%m/%d/%Y %I:%M %p",
                time.localtime(file_stats[stat.ST_CTIME]))
            modified_time = time.strftime(
                "%m/%d/%Y %I:%M %p",
                time.localtime(file_stats[stat.ST_MTIME]))
            file_size = file_stats[stat.ST_SIZE]
            if file_size > 1024:
                file_size = file_size / 1024.0
                file_size = "%.2f KB" % file_size

            self.file_list.append(FileInfo(path,
                                           creation_time,
                                           modified_time,
                                           file_size))

        self.olv.SetObjects(self.file_list)

    def setFiles(self):
        """"""

        self.olv.SetColumns([
            ColumnDefn("Name", "left", 220, "name"),
            ColumnDefn("Date created", "left", 150, "date_created"),
```

```
            ColumnDefn("Date modified", "left", 150, "date_modified"),
            ColumnDefn("Size", "left", 100, "size")
            ])
        self.olv.SetObjects(self.file_list)

class MainFrame(wx.Frame):
    """"""

    def __init__(self):
        """Constructor"""
        wx.Frame.__init__(self, None,
                          title="OLV DnD Tutorial", size=(800,600))
        panel = MainPanel(self)
        self.Show()

def main():
    """"""

    app = wx.App(False)
    frame = MainFrame()
    app.MainLoop()

if __name__ == "__main__":
    main()
```

Most of this stuff you've seen before. We have our **FileDropTarget** subclass, we connect the panel to it, and then we connect the ObjectListView widget to the drop target instance. We also have a generic class for holding our file-related data. If you run this program and drop folders into it, you won't receive the correct file size. You would probably need to walk the folder and add up the sizes of the files therein to get that to work. Feel free to fix that on your own. Anyway, the meat of the program is in the updateDisplay method. Here we grab the file's vital statistics and convert them into more readable formats as most people don't understand dates that are in seconds since the epoch. Once we've massaged the data a bit, we display it. Now wasn't that pretty cool?

You should now know how to do at least three different types of DnD in wxPython. Ideally, you will use this new information responsibly and create some fresh open source applications in the near future. Good luck!

Recipe 9-2. How to Drag and Drop a File from Your App to the OS

Problem

A somewhat common use case that you will come across is the need to be able to drag and drop a file from your own custom application to the file system. In the previous recipe you saw an example of dragging files into your application. Now we'll be looking at dragging them out.

Solution

Name	Ext	Size	Modified
cat.jpg	.jpg	95082 B	2016-08-16 20:43
cat_o.jpg	.jpg	235491 B	2016-08-16 20:34
config.ini	.ini	369 B	2016-08-22 20:35
darkMode.py	.py	1985 B	2016-08-22 20:31
darkMode.pyc	.pyc	2163 B	2016-08-22 20:31
generic.py	.py	2464 B	2016-08-22 20:40
get_titles.py	.py	245 B	2016-08-17 20:44
wxcook.wpr	.wpr	537 B	2016-08-16 20:13
wxcook.wpu	.wpu	19199 B	2016-08-22 20:40

Figure 9-5. *A custom DnD application*

You will probably want to use a **wx.ListCtrl** or an **ObjectListView** widget as they would be the most common widgets to display file information with. For this example, we will use the wx.ListCtrl. Let's take a look at some code.

```
import wx
import os
import time

class MyListCtrl(wx.ListCtrl):

    def __init__(self, parent, id):
        wx.ListCtrl.__init__(self, parent, id,
                        style=wx.LC_REPORT)
```

```
files = os.listdir('.')

self.InsertColumn(0, 'Name')
self.InsertColumn(1, 'Ext')
self.InsertColumn(2, 'Size',
                  wx.LIST_FORMAT_RIGHT)
self.InsertColumn(3, 'Modified')

self.SetColumnWidth(0, 220)
self.SetColumnWidth(1, 70)
self.SetColumnWidth(2, 100)
self.SetColumnWidth(3, 420)

j = 0
for i in files:
    (name, ext) = os.path.splitext(i)

    size = os.path.getsize(i)
    sec = os.path.getmtime(i)
    self.InsertStringItem(j, "{}{}".format(name, ext))
    self.SetStringItem(j, 1, ext)
    self.SetStringItem(j, 2, str(size) + ' B')
    self.SetStringItem(
        j, 3, time.strftime('%Y-%m-%d %H:%M',
                            time.localtime(sec)))

    if os.path.isdir(i):
        self.SetItemImage(j, 1)
    elif 'py' in ext:
        self.SetItemImage(j, 2)
    elif 'jpg' in ext:
        self.SetItemImage(j, 3)
    elif 'pdf' in ext:
        self.SetItemImage(j, 4)
    else:
        self.SetItemImage(j, 0)
```

```
        if (j % 2) == 0:
            self.SetItemBackgroundColour(j, 'light blue')
        j = j + 1

class DnDFrame(wx.Frame):

    def __init__(self):
        wx.Frame.__init__(self, None, title='DnD Files')
        panel = wx.Panel(self)

        p1 = MyListCtrl(panel, -1)
        p1.Bind(wx.EVT_LIST_BEGIN_DRAG, self.onDrag)
        sizer = wx.BoxSizer()
        sizer.Add(p1, 1, wx.EXPAND)
        panel.SetSizer(sizer)

        self.Center()
        self.Show(True)

    def onDrag(self, event):
        """"""
        data = wx.FileDataObject()
        obj = event.GetEventObject()
        id = event.GetIndex()
        filename = obj.GetItem(id).GetText()
        dirname = os.path.dirname(os.path.abspath(
            os.listdir(".")[0]))
        fullpath = os.path.join(dirname, filename)

        data.AddFile(fullpath)

        dropSource = wx.DropSource(obj)
        dropSource.SetData(data)
        result = dropSource.DoDragDrop()
        print(fullpath)

if __name__ == '__main__':
    app = wx.App(False)
    frame = DnDFrame()
    app.MainLoop()
```

How It Works

There are a couple of important points here. First, you need to bind to **EVT_LIST_ BEGIN_DRAG** to catch the appropriate event. Then, in your handler, you need to create a **wx.FileDataObject** object and use its **AddFile** method to append a full path to its internal file list. According to the wxPython documentation, **AddFile** is Windows-only; however, since Robin Dunn (creator of wxPython) recommends this method, I went with it. I will note that it also worked for me on Xubuntu 14.04. Anyway, we also need to define the **DropSource** and call its **DoDragDrop** method and you're done.

At this point you should have an idea of how you might make your own application be able to drag a file from it to your Desktop. It's really slick and I think it's a really neat little addition to your application.

CHAPTER 10

Working with Frames

Recipe 10-1. Using wx.Frame Styles

Problem

The wxPython Frame widget is used in almost all wxPython applications. It has the Minimize, Maximize, and Close buttons on it as well as the caption along the top that identifies the application. The **wx.Frame** class allows you to modify its styles in such a way that you can remove or disable various buttons and features. In this chapter, we will look at some of the ways that you can change the behavior of the wx.Frame widget. Specifically, I will cover the following:

- Different ways to create a default frame

- How to create a frame without a caption (i.e., no title bar)

- How to create a frame with a disabled Close button

- How to create a frame without a Maximize or Minimize button

- How to create a frame that cannot be resized

- How to create a frame without the system menu

- How to make your frame stay on top of other windows

© Mike Driscoll 2018
M. Driscoll, *wxPython Recipes*, https://doi.org/10.1007/978-1-4842-3237-8_10

Solution(s)

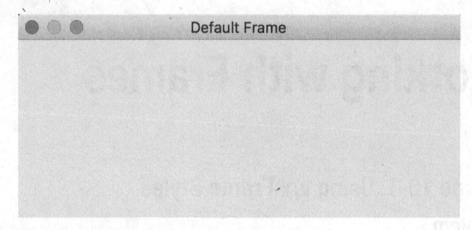

Figure 10-1.   *The default frame style*

It's always a good idea to look at how the default style works and then modify that to see what happens. So let's start with the frame's default style: wx.DEFAULT_FRAME_STYLE. You can create a frame that uses **wx.DEFAULT_FRAME_STYLE** (or its equivalent) in three different ways. The first and easiest is to just do something like the following:

```
import wx

class DefaultFrame(wx.Frame):
    """
    The default frame
    """

    def __init__(self):
        """Constructor"""
        wx.Frame.__init__(self, None, title="Default Frame")
        panel = wx.Panel(self)
        self.Show()

if __name__ == "__main__":
    app = wx.App(False)
    frame = DefaultFrame()
    app.MainLoop()
```

How It Works

This will create a normal frame with all the normal functionality any user would expect. Now let's change it slightly by passing it the wx.DEFAULT_FRAME_STYLE.

```python
import wx

class DefaultFrame(wx.Frame):
    """
    The default frame
    """

    def __init__(self):
        """Constructor"""
        wx.Frame.__init__(self, None, title="Default Frame",
                          style=wx.DEFAULT_FRAME_STYLE)
        panel = wx.Panel(self)
        self.Show()

if __name__ == "__main__":
    app = wx.App(False)
    frame = DefaultFrame()
    app.MainLoop()
```

This code does EXACTLY the same thing as the previous code. Now if you do a little research, you'll find out that wx.DEFAULT_FRAME_STYLE is the equivalent of passing the following:

```python
wx.MINIMIZE_BOX | wx.MAXIMIZE_BOX | wx.RESIZE_BORDER | wx.SYSTEM_MENU
    | wx.CAPTION | wx.CLOSE_BOX | wx.CLIP_CHILDREN
```

So let's modify our code one more time to show how that would work.

```python
import wx

class DefaultFrame(wx.Frame):
    """
    The default frame
    """
```

153

```
    def __init__(self):
        """Constructor"""
        default = (wx.MINIMIZE_BOX | wx.MAXIMIZE_BOX | wx.RESIZE_BORDER
                   | wx.SYSTEM_MENU | wx.CAPTION | wx.CLOSE_BOX
                   | wx.CLIP_CHILDREN)
        wx.Frame.__init__(self, None, title="Default Frame", style=default)
        panel = wx.Panel(self)
        self.Show()

if __name__ == "__main__":
    app = wx.App(False)
    frame = DefaultFrame()
    app.MainLoop()
```

That was easy. Now we're ready to start experimenting!

Create a Frame Without a Caption

Figure 10-2. *A frame with no caption*

Let's create a frame that doesn't have a caption (see Figure 10-2). The caption is what holds the buttons along the top of the frame along with the title of the application.

154

```python
import wx

class NoCaptionFrame(wx.Frame):
    """"""

    def __init__(self):
        """Constructor"""
        no_caption = (wx.MINIMIZE_BOX | wx.MAXIMIZE_BOX | wx.RESIZE_BORDER
                      | wx.SYSTEM_MENU | wx.CLOSE_BOX | wx.CLIP_CHILDREN)
        wx.Frame.__init__(self, None, title="No Caption", style=no_caption)
        panel = wx.Panel(self)
        self.Show()

if __name__ == "__main__":
    app = wx.App(False)
    frame = NoCaptionFrame()
    app.MainLoop()
```

When this code is run, the panel is squashed up in the upper left-hand corner of the frame. You can resize the frame and the panel will "snap" into place, but it's kind of weird looking. You might also note that you cannot close this application since there is no Close button on it. You will need to kill your Python process to close this application.

Note   This particular piece of code does not remove the caption on Mac OS X El Capitan.

Create a Frame with a Disabled Close Button

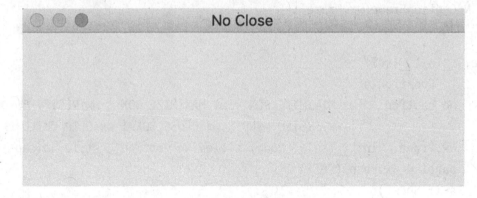

Figure 10-3. *A frame with a disabled Close button*

Some programmers think they need a frame where there's no Close button. Well you can't really remove the Close button (on Windows) and keep the other buttons at the same time, but you can disable the Close button. On Linux, the Close button actually does get removed. Here's the code.

```python
import wx

class NoCloseFrame(wx.Frame):
    """
    This frame has no close box and the close menu is disabled
    """

    def __init__(self):
        """Constructor"""
        no_close = (wx.MINIMIZE_BOX | wx.MAXIMIZE_BOX | wx.RESIZE_BORDER
                    | wx.SYSTEM_MENU | wx.CAPTION | wx.CLIP_CHILDREN)
        wx.Frame.__init__(self, None, title="No Close", style=no_close)
        panel = wx.Panel(self)
        self.Show()

if __name__ == "__main__":
    app = wx.App(False)
    frame = NoCloseFrame()
    app.MainLoop()
```

Of course, on Windows you cannot close this application either, so this is a rather annoying application. You'll probably want to add a wx.Button that can close it instead. On Linux, you can close it by double-clicking the top left corner.

Create a Frame Without Maximize/Minimize

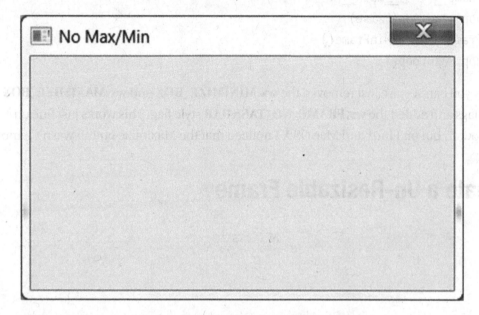

Figure 10-4. *A frame without a Maximize or Minimize button*

Sometimes you'll want to create an application that you cannot minimize or maximize. If you're going to go that far, let's make an application that also doesn't show up in the taskbar!

```
import wx

class NoMaxMinFrame(wx.Frame):
    """
    This frame does not have maximize or minimize buttons
    """

    def __init__(self):
        """Constructor"""
        no_caption = (wx.RESIZE_BORDER | wx.SYSTEM_MENU | wx.CAPTION
```

```
                    | wx.CLOSE_BOX | wx.CLIP_CHILDREN
                    | wx.FRAME_NO_TASKBAR)
        wx.Frame.__init__(self, None, title="No Max/Min", style=no_caption)
        panel = wx.Panel(self)
        self.Show()
if __name__ == "__main__":
    app = wx.App(False)
    frame = NoMaxMinFrame()
    app.MainLoop()
```

As you can see, we just removed the **wx.MINIMIZE_BOX** and **wx.MAXIMIZE_BOX** style flags and added the **wx.FRAME_NO_TASKBAR** style flag. This works just fine on Windows 7, but on Linux and Mac OS X I noticed that the Maximize button wasn't removed.

Create a Un-Resizable Frame

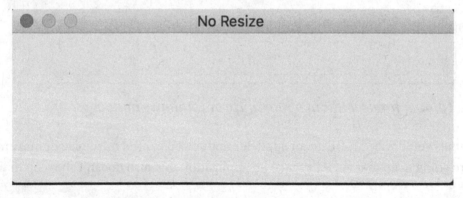

Figure 10-5. *A frame that cannot be resized*

Occasionally you'll want to create a frame that cannot be resized. You could use **SetSizeHints** or you could just set some frame style flags. We'll be doing the latter here.

```
import wx

class NoResizeFrame(wx.Frame):
    """

    This frame cannot be resized. It can only be minimized
    and closed
    """
```

```
    def __init__(self):
        """Constructor"""
        no_resize = wx.DEFAULT_FRAME_STYLE & ~ (wx.RESIZE_BORDER |
                                                wx.MAXIMIZE_BOX)
        wx.Frame.__init__(self, None, title="No Resize", style=no_resize)
        panel = wx.Panel(self)
        self.Show()

if __name__ == "__main__":
    app = wx.App(False)
    frame = NoResizeFrame()
    app.MainLoop()
```

Note that here we use bitwise operators to remove three style flags from the wx.DEFAULT_FRAME_STYLE. As you can see, this gives us a frame that we cannot resize in any way.

Create a Frame Without a System Menu

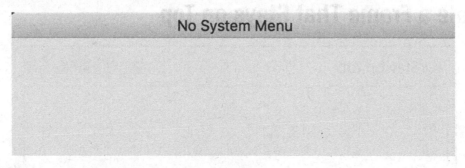

Figure 10-6. *A frame without a system menu*

This is a rather silly requirement, but I've seen people ask for it. Basically, they want to remove *all* the buttons, but leave the title. Here's how to do that.

```
import wx

class NoSystemMenuFrame(wx.Frame):
    """

    There is no system menu, which means the title bar is there, but
    no buttons and no menu when clicking the top left hand corner
```

```
    of the frame
    """

    def __init__(self):
        """Constructor"""
        no_sys_menu = wx.CAPTION
        wx.Frame.__init__(self, None, title="No System Menu",
                            style=no_sys_menu)
        panel = wx.Panel(self)
        self.Show()

if __name__ == "__main__":
    app = wx.App(False)
    frame = NoSystemMenuFrame()
    app.MainLoop()
```

You will note that all we changed was the reduction of the style flags down to just one: **wx.CAPTION**.

Create a Frame That Stays on Top

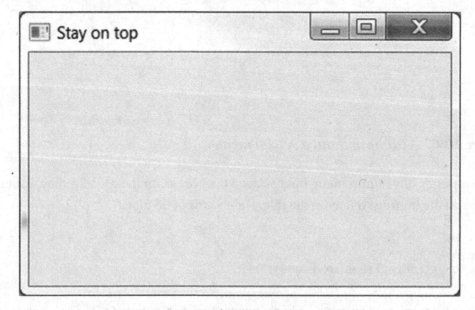

Figure 10-7. *A frame that stays on top of other applications*

A lot of programmers ask about this one. They want their application to stay on top of all the others. While there isn't a completely foolproof way to accomplish this, the little recipe that follows will work most of the time:

```python
import wx


class StayOnTopFrame(wx.Frame):
    """
    A frame that stays on top of all the others
    """

    def __init__(self):
        """Constructor"""
        on_top = wx.DEFAULT_FRAME_STYLE | wx.STAY_ON_TOP
        wx.Frame.__init__(self, None, title="Stay on top", style=on_top)
        panel = wx.Panel(self)
        self.Show()

if __name__ == "__main__":
    app = wx.App(False)
    frame = StayOnTopFrame()
    app.MainLoop()
```

Here we just use the default style flag and add on **wx.STAY_ON_TOP**.

Note   This example does not work on Mac OS X El Capitan.

At this point, you should know how to edit almost all the frame's styles. There are a couple of other style flags that are OS dependent (like wx.ICONIZE) or just aren't that useful. To learn about those flags, I recommend checking out the documentation. In the meantime, go forth and use your knowledge wisely.

Recipe 10-2. Making Your Frame Maximize or Full Screen

Problem

Sometimes you will create an application that you want to load so that it's maximized right when it opens. While we will look at how that is accomplished in this recipe, we will also take it one step further and learn how to make our application full screen. A full screen application will actually run in such a way that you cannot see anything else on that screen (i.e., not even the taskbar).

Solution

As I mentioned in the introduction, occasionally you will want your wxPython application to be maximized when you first load it. Or perhaps you'll want to have a subframe maximized. This is really easy to do in wxPython, but there is a little "gotcha" to watch out for. Let's look at the code before we discuss the gotcha though.

```python
import wx


class MyPanel(wx.Panel):
    """"""


    def __init__(self, parent):
        """"""
        wx.Panel.__init__(self, parent)

class MyFrame(wx.Frame):
    """"""


    def __init__(self):
        """"""
        wx.Frame.__init__(self, None, title="Test Maximize")
        panel = MyPanel(self)
        self.Show()
        self.Maximize(True)
```

```
if __name__ == "__main__":
    app = wx.App(False)
    frame = MyFrame()
    app.MainLoop()
```

How It Works

Here we have a pretty standard setup using two classes, one a subclass of wx.Panel and the other a subclass of wx.Frame. To get it to Maximize, we just call the frame's Maximize() method. Here's where the gotcha comes in though. If you call Maximize before you call Show(), you may see a glitch. For example, when I called Maximize first on Windows 7, the panel didn't stretch to fully cover the frame correctly (see the screenshot in Figure 10-8).

Figure 10-8. *A glitch in maximizing the frame*

As you can see, the frame is showing a little on the right-hand side and along the bottom (the darker gray). So if you run the aforementioned code, the panel will cover the frame like it's supposed to and it will look uniform. I am only aware of this problem on Windows. It works fine on Mac OS X El Capitan.

Occasionally you might need to also call your frame's **Raise()** method to make it show up on top or at least cause the taskbar to blink a bit to get the user's attention.

Making Your Application Full Screen

Personally, I haven't found many good use cases for going full screen (i.e., covering up the entire screen) except for maybe a screen saver type of application or perhaps a photo viewer. But regardless, following is the usual way to accomplish this task:

```python
import wx

class MyPanel(wx.Panel):
    """"""

    def __init__(self, parent):
        """Constructor"""
        wx.Panel.__init__(self, parent)

        self.Bind(wx.EVT_KEY_DOWN, self.onKey)

    def onKey(self, event):
        """
        Check for ESC key press and exit is ESC is pressed
        """
        key_code = event.GetKeyCode()
        if key_code == wx.WXK_ESCAPE:
            self.GetParent().Close()
        else:
            event.Skip()

class MyFrame(wx.Frame):
    """"""

    def __init__(self):
        """Constructor"""
        wx.Frame.__init__(self, None, title="Test FullScreen")
        panel = MyPanel(self)
        self.ShowFullScreen(True)

if __name__ == "__main__":
    app = wx.App(False)
    frame = MyFrame()
    app.MainLoop()
```

Note that because the application is full screen, there is no title bar with a Close button, so there's no good way to close the application. Thus I added an event handler for key events such that the user can press ESC to close the application.

Note   This example may not work on all platforms.

At this point, you should be familiar with how to make your own wxPython application go into a maximized state or even full screen right after starting. I think Mac users will probably find this particular recipe the most useful as I have seen a lot of Mac power users who like to full screen their applications.

Recipe 10-3. Ensuring Only One Instance per Frame

Problem

The other day, I came across an interesting StackOverflow question where the fellow was trying to figure out how to open a subframe only once. Basically he wanted a single instance of the subframe (and other subframes). After digging around a bit on Google, I found an old thread from the wxPython Google Group that had an interesting approach to doing what was needed.

Solution

Basically it required a bit of meta-programming, but it was a fun little exercise that I thought the readers of this book would find it interesting. Here's the code.

```python
import wx

class MyPanel(wx.Panel):
    """"""

    def __init__(self, parent):
        """Constructor"""
        wx.Panel.__init__(self, parent)
```

```python
class SingleInstanceFrame(wx.Frame):
    """"""

    instance = None
    init = 0

    def __new__(self, *args, **kwargs):
        """"""
        if self.instance is None:
            self.instance = wx.Frame.__new__(self)
        elif not self.instance:
            self.instance = wx.Frame.__new__(self)

        return self.instance

    def __init__(self):
        """Constructor"""
        print(id(self))
        if self.init:
            return
        self.init = 1

        wx.Frame.__init__(self, None, title="Single Instance Frame")
        panel = MyPanel(self)
        self.Show()

class MainFrame(wx.Frame):
    """"""

    def __init__(self):
        """Constructor"""
        wx.Frame.__init__(self, None, title="Main Frame")
        panel = MyPanel(self)
        btn = wx.Button(panel, label="Open Frame")
        btn.Bind(wx.EVT_BUTTON, self.open_frame)
        self.Show()
```

```
    def open_frame(self, event):
        frame = SingleInstanceFrame()

if __name__ == '__main__':
    app = wx.App(False)
    frame = MainFrame()
    app.MainLoop()
```

The meat of this code is in the **SingleInstanceFrame** class, specifically in the __ new__ method. Here we check to see if the variable **self.instance** is set to **None**. If so, we create a new instance. We will also create a new instance if the user closes the frame. This is what the **elif** statement is for. It checks to see if the instance has been deleted and if it has, it creates a new instance.

You will also notice that we have a variable called **self.init**. This is used to check if the instance has already been initialized. If so, __**init**__ will just return instead of re-instantiating everything. Anyway, I hope you found that enlightening.

This recipe demonstrates the **singleton** pattern of programming which proves to be quite useful in solving this problem. When you want only one frame to be opened on a button press, using the singleton pattern is the way to go.

CHAPTER 11

wxPython and the System Tray

Recipe 11-1. Creating Taskbar Icons

Problem

Have you ever wondered how to create those little status icons in the Windows System Tray that usually appear on the lower right of your screen? The wxPython toolkit provides a pretty simple way to do just that and this chapter will walk you through the process.

You will need to find an icon file to use or create a Python image file via the img2py utility that was mentioned in Recipe 2-2 back in Chapter 2.

Solution

We will look at how to create the **TaskBarIcon** in both Classic wxPython and in the new wxPython 4 (Phoenix).

Creating the TaskBarIcon in Classic

Creating a **TaskBarIcon** subclass is your first step to using it in your application. The subclass is not particularly hard to create, but you do need to know which methods to override to make it work correctly. Let's look at an example for wxPython Classic.

```
import wx

class PythonIcon(wx.TaskBarIcon):
    TBMENU_RESTORE = wx.NewId()
    TBMENU_CLOSE   = wx.NewId()
```

M. Driscoll, *wxPython Recipes*, https://doi.org/10.1007/978-1-4842-3237-8_11

```python
    TBMENU_CHANGE  = wx.NewId()
    TBMENU_REMOVE  = wx.NewId()

    def __init__(self, frame):
        wx.TaskBarIcon.__init__(self)
        self.frame = frame

        # Set the image
        icon = wx.Icon('python.ico', wx.BITMAP_TYPE_ICO)

        self.SetIcon(icon, "Python")

        # bind some events
        self.Bind(wx.EVT_MENU, self.OnTaskBarClose, id=self.TBMENU_CLOSE)
        self.Bind(wx.EVT_TASKBAR_LEFT_DOWN, self.OnTaskBarLeftClick)

    def CreatePopupMenu(self, evt=None):
        """

        This method is called by the base class when it needs to popup
        the menu for the default EVT_RIGHT_DOWN event.  Just create
        the menu how you want it and return it from this function,
        the base class takes care of the rest.
        """

        menu = wx.Menu()
        menu.Append(self.TBMENU_RESTORE, "Open Program")
        menu.Append(self.TBMENU_CHANGE, "Show all the Items")
        menu.AppendSeparator()
        menu.Append(self.TBMENU_CLOSE,   "Exit Program")
        return menu

    def OnTaskBarActivate(self, evt):
        """"""

        pass

    def OnTaskBarClose(self, evt):
        """

        Destroy the taskbar icon and frame from the taskbar icon itself
        """

        self.frame.Close()
```

```
def OnTaskBarLeftClick(self, evt):
    """

    Create the right-click menu
    """

    menu = self.CreatePopupMenu()
    self.PopupMenu(menu)
    menu.Destroy()
```

How It Works

This first class is based on one that you can find in the wxPython demo package. As mentioned earlier, you will note that we are subclassing **wx.TaskBarIcon**. We set its icon to something and also set its mouse-over help string. If you mouse-over the image in your toolbar, you should see the text appear. Then we bind a few events. One event will open a pop-up menu on a right-click. Yes, I know it says you're binding to the left-click button, but that's not how it works in this case. Anyway we also set it up such that when you right-click, you can choose to do a few options. We only have a couple of the options actually do anything though. You will note that we call the frame's **Close** method to close the frame.

Let's actually add a class that utilizes our task bar icon.

```
class MyForm(wx.Frame):

    def __init__(self):
        wx.Frame.__init__(self, None, title="TaskBarIcon Tutorial",
            size=(500,500))
        panel = wx.Panel(self)
        self.tbIcon = PythonIcon(self)
        self.Bind(wx.EVT_CLOSE, self.onClose)

    def onClose(self, evt):
        """

        Destroy the taskbar icon and the frame
        """

        self.tbIcon.RemoveIcon()
        self.tbIcon.Destroy()
        self.Destroy()
```

```
if __name__ == "__main__":
    app = wx.App(False)
    frame = MyForm().Show()
    app.MainLoop()
```

Here we basically just instantiate the **TaskBarIcon** class that we created earlier and we bind the frame to EVT_CLOSE. You might wonder about this. There are some "gotchas" with using the TaskBarIcon on Windows. If I just tell the frame to close, it closes just fine, but the icon remains and Python just kind of hangs in la la land. If you only allow the user to close using the task bar icon's right-click menu, then you could just add a **RemoveIcon** method and a **self.Destroy()** there and you'd be good to go (for some reason, RemoveIcon isn't enough to get rid of the TaskBarIcon, so you also need to tell it to Destroy itself too) But if you allow the user to press the little "X" in the upper right-hand corner, then you'll need to catch EVT_CLOSE and deal with it appropriately. When you do catch this event, you cannot just call **self.Close()** or you'll end up in an infinite loop, which is why we call **self.Destroy()** instead.

Creating the TaskBarIcon in wxPython 4

Creating a TaskBarIcon in wxPython 4 is slightly different than it was in Classic due to the fact that the TaskBarIcon class was moved to wx.adv. For completeness, I am including an updated example for wxPython 4 in the code that follows:

```
import wx
import wx.adv

class PythonIcon(wx.adv.TaskBarIcon):
    TBMENU_RESTORE = wx.NewId()
    TBMENU_CLOSE   = wx.NewId()
    TBMENU_CHANGE  = wx.NewId()
    TBMENU_REMOVE  = wx.NewId()

    def __init__(self, frame):
        wx.adv.TaskBarIcon.__init__(self)
        self.frame = frame
```

```python
        # Set the image
        icon = wx.Icon('python.ico', wx.BITMAP_TYPE_ICO)

        self.SetIcon(icon, "Python")

        # bind some events
        self.Bind(wx.EVT_MENU, self.OnTaskBarClose, id=self.TBMENU_CLOSE)
        self.Bind(wx.adv.EVT_TASKBAR_LEFT_DOWN, self.OnTaskBarLeftClick)

    def CreatePopupMenu(self, evt=None):
        """

        This method is called by the base class when it needs to popup
        the menu for the default EVT_RIGHT_DOWN event.  Just create
        the menu how you want it and return it from this function,
        the base class takes care of the rest.
        """

        menu = wx.Menu()
        menu.Append(self.TBMENU_RESTORE, "Open Program")
        menu.Append(self.TBMENU_CHANGE, "Show all the Items")
        menu.AppendSeparator()
        menu.Append(self.TBMENU_CLOSE,    "Exit Program")
        return menu

    def OnTaskBarActivate(self, evt):
        """"""

        pass

    def OnTaskBarClose(self, evt):
        """

        Destroy the taskbar icon and frame from the taskbar icon itself
        """

        self.frame.Close()

    def OnTaskBarLeftClick(self, evt):
        """
```

```
        Create the right-click menu
        """

        menu = self.CreatePopupMenu()
        self.PopupMenu(menu)
        menu.Destroy()

class MyForm(wx.Frame):

    def __init__(self):
        wx.Frame.__init__(self, None, title="TaskBarIcon Tutorial",
            size=(500,500))
        panel = wx.Panel(self)
        self.tbIcon = PythonIcon(self)
        self.Bind(wx.EVT_CLOSE, self.onClose)

    def onClose(self, evt):
        """

        Destroy the taskbar icon and the frame
        """

        self.tbIcon.RemoveIcon()
        self.tbIcon.Destroy()
        self.Destroy()

if __name__ == "__main__":
    app = wx.App(False)
    frame = MyForm().Show()
    app.MainLoop()
```

The main difference here is where we import **wx.adv** and then use that when we define and initialize the **TaskBarIcon**. The other change is in the binding of the **EVT_TASKBAR_LEFT_DOWN** which was also moved into wx.adv. Once that's done, the rest of the code remains the same and everything just works!

Now you should be able to create your own application that includes a TaskBarIcon. I highly recommend looking at the wxPython demo to see what else you can do with it. I think adding an icon can add a bit of polish to your application, especially if you need to have it running hidden for a while and then make it pop up at the user's command.

Recipe 11-2. Minimizing to the System Tray

Problem

This recipe is on a topic that I know users ask about every once in a while. Making wxPython minimize the frame to the system tray is really quite simple. We'll start out by looking at the code to create a **TaskBarIcon** and then we'll move on to creating a simple application that can be minimized to the system tray.

Note   This recipe does not work on Mac OS.

Solution

Creating a task bar icon is very easy to do in wxPython, especially if you already have an icon file.

Let's take a look at one simple approach.

```python
import wx

class CustomTaskBarIcon(wx.TaskBarIcon):
    """"""

    def __init__(self, frame):
        """Constructor"""
        wx.TaskBarIcon.__init__(self)
        self.frame = frame

        icon = wx.Icon('python.ico', wx.BITMAP_TYPE_ICO)

        self.SetIcon(icon, "Restore")

        self.Bind(wx.EVT_TASKBAR_LEFT_DOWN, self.OnTaskBarLeftClick)

    def OnTaskBarActivate(self, evt):
        """"""
        pass

    def OnTaskBarClose(self, evt):
        """
```

```
        Destroy the taskbar icon and frame from the taskbar icon itself
        """
        self.frame.Close()

    def OnTaskBarLeftClick(self, evt):
        """
        Create the right-click menu
        """
        self.frame.Show()
        self.frame.Restore()
```

How It Works

As you can see here, all we needed to do was pass the path of the icon file to wx.Icon and tell it what file type we gave it. Then we just call the **wx.TaskBarIcon's SetIcon()** method to set the icon. If you don't have an icon file, then you could use the following alternate method to create one from another image type:

```
img = wx.Image("24x24.png", wx.BITMAP_TYPE_ANY)

bmp = wx.BitmapFromImage(img)

self.icon = wx.EmptyIcon()

self.icon.CopyFromBitmap(bmp)

self.SetIcon(self.icon, "Restore")
```

In this case, we have to jump through a couple of hoops to turn a PNG file into a format that can be used by wx's icon methods. You'll note that we bind to EVT_TASKBAR_LEFT_DOWN so that when the user clicks the icon, we can restore the window.

Note   As mentioned in the previous recipe, you will need to update this code to make it work in wxPython 4 as the TaskBarIcon class was moved into **wx.adv**. If you are using wxPython 4, then you'll want the code to look as follows:

```python
# custTray.py

import wx
import wx.adv

class CustomTaskBarIcon(wx.adv.TaskBarIcon):
    """"""

    def __init__(self, frame):
        """Constructor"""
        wx.adv.TaskBarIcon.__init__(self)
        self.frame = frame

        icon = wx.Icon('python.ico', wx.BITMAP_TYPE_ICO)

        self.SetIcon(icon, "Restore")

        self.Bind(wx.adv.EVT_TASKBAR_LEFT_DOWN, self.OnTaskBarLeftClick)

    def OnTaskBarActivate(self, evt):
        """"""
        pass

    def OnTaskBarClose(self, evt):
        """
        Destroy the taskbar icon and frame from the taskbar icon itself
        """
        self.frame.Close()

    def OnTaskBarLeftClick(self, evt):
        """
        Create the right-click menu
        """
        self.frame.Show()
        self.frame.Restore()
```

There are examples of both in the book's code examples. Let's move on to creating the application that actually minimizes!

Making the Application Minimize to Tray

Now we're ready to create an application that can minimize to the system tray. Let's write some code.

```python
import custTray
import wx

class MainFrame(wx.Frame):
    """"""

    def __init__(self):
        """Constructor"""
        wx.Frame.__init__(self, None, title="Minimize to Tray")
        panel = wx.Panel(self)
        self.tbIcon = custTray.CustomTaskBarIcon(self)

        self.Bind(wx.EVT_ICONIZE, self.onMinimize)
        self.Bind(wx.EVT_CLOSE, self.onClose)

        self.Show()

    def onClose(self, evt):
        """
        Destroy the taskbar icon and the frame
        """
        self.tbIcon.RemoveIcon()
        self.tbIcon.Destroy()
        self.Destroy()

    def onMinimize(self, event):
        """
        When minimizing, hide the frame so it "minimizes to tray"
        """
        if self.IsIconized():
            self.Hide()

def main():
    """"""
```

```
    app = wx.App(False)
    frame = MainFrame()
    app.MainLoop()

if __name__ == "__main__":
    main()
```

Here we have two event bindings: one for EVT_CLOSE and the other for EVT_ICONIZE. The latter fires when the user minimizes the frame, so we use that to minimize to the tray, which is really just hiding the frame. The other event fires when you close the frame and it's a little more important. Why? Well you need to catch the close event in case the user tries to close the application via the tray icon. And you need to make sure you remove the icon *and* destroy it or your application will appear to close but actually just hang in the background.

Now you know how to minimize your wxPython application to the system tray area. I've used this for a simple e-mail checking program before. You could use it for lots of other things, such as a monitor that responds to events by raising the frame to prominence.

## CHAPTER 12

Fun with Panels

Recipe 12-1. Making a Panel Self-Destruct

Problem

A few years ago I saw a question on the popular StackOverflow web site asking how to dynamically destroy and create panels after a certain amount of time has passed. It was such an interesting idea that I decided to go ahead and write about how to do it. All you really need is a **wx.Timer** and the panel object. For this piece of code, I used a panel that displays a countdown with a **wx.StaticText** widget, destroys itself, and is promptly replaced with another panel.

Solution

Let's take a look at the following code to do this little piece of magic:

```python
import wx

class PanelOne(wx.Panel):
    """"""

    def __init__(self, parent):
        """Constructor"""
        wx.Panel.__init__(self, parent)

        msg = "This panel will self-destruct in 10 seconds"
        self.countdown = wx.StaticText(self, label=msg)

class PanelTwo(wx.Panel):
    """"""
```

© Mike Driscoll 2018
M. Driscoll, *wxPython Recipes*, https://doi.org/10.1007/978-1-4842-3237-8_12

```python
    def __init__(self, parent):
        """Constructor"""
        wx.Panel.__init__(self, parent)

        txt = wx.StaticText(self, label="Panel Two")

class MainFrame(wx.Frame):
    """"""

    def __init__(self):
        """Constructor"""
        wx.Frame.__init__(self, None, title="Panel Smacker")
        self.panelOne = PanelOne(self)
        self.time2die = 10

        self.timer = wx.Timer(self)
        self.Bind(wx.EVT_TIMER, self.update, self.timer)
        self.timer.Start(1000)

        self.sizer = wx.BoxSizer(wx.VERTICAL)
        self.sizer.Add(self.panelOne, 1, wx.EXPAND)
        self.SetSizer(self.sizer)

    def update(self, event):
        """"""

        if self.time2die < 0:
            self.panelOne.Destroy()
            self.panelTwo = PanelTwo(self)
            self.sizer.Add(self.panelTwo, 1, wx.EXPAND)
            self.Layout()
            self.timer.Stop()
        else:
            msg = "This panel will self-destruct in %s seconds" % self.
            time2die
            self.panelOne.countdown.SetLabel(msg)
        self.time2die -= 1
```

```
if __name__ == "__main__":
    app = wx.App(False)
    frame = MainFrame()
    frame.Show()
    app.MainLoop()
```

How It Works

When you run this code, you should see something like the image in Figure 12-1.

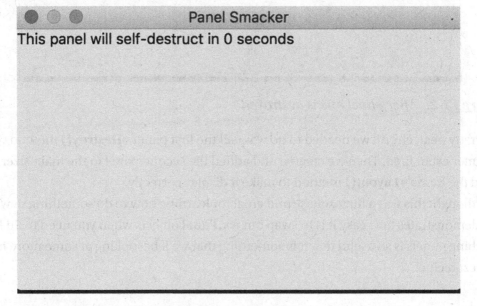

Figure 12-1. *Before panel destruction*

It will then count down for ten seconds and you'll see the panel change into something like the image in Figure 12-2.

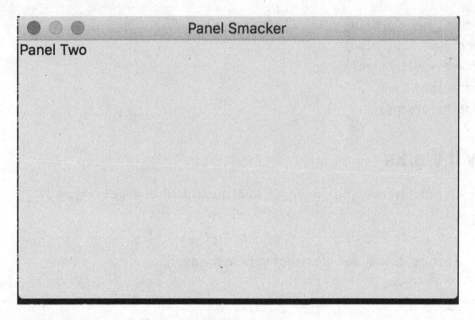

Figure 12-2. *After panel one is destroyed*

Pretty neat, eh? All we needed to do was call the first panel's **Destroy()** method when the timer event fired. Then we created and added the second panel to the main sizer and called the frame's **Layout()** method to make it display correctly.

I thought this was a fun exercise and great for learning how to do something new. It also demonstrates how easy it is to swap out **wx.Panel** objects when you need to. In fact, switching panels is so useful that it is something that we'll be looking at some more in the next recipe!

Recipe 12-2. How to Switch Between Panels

Problem

Every couple of months, I'll see someone asking how to switch between two views or panels in a wxPython application that they're working on. Since this is such a common question and because someone asked it recently on the wxPython channel on IRC, I wrote up a quick script that shows how it's done. Note that, in most cases, the user will probably find one of the many notebook widgets to be more than sufficient for their needs. Anyway, let's take a look at how to do this thing!

Solution

In this example, we'll use a menu to toggle between two panels. The first panel will have just a text control on it and the second panel will just have a grid widget.

Figure 12-3 shows the first panel.

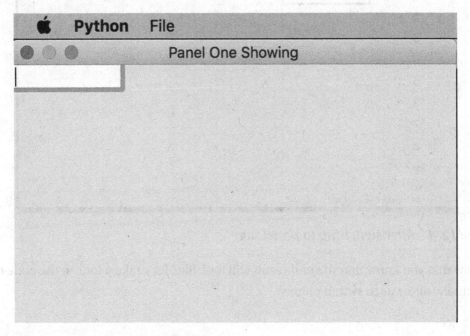

Figure 12-3. *Before switching panels*

And Figure 12-4 shows the panel you can switch to.

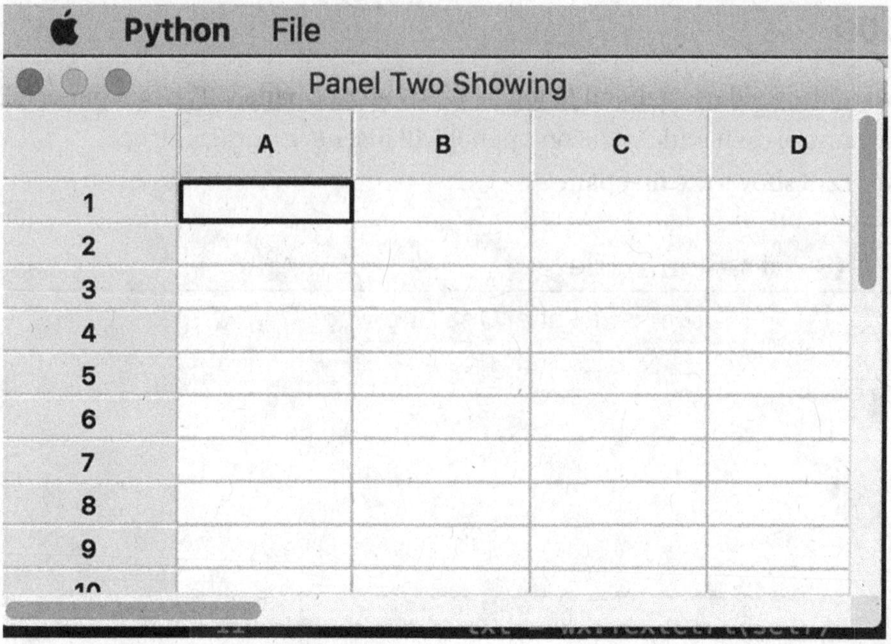

Figure 12-4. *After switching to panel two*

Now that you know that the end result will look like, let's take a look at the code that will actually allow us to switch panels.

```python
import wx
import wx.grid as gridlib

class PanelOne(wx.Panel):
    """"""

    def __init__(self, parent):
        """Constructor"""
        wx.Panel.__init__(self, parent=parent)
        txt = wx.TextCtrl(self)

class PanelTwo(wx.Panel):
    """"""

    def __init__(self, parent):
        """Constructor"""
        wx.Panel.__init__(self, parent=parent)
```

```
        grid = gridlib.Grid(self)
        grid.CreateGrid(25,12)

        sizer = wx.BoxSizer(wx.VERTICAL)
        sizer.Add(grid, 0, wx.EXPAND)
        self.SetSizer(sizer)

class MyForm(wx.Frame):

    def __init__(self):
        wx.Frame.__init__(self, None, wx.ID_ANY,
                        "Panel Switcher Tutorial")

        self.panel_one = PanelOne(self)
        self.panel_two = PanelTwo(self)
        self.panel_two.Hide()

        self.sizer = wx.BoxSizer(wx.VERTICAL)
        self.sizer.Add(self.panel_one, 1, wx.EXPAND)
        self.sizer.Add(self.panel_two, 1, wx.EXPAND)
        self.SetSizer(self.sizer)

        menubar = wx.MenuBar()
        fileMenu = wx.Menu()
        switch_panels_menu_item = fileMenu.Append(
            wx.ID_ANY,
            "Switch Panels",
            "Some text")
        self.Bind(wx.EVT_MENU, self.onSwitchPanels,
                switch_panels_menu_item)
        menubar.Append(fileMenu, '&File')
        self.SetMenuBar(menubar)

    def onSwitchPanels(self, event):
        """

        Event handler called when we want to switch panels
        """

        if self.panel_one.IsShown():
            self.SetTitle("Panel Two Showing")
```

```
            self.panel_one.Hide()
            self.panel_two.Show()
        else:
            self.SetTitle("Panel One Showing")
            self.panel_one.Show()
            self.panel_two.Hide()
        self.Layout()

# Run the program
if __name__ == "__main__":
    app = wx.App(False)
    frame = MyForm()
    frame.Show()
    app.MainLoop()
```

How It Works

The only code that we care about is located in the **onSwitchPanels** event handler. Here we use a conditional to check which panel is showing and then Hide the current one and Show the other. We also set the frame's title to make it obvious which panel is which. We also need to call the frame's **Layout()** method to make the panels visible. Otherwise, you might see some weird visual anomalies like nothing really showing in the frame unless you resize it slightly.

Now you know how to switch panels too. If you plan to do a lot of visual work, like adding or deleting widgets, then you might want to look into the Freeze and Thaw methods and then use Layout. They help hide the flickering that can be seen when you modify a panel's children.

Another common method of switching panels is to use tabs. The wxPython package has a **wx.Notebook** widget that is made for just this sort of thing. In fact, wxPython includes several other "Book" controls, such as **wx.Toolbook** and the **AUI Notebook**. Check out the wxPython demo to see them in action!

CHAPTER 13

Using Objects in Widgets

Recipe 13-1. Using ObjectListView Instead of ListCtrl

Problem

The wxPython ListCtrl is a very handy widget. Unfortunately, it can be a pain to use as well. This discovery caused Phillip Piper, missionary to Mozambique, to write **ObjectListView**, a wrapper for the wx.ListCtrl. It is now maintained by others in the wxPython community.

ObjectListView actually adds functionality because it uses objects to create its rows, and thus, it makes getting information from multiple columns much easier. Mr. Piper also added lots of other conveniences that make adding custom editors easier, alternating the color of rows, automatically sorting rows, and much, much more! This chapter will help you learn some of the basics of using ObjectListView so that you'll be able to use it in your future projects. It is not meant to be an exhaustive look at the control as it is actually very well documented.

It should be noted that ObjectListView is not a drop-in replacement for a standard list control. The setup is quite a bit different. Fortunately, you can install ObjectListView with pip:

pip install objectlistview

© Mike Driscoll 2018
M. Driscoll, *wxPython Recipes*, https://doi.org/10.1007/978-1-4842-3237-8_13

Solution

Let's look at a fairly simple example. We'll start by creating a simple class that ObjectListView will use as its data model.

```
class Book(object):
    """

    Model of the Book object

    Contains the following attributes:
    'ISBN', 'Author', 'Manufacturer', 'Title'
    """

    def __init__(self, title, author, isbn, mfg):
        self.isbn = isbn
        self.author = author
        self.mfg = mfg
        self.title = title
```

You can put this code into a separate file or add it to the wxPython code that we'll be looking at next. All this class does is define our data model, which will match up with the columns in our ObjectListView widget. Now we're ready to look at the wxPython code.

```
import wx
from ObjectListView import ObjectListView, ColumnDefn

class MainPanel(wx.Panel):

    def __init__(self, parent):
        wx.Panel.__init__(self, parent=parent, id=wx.ID_ANY)
        self.products = [Book("wxPython in Action", "Robin Dunn",
                              "1932394621", "Manning"),
                         Book("Hello World", "Warren and Carter Sande",
                              "1933988495", "Manning")
                        ]

        self.dataOlv = ObjectListView(self, wx.ID_ANY,
style=wx.LC_REPORT|wx.SUNKEN_BORDER)
        self.setBooks()
```

```python
        # Allow the cell values to be edited when double-clicked (see
        # explanation after the code)
        self.dataOlv.cellEditMode = ObjectListView.CELLEDIT_SINGLECLICK

        # create an update button
        updateBtn = wx.Button(self, wx.ID_ANY, "Update OLV")
        updateBtn.Bind(wx.EVT_BUTTON, self.updateControl)

        # Create some sizers
        mainSizer = wx.BoxSizer(wx.VERTICAL)

        mainSizer.Add(self.dataOlv, 1, wx.ALL|wx.EXPAND, 5)
        mainSizer.Add(updateBtn, 0, wx.ALL|wx.CENTER, 5)
        self.SetSizer(mainSizer)

    def updateControl(self, event):
        """

            Update the object list view widget
        """
        print("updating...")
        product_dict = [
            {"title":"Core Python Programming", "author":"Wesley Chun",
             "isbn":"0132269937", "mfg":"Prentice Hall"},
            {"title":"Python Programming for the Absolute Beginner",
             "author":"Michael Dawson", "isbn":"1598631128",
             "mfg":"Course Technology"},
            {"title":"Learning Python", "author":"Mark Lutz",
             "is       data = self.products + product_dict
        self.dataOlv.SetObjects(data)

    def setBooks(self, data=None):
        self.dataOlv.SetColumns([
            ColumnDefn("Title", "left", 220, "title"),
            ColumnDefn("Author", "left", 200, "author"),
            ColumnDefn("ISBN", "right", 100, "isbn"),
            ColumnDefn("Mfg", "left", 180, "mfg")
        ])
```

```
        self.dataOlv.SetObjects(self.products)
class MainFrame(wx.Frame):

    def __init__(self):
        wx.Frame.__init__(self, parent=None, id=wx.ID_ANY,
                          title="ObjectListView Demo", size=(800,600))
        panel = MainPanel(self)

class GenApp(wx.App):

    def __init__(self, redirect=False, filename=None):
        wx.App.__init__(self, redirect, filename)

    def OnInit(self):
        # create frame here
        frame = MainFrame()
        frame.Show()
        return True

def main():
    """

    Run the demo
    """

    app = GenApp()
    app.MainLoop()

if __name__ == "__main__":
    main()
```

How It Works

If you run this code, you should end up seeing an application that looks like the image in Figure 13-1.

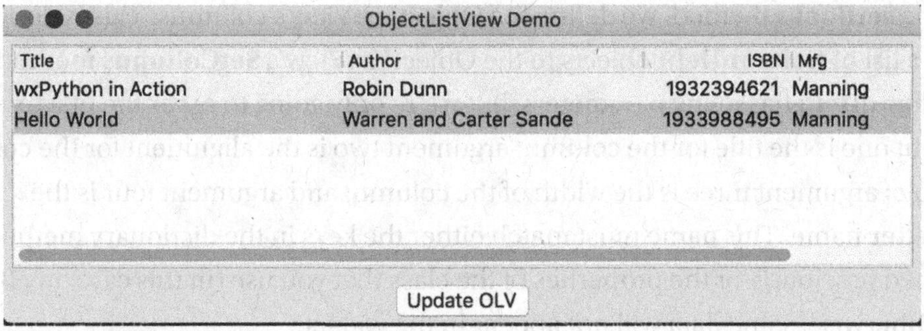

Figure 13-1. *An example of the ObjectListView widget in action*

Now let's take a look at what all this does. First, I create a generic **Book** class with some properties: **isbn, author, mfg,** and **title**. We'll use this class for creating rows in the ObjectListView. Next we create a standard panel and put an ObjectListView and a button widget on it. You'll also notice that there's a short list of "Book" objects. The ObjectListView is set to report mode with the LC_REPORT style flag. It has other modes too, but I won't be covering those. The report mode looks most like the details mode in Windows Explorer.

The next piece is a little weird.

```
self.dataOlv.cellEditMode = ObjectListView.CELLEDIT_SINGLECLICK
```

This code tells our widget to allow editing of all the cells in the row (except the first) by double-clicking them. I don't know why it was designed this way as it looks like all you should have to do is single-click one. Even the documentation says that a single click should be enough. Maybe it's a Windows limitation. Anyway, to edit the first cell of any row, just select it and hit F2.

The last few lines in the initialization method just put the widgets into sizers. The next piece of interesting code is in the **updateControl** method, where we actually update our ObjectListView's contents. I show two different ways to do the update here. The first is to just use the product list of Book objects and call the ObjectListView's **SetObjects** method with the list passed in. The second way is to use a dictionary. The dictionary's keys must match the ColumnDefn's **valueGetter** name (which we'll see in the **setBooks** method). The dictionary values can be whatever you want. In my example, I actually combine the list of Book objects and the list of dictionaries and call **SetObjects** on the result.

In the **setBooks** method, we define the ObjectListView's columns. This is done by passing a list of **ColumnDefn** objects to the ObjectListView's **SetColumns** method. The **ColumnDefn** has many parameters, but we're only going to cover the first four. Argument one is the title for the column; argument two is the alignment for the column as a whole; argument three is the width of the column; and argument four is the **valueGetter** name. This name must match either the keys in the dictionary method mentioned previously or the properties of the class that you use (in this case, my Book class). Otherwise, some data will not appear in the widget.

If you want to learn about accessing some of the row object's data, then add another button to this application and bind it to the following function:

```python
def getRowInfo(self, event):
    """"""
    rowObj = self.dataOlv.GetSelectedObject()
    print(rowObj.author)
    print(rowObj.title)
```

Now you can select a row and use the ObjectListView's GetSelectedObject method to get the row object. Once you have that, you can access the object's properties, like the author and title and whatever else you have defined. This is much easier than the ListCtrl where you have to get the column and row to find the information for each item.

That covers the basics of using an ObjectListCtrl. Be sure to download the source as it has a bunch of interesting demos including one that allows the user to edit some cells with an owner-drawn combobox! The documentation is also quite thorough and well put together. If I ever need a ListCtrl, I always opt for using the ObjectListView as I feel it has a lot more features and is just easier to use.

Recipe 13-2. Storing Objects in ComboBox or ListBox
Problem

This recipe came about because of a discussion on the wxPython IRC channel about how to store objects in **wx.ListBox**. Then, later on that day, there was a question on StackOverflow about the same thing, but in relation to the **wx.ComboBox**. Fortunately, both of these widgets inherit from wx.ItemContainer and contain the Append method, which allows you to associate an object with an item in these widgets. In this chapter, you will find out how it is done.

Solution

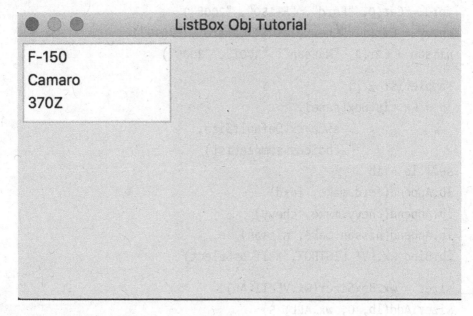

Figure 13-2. *Adding objects to wx.ListBox*

We'll start with the ListBox (see Figure 13-2). Let's just jump into the code as I think you
will understand it faster that way.

```python
import wx

class Car(object):
    """"""

    def __init__(self, id, model, make, year):
        """Constructor"""
        self.id = id
        self.model = model
        self.make = make
        self.year = year

class MyForm(wx.Frame):

    def __init__(self):
        wx.Frame.__init__(self, None, title="ListBox Obj Tutorial")
```

```python
        panel = wx.Panel(self, wx.ID_ANY)

        ford = Car(0, "Ford", "F-150", "2008")
        chevy = Car(1, "Chevrolet", "Camaro", "2010")
        nissan = Car(2, "Nissan", "370Z", "2005")

        sampleList = []
        lb = wx.ListBox(panel,
                        size=wx.DefaultSize,
                        choices=sampleList)
        self.lb = lb
        lb.Append(ford.make, ford)
        lb.Append(chevy.make, chevy)
        lb.Append(nissan.make, nissan)
        lb.Bind(wx.EVT_LISTBOX, self.onSelect)

        sizer = wx.BoxSizer(wx.VERTICAL)
        sizer.Add(lb, 0, wx.ALL, 5)
        panel.SetSizer(sizer)

    def onSelect(self, event):
        """"""

        selection = self.lb.GetStringSelection()
        if selection:
            print("You selected: " + selection)
            obj = self.lb.GetClientData(self.lb.GetSelection())
            text = """
            The object's attributes are:
            %s  %s    %s  %s

            """ % (obj.id, obj.make, obj.model, obj.year)
            print(text)

if __name__ == "__main__":
    app = wx.App(False)
    frame = MyForm()
    frame.Show()
    app.MainLoop()
```

How It Works

Now, how does this work? Let's take some time and unpack this example. First, we'll create a super-simple Car class where we define four attributes: an ID, model, make, and year. Then we create a simple frame with a panel and the **ListBox** widget. As you can see, we use the ListBox's inherited Append method to add each Car object's "make" string and then the object itself. This allows us to associate each item in the list box to an object. Finally, we bind the ListBox to **EVT_LISTBOX** so we can find out how to access that object when we select an item from the widget.

To see how this is accomplished, check out the **onSelect** method. Here we can see that we need to call the ListBox's **GetClientData** method and pass it the current selection. This will return the object that we associated earlier. Now we can access each of the method's attributes. In this example, we just print all that out to stdout. Now let's look at how it is done with the wx.ComboBox.

Adding Objects to the wx.ComboBox

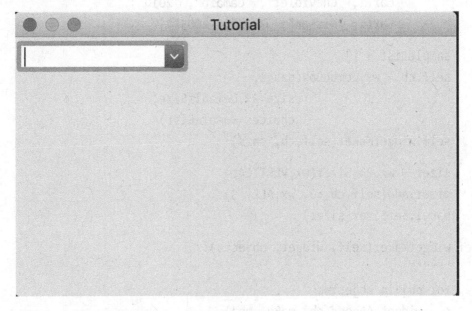

Figure 13-3. *Adding objects to wx.ComboBox*

The code for the wx.ComboBox is practically the same, so for fun we'll do a little refactoring. Take a look.

```python
import wx

class Car:
    """"""

    def __init__(self, id, model, make, year):
        """Constructor"""
        self.id = id
        self.model = model
        self.make = make
        self.year = year

class MyForm(wx.Frame):

    def __init__(self):
        wx.Frame.__init__(self, None, title="Tutorial")

        panel = wx.Panel(self, wx.ID_ANY)

        cars = [Car(0, "Ford", "F-150", "2008"),
                Car(1, "Chevrolet", "Camaro", "2010"),
                Car(2, "Nissan", "370Z", "2005")]

        sampleList = []
        self.cb = wx.ComboBox(panel,
                              size=wx.DefaultSize,
                              choices=sampleList)
        self.widgetMaker(self.cb, cars)

        sizer = wx.BoxSizer(wx.VERTICAL)
        sizer.Add(self.cb, 0, wx.ALL, 5)
        panel.SetSizer(sizer)

    def widgetMaker(self, widget, objects):
        """"""

        for obj in objects:
            widget.Append(obj.make, obj)
        widget.Bind(wx.EVT_COMBOBOX, self.onSelect)
```

```python
    def onSelect(self, event):
        """"""
        print("You selected: " + self.cb.GetStringSelection())
        obj = self.cb.GetClientData(self.cb.GetSelection())
        text = """
        The object's attributes are:
        %s %s    %s %s

        """ % (obj.id, obj.make, obj.model, obj.year)
        print(text)

if __name__ == "__main__":
    app = wx.App(False)
    frame = MyForm()
    frame.Show()
    app.MainLoop()
```

In this example, the steps are exactly the same. But what if we had multiple ComboBoxes that we had to do this sort of thing for? That would be a lot of redundant code. Thus, we'll write up a simple helper method called **widgetMaker** that will do the appending and event binding for us. We could make it build the widget, add it to a sizer, and other things too, but we'll keep it simple for this example. Anyway, to make it work, we pass in the ComboBox widget along with a list of objects that we want to add to the widget. The **widgetMaker** will append those objects to the ComboBox for us. The rest of the code is the same, except for the slightly different event that we needed to bind to.

As you can see, this is a pretty straightforward little exercise, but it makes your graphical user interfaces more robust. You might do this for database applications. I can see myself using this with SqlAlchemy result sets. Be creative and I'm sure you'll find good uses for it as well.

CHAPTER 14

XML and XRC

Recipe 14-1. Extracting XML from the RichTextCtrl

Problem

The **RichTextCtrl** gives you the ability to use styled text. It also provides a few different handlers to save the data it contains into various formats. One of those happens to be XML. In this recipe, we will learn how to extract XML from the **RichTextCtrl**.

Solution

The RichTextCtrl is a part of **wx.richtext** which you will need to import in addition to the wx module. It's easiest to understand if we just go ahead and code an example.

```python
# wxPython Classic version

import wx
import wx.richtext

from StringIO import StringIO

class MyFrame(wx.Frame):

    def __init__(self):
        wx.Frame.__init__(self, None, title='Richtext Test')

        sizer = wx.BoxSizer(wx.VERTICAL)
        self.rt = wx.richtext.RichTextCtrl(self)
        self.rt.SetMinSize((300,200))
```

© Mike Driscoll 2018
M. Driscoll, *wxPython Recipes*, https://doi.org/10.1007/978-1-4842-3237-8_14

```
        save_button = wx.Button(self, label="Save")
        save_button.Bind(wx.EVT_BUTTON, self.on_save)

        sizer = wx.BoxSizer(wx.VERTICAL)
        sizer.Add(self.rt, 1, wx.EXPAND|wx.ALL, 6)
        sizer.Add(save_button, 0, wx.EXPAND|wx.ALL, 6)

        self.SetSizer(sizer)
        self.Show()

    def on_save(self, event):
        out = StringIO()
        handler = wx.richtext.RichTextXMLHandler()
        rt_buffer = self.rt.GetBuffer()
        handler.SaveStream(rt_buffer, out)
        self.xml:content = out.getvalue()
        print(self.xml:content)

if __name__ == "__main__":
    app = wx.App(False)
    frame = MyFrame()
    app.MainLoop()
```

How It Works

Let's break this down a bit. First we create our lovely application and add an instance of the **RichTextCtrl** widget to the frame along with a button for saving whatever we happen to write in said widget. Next we set up the binding for the button and lay out the widgets. Finally, we create our event handler. This is where the magic happens. Here we create the **RichTextXMLHandler** and grab the RichTextCtrl's buffer so we can write out the data. But instead of writing to a file, we write to a file-like object, which is our **StringIO** instance. We do this so we can write the data to memory and then read it back out. The reason we do this is because the person on StackOverflow wanted a way to extract the XML that the RichTextCtrl generates and write it to a database. We could have written it to disk first and then read that file, but this is less messy and faster.

Note, however, that if someone had written a novel into the RichTextCtrl, then, it would have been a *bad* idea! While it's not likely that we would run out of room, there are certainly plenty of text files that exceed your computer's memory. If you know that the file you are loading is going to take up a lot of memory, then you wouldn't go this route. Instead, you would read and write the data in chunks. Anyway, this code works for what we wanted to do. I hope you found this useful. It was certainly fun to figure out.

Unfortunately, this code example doesn't work in **wxPython 4**. In this next section, we will update the example so that it will!

Updating for wxPython 4

The first problem you'll encounter when running the previous example in Phoenix is that the **SaveStream** method no longer exists. You will need to use **SaveFile** instead. The other problem is actually one introduced by Python 3. If you run this code in Python 3, you will find that the **StringIO** module doesn't exist and you'll need to use io instead. So, for our next example, I updated the code to support both Python 3 and wxPython 4. Let's see how it differs.

```python
# wxPython 4 / Python 3 Version

import wx
import wx.richtext

from io import BytesIO

class MyFrame(wx.Frame):

    def __init__(self):
        wx.Frame.__init__(self, None, title='Richtext Test')

        sizer = wx.BoxSizer(wx.VERTICAL)
        self.rt = wx.richtext.RichTextCtrl(self)
        self.rt.SetMinSize((300,200))

        save_button = wx.Button(self, label="Save")
        save_button.Bind(wx.EVT_BUTTON, self.on_save)

        sizer = wx.BoxSizer(wx.VERTICAL)
        sizer.Add(self.rt, 1, wx.EXPAND|wx.ALL, 6)
        sizer.Add(save_button, 0, wx.EXPAND|wx.ALL, 6)
```

```
        self.SetSizer(sizer)
        self.Show()

    def on_save(self, event):
        out = BytesIO()
        handler = wx.richtext.RichTextXMLHandler()
        rt_buffer = self.rt.GetBuffer()
        handler.SaveFile(rt_buffer, out)
        self.xml:content = out.getvalue()
        print(self.xml:content)

if __name__ == "__main__":
    app = wx.App(False)
    frame = MyFrame()
    app.MainLoop()
```

The main differences lie in the imports section at the beginning and the **on_save** method. You will note that we are using the **io** module's **BytesIO** class. Then we grab the rest of the data the same way as before except for where we swap **SaveStream** with **SaveFile**. The XML that is printed out is a binary string, so if you plan to parse that, then you may need to cast that result into a string. I've had some XML parsers that wouldn't work correctly with binary strings.

While this recipe only covers extracting XML, you could easily extend it to extract the other formats that RichTextCtrl supports, such as HTML or the Rich Text Format (RTF) itself. This can be a useful tool to have should you need to save the data in your application to a database or some other data storage.

Recipe 14-2. An Introduction to XRC

Problem

Have you ever wondered if you could create a wxPython program using XML? Well, I never did either, but there is a way and its name is XRC. In fact, wxPython comes with an editor called XRCed that you can use to layout your GUI (graphical user interface) and generate the XML code with. In this chapter, we'll give you a quick walk-through of XRC and how to use it to create a couple of GUI skeletons. We will look at two examples that use only XRC controls and then a third that mixes in some additional non-XRC widgets.

Solution

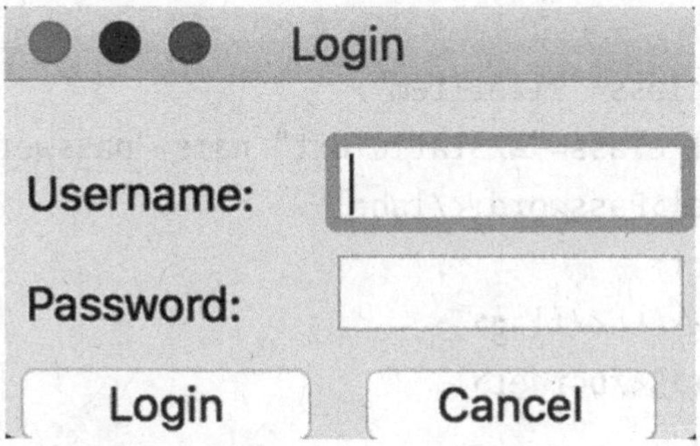

Figure 14-1. *A log-in dialog generated with XRC/XML*

A common dialog that we often see is a log-in dialog. wxPython includes an XRC Editor in its **Documentation and Demos** package called **XRCed,** which I used to create the following XML code:

```xml
<?xml version="1.0" encoding="cp1252"?>
<resource>
  <object class="wxFrame" name="mainFrame">
    <object class="wxPanel" name="panel">
      <object class="wxBoxSizer">
        <orient>wxVERTICAL</orient>
        <object class="sizeritem">
          <object class="wxStaticText" name="handle">
            <label/>
          </object>
        </object>
        <object class="sizeritem">
          <object class="wxFlexGridSizer">
            <object class="sizeritem">
              <object class="wxStaticText" name="userLbl">
                <label>Username:</label>
              </object>
              <flag>wxALL</flag>
              <border>5</border>
            </object>
```

```xml
        <object class="sizeritem">
          <object class="wxTextCtrl" name="userTxt"/>
        </object>
        <object class="sizeritem">
          <object class="wxStaticText" name="passwordLbl">
            <label>Password:</label>
          </object>
          <flag>wxALL</flag>
          <border>5</border>
        </object>
        <object class="sizeritem">
          <object class="wxTextCtrl" name="passwordTxt">
            <style>wxTE_PROCESS_ENTER|wxTE_PASSWORD</style>
          </object>
        </object>
        <object class="sizeritem">
          <object class="wxButton" name="loginBtn">
            <label>Login</label>
          </object>
          <flag>wxALL|wxALIGN_CENTRE</flag>
          <border>5</border>
        </object>
        <object class="sizeritem">
          <object class="wxButton" name="cancelBtn">
            <label>Cancel</label>
          </object>
          <flag>wxALL|wxALIGN_CENTRE</flag>
          <border>5</border>
        </object>
        <cols>2</cols>
        <rows>3</rows>
        <vgap>4</vgap>
        <hgap>2</hgap>
      </object>
      <border>5</border>
```

```
        </object>
      </object>
      <style/>
    </object>
    <size>200,100</size>
    <title>Login</title>
    <centered>1</centered>
  </object>
</resource>
```

How It Works

To use XRC code in your wxPython, all you need to do is "import wx.xrc" or use "from wx import xrc." Let's see what the Python code looks like.

```python
import wx
from wx import xrc

class MyApp(wx.App):
    def OnInit(self):
        res = xrc.XmlResource("login.xrc")

        frame = res.LoadFrame(None, 'mainFrame')

        frame.Show()
        return True

if __name__ == "__main__":
    app = MyApp(False)
    app.MainLoop()
```

In the foregoing code, we use xrc's **XmlResource** method to open our XML file and load it in our program. Next, we use the resulting variable to load specific widgets from the file. In this case, we load just the frame by calling **LoadFrame**. Note that we passed **None** into the **LoadFrame** call. That first argument is the parent argument and since this frame shouldn't have a parent, we passed it **None**. Finally, we call the frame's Show method so we can actually see our program. That's all there is to it! Now let's move on to something a little bit more complex.

Creating a Notebook with XRC

Creating a Notebook widget is a little trickier than just creating a frame. For one thing, when using a Notebook, you usually stick multiple panels on it. This can get confusing if your panels are complex. Thus, we'll look at how to create a simple notebook and a slightly more complex version. Let's start with the simple one first. If you want to follow along, open **XRCed** and see if you can copy the layout in the screenshot shown in Figure 14-2.

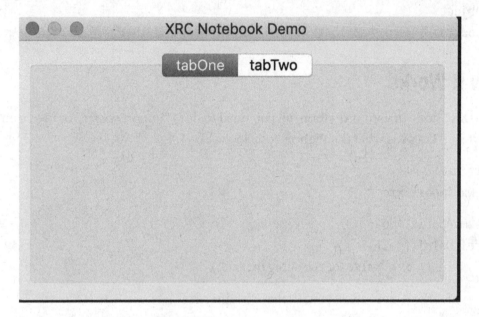

Figure 14-2. *A notebook created with XRC*

The trick to adding pages to your notebook in XRCed is that you need to select the child panel and choose the NotebookPage tab that appears on the right. In there you can set the labels for the tabs. Let's take a look at the generated XML.

```
<?xml version="1.0" ?>
<resource>
  <object class="wxFrame" name="DemoFrame">
    <object class="wxPanel" name="DemoPanel">
      <object class="wxBoxSizer">
        <orient>wxVERTICAL</orient>
        <object class="sizeritem">
          <object class="wxNotebook" name="DemoNotebook">
            <object class="notebookpage">
```

```
            <object class="wxPanel" name="tabOne"/>
            <label>tabOne</label>
          </object>
          <object class="notebookpage">
            <object class="wxPanel" name="tabTwo"/>
            <label>tabTwo</label>
          </object>
        </object>
        <option>1</option>
        <flag>wxALL|wxEXPAND</flag>
        <border>5</border>
      </object>
    </object>
  </object>
  <title>XRC Notebook Demo</title>
</object>
</resource>
```

It's pretty much the same as the code we saw previously. Note that we can embed sizer flags in the XML itself (e.g., **wxALL|wx.EXPAND**). That's pretty neat! The code to load this notebook is almost exactly the same as the code we used for the log-in dialog earlier.

```python
# notebookXrcDemo.py
import wx
from wx import xrc

class MyApp(wx.App):
    def OnInit(self):
        self.res = xrc.XmlResource("notebook.xrc")

        self.frame = self.res.LoadFrame(None, 'DemoFrame')

        self.frame.Show()
        return True

if __name__ == "__main__":
    app = MyApp(False)
    app.MainLoop()
```

The only differences here are the names of the frame and the XRC file. Now let's move on to our slightly more complex notebook example. In this example, we will create a notebook XRC file and two panel XRC files that we can use as tabs for the notebook. Our new notebook's XML is pretty much like the old one, so we'll skip that. But let's take a moment to check out the panel XRC code. Following is the first one:

```
<?xml version="1.0" ?>
<resource>
  <object class="wxPanel" name="panelOne">
    <object class="wxBoxSizer">
      <orient>wxVERTICAL</orient>
      <object class="sizeritem">
        <object class="wxTextCtrl" name="txtOne"/>
        <option>0</option>
        <flag>wxALL</flag>
        <border>5</border>
      </object>
      <object class="sizeritem">
        <object class="wxTextCtrl" name="txtTwo"/>
        <option>0</option>
        <flag>wxALL</flag>
        <border>5</border>
      </object>
    </object>
  </object>
</resource>
```

You will note that this panel is loaded up as **TabOne** (note the capital T) and includes two text controls. The other panel XRC code looks like the following:

```
<?xml version="1.0" ?>
<resource>
  <object class="wxPanel" name="panelTwo">
    <object class="wxBoxSizer">
      <orient>wxVERTICAL</orient>
      <object class="sizeritem">
        <object class="wxListCtrl" name="list_ctrl">
```

```
        <style>wxNO_BORDER|wxLC_REPORT|wxLC_EDIT_LABELS</style>
      </object>
      <option>1</option>
      <flag>wxEXPAND</flag>
    </object>
   </object>
  </object>
</resource>
```

This piece of XML just creates a super-simple empty ListCtrl instance that is expanded to fill the panel. Now we'll turn our attention to the Python code that loads up these XRC files.

```python
# notebookXrcDemo2.py
import wx
from wx import xrc

class MyApp(wx.App):
    def OnInit(self):
        res = xrc.XmlResource("notebook2.xrc")
        frame = res.LoadFrame(None, "DemoFrame")
        panel = xrc.XRCCTRL(frame, "DemoPanel")
        notebook = xrc.XRCCTRL(panel, "DemoNotebook")

        # load another xrc file
        res = xrc.XmlResource("panelOne.xrc")
        tabOne = res.LoadPanel(notebook, "panelOne")
        notebook.AddPage(tabOne, "TabOne")

        # load the last xrc file
        res = xrc.XmlResource("panelTwo.xrc")
        tabTwo = res.LoadPanel(notebook, "panelTwo")
        notebook.AddPage(tabTwo, "tabTwo")

        frame.Show()
        return True
```

```
if __name__ == "__main__":
    app = MyApp(False)
    app.MainLoop()
```

Here we just extract the frame, panel, and notebook objects from the first XRC file and use those as our basis for adding other controls. Loading the other two panels is a cinch as we just do what we did to load the original panel. Then we add our new panels to the notebook using the familiar **AddPage** methodology. Once that's done, we show the frame and we're done! The second panel has an empty ListCtrl in it and when I first created it, I kept getting error messages because I forgot to set its style. Make sure you tell it that you want it to be in List, Report, or one of its other modes or you'll have issues too.

Adding Controls Outside XRC

Figure 14-3. Adding controls that aren't included in XRC

One of the issues with XRC is that it only supports a small subset of the widgets available. Fortunately, there are ways to "teach" XRC how to use new controls, but that is beyond the scope of this introductory chapter. Instead, I'll show you how to add the controls outside XRC. The concept is the same as using normal widgets, so it's really easy to

understand. In fact, we're going to take the second notebook example and add a
PlateButton to it.

```python
# notebookXrcDemo3.py
import wx
from wx import xrc
import wx.lib.platebtn as platebtn

class MyApp(wx.App):
    def OnInit(self):
        self.res = xrc.XmlResource("notebook2.xrc")

        frame = self.res.LoadFrame(None, 'DemoFrame')
        panel = xrc.XRCCTRL(frame, "DemoPanel")
        notebook = xrc.XRCCTRL(panel, "DemoNotebook")

        sizer = wx.BoxSizer(wx.VERTICAL)
        btn = platebtn.PlateButton(panel, label="Test", style=platebtn.
        PB_STYLE_DEFAULT)
        sizer.Add(notebook, 1, wx.ALL|wx.EXPAND, 5)
        sizer.Add(btn)
        panel.SetSizer(sizer)

        frame.Show()
        return True

if __name__ == "__main__":
    app = MyApp(False)
    app.MainLoop()
```

Notice that all we had to do was take the XRC Panel widget and make it the
PlateButton's parent. Then we added the notebook and the button to a vertically
oriented sizer. Now we know how to combine normal widgets with XRC widgets in our
applications.

At this point you should understand how to use XRC to create your user interface in
wxPython. It's quite flexible and helps you to separate out your logic from your view so
you can follow the model-view-controller paradigm. I hope you've learned a lot from this
recipe and will find it helpful in your own work.

Recipe 14-3. An Introduction to XRCed

Problem

If you're new to wxPython but not new to XML, you might find this recipe useful to you. Why? Because wxPython supports **XRC**, an XML file format that describes the GUI in XML, duh. In fact, wxPython's **Documentation & Demos** package includes an editor just for creating and manipulating these files, which is called, XRCed. This chapter will take you on a journey to see XRCed's features and general usage.

One confusing aspect of **XRCed** is that it used to be a project separate from wxPython and its web site still exists here. I've been told that the old version from that web site works really well with screen readers compared to the new version that is shipped with the demo package. So if you have sight problems, you might find that version more suitable. Of course, the old version hasn't been updated since 2007 . . . so pick your poison.

Solution

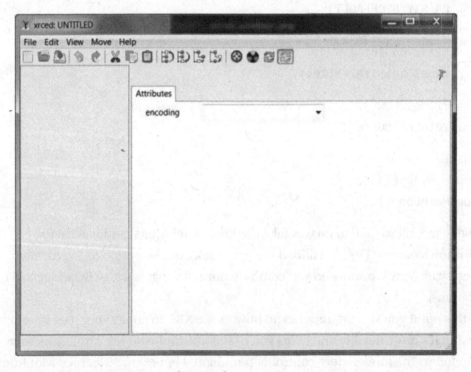

Figure 14-4. *The main screen of XRCed*

Once you have the Demo application installed, run the tool called XRC Resource Editor. The main screen is what you see in the screenshot in Figure 14-4 screenshot. You will also see a second, smaller window that looks like the following in Figure 14-5:

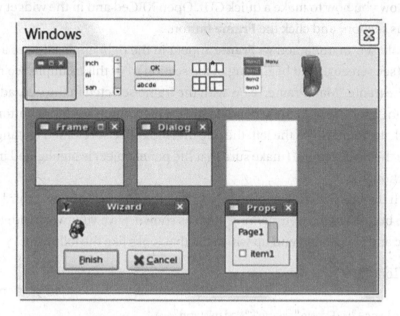

Figure 14-5. *XRCed's widget window*

This secondary window allows you to add various widgets to your interface. To really understand how this works, we should make a simple application!

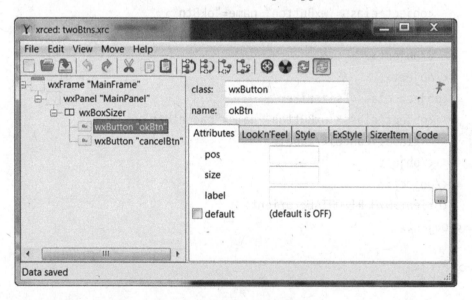

Figure 14-6. *Creating an application with two buttons*

215

How It Works

Let's create a simple two-button application with XRCed. It won't do anything, but it will show you how to make a quick GUI. Open XRCed and in the widget window (see previous section) and click the **Frame** button.

You should see an unnamed **wxFrame** appear in the right application as a root in a tree widget (see screenshot at beginning of the section). For this example, we're going to give name the frame "MainFrame." Now with the frame selected in the tree, add a panel named "MainPanel." Next, in the second floating screen, there's a row of buttons along the top. Click the fourth from the left, the one that looks like several red rectangles, and then choose the BoxSizer one (make sure that the panel object is highlighted in the other screen first though).

Now with the box sizer tree item selected, click the floating window's third button and add two buttons to the tree, naming them as shown. Save your work with the name **twoBtns.xrc** and you should end up with a file that looks like the following:

```xml
<?xml version="1.0" ?>
<resource>
  <object class="wxFrame" name="MainFrame">
    <object class="wxPanel" name="MainPanel">
      <object class="wxBoxSizer">
        <object class="sizeritem">
          <object class="wxButton" name="okBtn">
            <label>OK</label>
          </object>
        </object>
        <object class="sizeritem">
          <object class="wxButton" name="cancelBtn">
            <label>Cancel</label>
          </object>
        </object>
        <orient>wxHORIZONTAL</orient>
      </object>
```

```
        </object>
    </object>
</resource>
```

It's shocking, but XRCed actually produces easy-to-read XML code. Now we just need to figure out how to load the XML with wxPython. Fortunately, it's actually quite easy. Check this out.

```python
import wx
from wx import xrc

class MyApp(wx.App):
    def OnInit(self):
        self.res = xrc.XmlResource("twoBtns.xrc")

        self.frame = self.res.LoadFrame(None, 'MainFrame')

        self.frame.Show()
        return True

if __name__ == "__main__":
    app = MyApp(False)
    app.MainLoop()
```

To load the XML, we need to import the **xrc** module from **wx**. Then we load the XML with the following line: **xrc.XmlResource("twoBtns.xrc")**. Note that we had to pass in the name (or path) of the xrc file. You'll probably need to change it to whatever you called your copy. Then, to load the frame, we call the xml resource object's **LoadFrame** method, passing it None (i.e., no parent) and the name that we gave the frame in the xrc file. This is where it's really easy to make a mistake. You HAVE to type the name of widget in the Python code exactly the same way that you did in the **xrc** file or it will not work (or it might work, but not in the way you expect). Yes, the name is case sensitive. Anyway, once that's done, you just do what you normally do in a wxPython file.

Creating Something More Complex

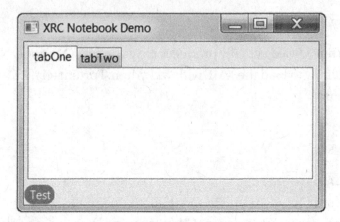

Figure 14-7. *Creating a wx.Notebook in XRCed*

The example in the previous section is pretty bare-bones. Let's take a look at how we can create part of the application in XRC and part of it in wxPython. In the screenshot in Figure 14-7, we have a notebook with two pages and a PlateButton underneath it. The notebook, frame, and panel are all made in XRC whereas the PlateButton is just normal wx. Following is the XML:

```
<?xml version="1.0" ?>
<resource>
  <object class="wxFrame" name="DemoFrame">
    <object class="wxPanel" name="DemoPanel">
      <object class="wxBoxSizer">
        <orient>wxVERTICAL</orient>
        <object class="sizeritem">
          <object class="wxNotebook" name="DemoNotebook">
            <object class="notebookpage">
              <object class="wxPanel" name="tabOne"/>
              <label>tabOne</label>
            </object>
            <object class="notebookpage">
              <object class="wxPanel" name="tabTwo"/>
              <label>tabTwo</label>
            </object>
```

```
        </object>
        <option>1</option>
        <flag>wxALL|wxEXPAND</flag>
        <border>5</border>
      </object>
    </object>
  </object>
  <title>XRC Notebook Demo</title>
  </object>
</resource>
```

Now let's add the PlateButton.

```python
import wx
from wx import xrc
import wx.lib.platebtn as platebtn

class MyApp(wx.App):
    def OnInit(self):
        self.res = xrc.XmlResource("notebook.xrc")

        frame = self.res.LoadFrame(None, 'DemoFrame')
        panel = xrc.XRCCTRL(frame, "DemoPanel")
        notebook = xrc.XRCCTRL(panel, "DemoNotebook")

        sizer = wx.BoxSizer(wx.VERTICAL)
        btn = platebtn.PlateButton(panel, label="Test",
                                   style=platebtn.PB_STYLE_DEFAULT)
        btn.Bind(wx.EVT_BUTTON, self.onButton)
        sizer.Add(notebook, 1, wx.ALL|wx.EXPAND, 5)
        sizer.Add(btn)
        panel.SetSizer(sizer)

        frame.Show()
        return True

    def onButton(self, event):
        """"""
        print("You pressed the button!")
```

```
if __name__ == "__main__":
    app = MyApp(False)
    app.MainLoop()
```

As you can see, that was as simple as it is to create the application in just plain wxPython. If there had been a wx.Button defined in XRC, we would do the same thing that we did for the panel to create a handle of it. Once we had the handle, we could bind events to the button as we would normally.

Using XRCed to Generate Python Code

The XRCed application includes a Python code generator that we can subclass for our own code. To start, we'll use the first simple example in this article and then we'll expand that example and show you how to bind events. In XRCed, load the first example and then go to File, Generate Python. Accept the defaults and click the **Generate** module button. You should now have some autogenerated code that looks like the following:

```
# This file was automatically generated by pywxrc.
# -*- coding: UTF-8 -*-

import wx
import wx.xrc as xrc

__res = None

def get_resources():
    """ This function provides access to the XML resources in this
    module."""
    global __res
    if __res == None:
        __init_resources()
    return __res

        class xrcMainFrame(wx.Frame):
        #!XRCED:begin-block:xrcMainFrame.PreCreate
            def PreCreate(self, pre):
                """ This function is called during the class's
                initialization.
```

```
        Override it for custom setup before the window is created
        usually to
        set additional window styles using SetWindowStyle() and
        SetExtraStyle().
        """

        pass

#!XRCED:end-block:xrcMainFrame.PreCreate


    def __init__(self, parent):
        # Two stage creation (see http://wiki.wxpython.org/index.
        cgi/TwoStageCreation)
        pre = wx.PreFrame()
        self.PreCreate(pre)
        get_resources().LoadOnFrame(pre, parent, "MainFrame")
        self.PostCreate(pre)

        # Define variables for the controls, bind event handlers


# ----------------------- Resource data ----------------------

    def __init_resources():
        global __res
        __res = xrc.EmptyXmlResource()

        __res.Load('twoBtns.xrc')
```

It's a little ugly, but if you can read normal wxPython, then you should be able to figure this out. Now let's create a subclass of this code. The main reason we want to do this is so that we can change the XRC file and the subsequent generated code and our subclass can basically just stay the same. It helps us to separate the model (the XML) from the view (the wxPython code).

Special note: The XRC example above doesn't work in wxPython 4!

Anyway, here's the simple example code that we can use with this XRC example in wxPython Classic:

```python
# twoBtns_xrc_subclass.py

import twoBtns_xrc
import wx

class XrcFrameSubClass(twoBtns_xrc.xrcMainFrame):
    """"""

    def __init__(self):
        """Constructor"""
        twoBtns_xrc.xrcMainFrame.__init__(self, parent=None)
        self.Show()

if __name__ == "__main__":
    app = wx.App(False)
    frame = XrcFrameSubClass()
    app.MainLoop()
```

Notice that we import the module "twoBtns_xrc," which is similar to what I called the XRCfile. XRCed adds the "_xrc" part to the Python file name. Once we have that imported, we can access the XRC Frame object and subclass it.

This covers the basics of using the XRCed application. Hopefully you know enough now to use it wisely and will be able to create some truly amazing code using these shortcuts. If you need help, be sure to check the links in the following section, email the wxPython mailing list or try bugging the wx guys on the IRC channel.

Recipe 14-4. How to Create a Grid in XRC

Problem

Some widgets are harder than others to figure out how to add to your application when using XRC. In this recipe, we will look at how to add a Grid widget to our application

Adding a Grid widget from **wx.grid.Grid** should be just like any other widget, but if you run the code below, you'll discover a weird issue:

```python
import wx
from wx import xrc

class MyApp(wx.App):
    def OnInit(self):
        self.res = xrc.XmlResource("grid.xrc")

        frame = self.res.LoadFrame(None, 'MyFrame')
        panel = xrc.XRCCTRL(frame, "MyPanel")
        grid = xrc.XRCCTRL(panel, "MyGrid")
        print(type(grid))
        grid.CreateGrid(25, 6)

        sizer = wx.BoxSizer(wx.VERTICAL)
        sizer.Add(grid, 1, wx.EXPAND|wx.ALL, 5)

        panel.SetSizer(sizer)

        frame.Show()
        return True

if __name__ == "__main__":
    app = MyApp(False)
    app.MainLoop()
```

You'll note that when you run this, the type that is printed out is a "**wx._windows. ScrolledWindow,**" not a **Grid** object. Thus you'll end up with the following traceback in Python 2:

AttributeError: 'ScrolledWindow' object has no attribute 'CreateGrid'

```
File "c:\Users\mdriscoll\Desktop\xrcGridDemo.py", line 26, in <module>
  app = MyApp(False)
File "C:\Python26\Lib\site-packages\wx-2.8-msw-unicode\wx\_core.py", line
7981, in __init__
  self._BootstrapApp()
File "C:\Python26\Lib\site-packages\wx-2.8-msw-unicode\wx\_core.py", line
7555, in _BootstrapApp
```

```
return _core_.PyApp__BootstrapApp(*args, **kwargs)
File "c:\Users\mdriscoll\Desktop\xrcGridDemo.py", line 14, in OnInit
  grid.CreateGrid(25, 6)
```

The traceback in Python 3 is quite similar, so it won't be reproduced here. Instead, we'll take a look at the XRC file that we tried to load in the previous example code.

```xml
<?xml version="1.0" ?>
<resource class="">
  <object class="wxFrame" name="MyFrame">
    <object class="wxPanel" name="MyPanel">
      <object class="wxGrid" name="MyGrid"/>
    </object>
    <title>XRC Grid</title>
  </object>
</resource>
```

As you can see, you should be getting a wxGrid back. What's the solution? You need to import wx.grid! According to Robin Dunn, creator of wxPython, following is the reason you need to do that: "You need to import wx.grid in your python code. When you do that then some internal data structures are updated with the type info for the grid classes, and this info is used when figuring out how to convert a C++ pointer to a Python object of the right type for the XRCCTRL return value."

Solution

So let's use this information to update our code in such a way that we can add a Grid to our application.

```python
import wx
import wx.grid
from wx import xrc

class MyApp(wx.App):
    def OnInit(self):
        self.res = xrc.XmlResource("grid.xrc")

        frame = self.res.LoadFrame(None, 'MyFrame')
```

```
        panel = xrc.XRCCTRL(frame, "MyPanel")
        grid = xrc.XRCCTRL(panel, "MyGrid")
        print(type(grid))
        grid.CreateGrid(25, 6)

        sizer = wx.BoxSizer(wx.VERTICAL)
        sizer.Add(grid, 1, wx.EXPAND|wx.ALL, 5)

        panel.SetSizer(sizer)

        frame.Show()
        return True

if __name__ == "__main__":
    app = MyApp(False)
    app.MainLoop()
```

How It Works

As Robin mentioned in his earlier quote, the reason this code worked versus the original
is that now we are import **wx.grid**. This is one of those times where working with a GUI
toolkit that wraps C++ can bite us, but overall I think you'll find that these sorts of issues
are few and far between.

When you run this code, it will look like the screen in Figure 14-8:

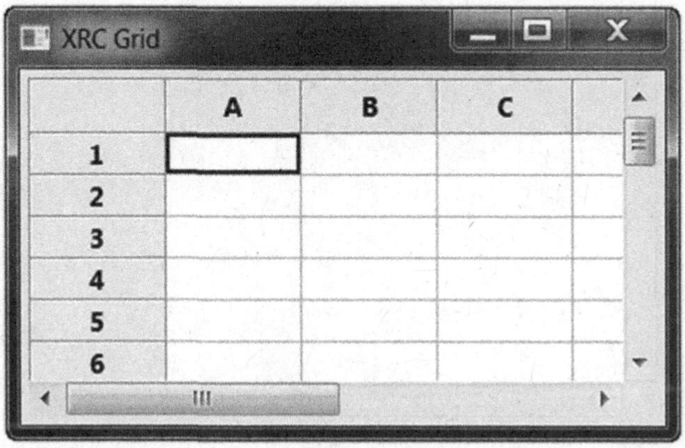

Figure 14-8. *Adding a grid widget to your application in XRCed*

Creating widgets in XRC can be challenging, but it's also a rewarding experience as it can really help you separate your logic from your user interface. In this recipe, we learned how to work around a fairly straightforward issue. As we saw in the previous recipe, adding a control that's not a part of XRC already is a bit harder.

CHAPTER 15

Working with Sizers

Recipe 15-1. How to Get Children Widgets from a Sizer

Problem

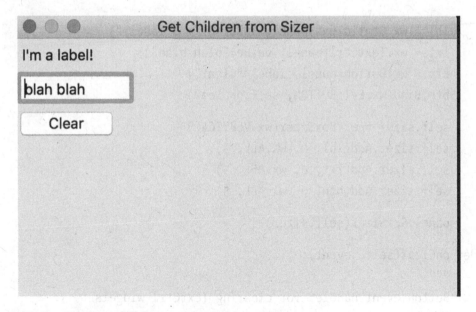

Figure 15-1. *Getting children widgets from a sizer*

In this recipe we will discover how to get the children widgets from a sizer object. In wxPython, you would expect to call the sizer's **GetChildren()** method. However, this returns a list of **SizerItem** objects rather than a list of the actual widgets themselves. You can see the difference if you call a wx.Panel's **GetChildren()** method which will actually give you a list of widgets.

© Mike Driscoll 2018
M. Driscoll, *wxPython Recipes*, https://doi.org/10.1007/978-1-4842-3237-8_15

Solution

The best way to figure these kinds of problems out is by experimenting with the code. Of course, this being a book, you probably don't want to see all the iterations I went through to finally get to the solution, so I'll just show you the end result.

```python
import wx

class MyApp(wx.Frame):
    """"""

    def __init__(self):
        """Constructor"""
        title = 'Get Children from Sizer'
        wx.Frame.__init__(self, None, title=title)
        panel = wx.Panel(self)

        lbl = wx.StaticText(panel, label="I'm a label!")
        txt = wx.TextCtrl(panel, value="blah blah")
        btn = wx.Button(panel, label="Clear")
        btn.Bind(wx.EVT_BUTTON, self.onClear)

        self.sizer = wx.BoxSizer(wx.VERTICAL)
        self.sizer.Add(lbl, 0, wx.ALL, 5)
        self.sizer.Add(txt, 0, wx.ALL, 5)
        self.sizer.Add(btn, 0, wx.ALL, 5)

        panel.SetSizer(self.sizer)

    def onClear(self, event):
        """
        Button event handler for clearing TextCtrl widgets
        """
        children = self.sizer.GetChildren()

        for child in children:
            widget = child.GetWindow()
            print(widget)
```

```
        if isinstance(widget, wx.TextCtrl):
            widget.Clear()

if __name__ == "__main__":
    app = wx.App(False)
    frame = MyApp()
    frame.Show()
    app.MainLoop()
```

How It Works

The important bit is in the **onClear** method. Here we need to call the **SizerItem's GetWindow()** method to return the actual widget instance. Once we have that, we can do stuff with the widget, such as change the label or value or, in this case, clear the text control. Try adding a **print(child)** call in the **for** loop to see that we are getting **SizerItems** instead of the widget itself. That can be quite illuminating and is a good way to test out if the code is working the way you expect. In fact, that is how I quickly discovered that I was doing it incorrectly.

This piece of code can be really handy to know how to do when you need to loop over some children widgets that need to be hidden. Or, if you have a form and you want to clear it, this is one of the easiest methods of doing so. Give it a try and do some experimentation to see how useful it can be.

Recipe 15-2. How to Center a Widget

Problem

Over the years, I see people ask about how to center a widget within their frame, panel, or dialog. The solution is actually quite easy. In most cases, you just need to nest a Horizontal BoxSizer inside of a Vertical BoxSizer with some spacers. In this chapter, I'll show you two or three different ways to accomplish this task.

Solution #1—Using Faux Spacers

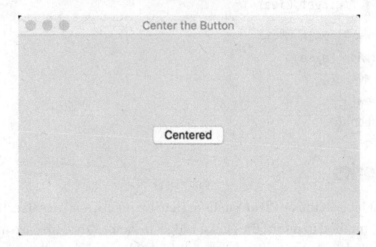

Figure 15-2. *Centering a button using faux spacers*

The first time I learned how to center widgets, I was told I could use a tuple for my spacer. The syntax looks a bit odd, but it works.

```python
import wx

class MainFrame(wx.Frame):
    """"""

    def __init__(self):
        """Constructor"""
        wx.Frame.__init__(self, None, title="Center the Button")
        panel = wx.Panel(self)

        h_sizer = wx.BoxSizer(wx.HORIZONTAL)
        main_sizer = wx.BoxSizer(wx.VERTICAL)

        btn = wx.Button(panel, label="Centered")
        h_sizer.Add(btn, 0, wx.CENTER)

        main_sizer.Add((0,0), 1, wx.EXPAND)
        main_sizer.Add(h_sizer, 0, wx.CENTER)
        main_sizer.Add((0,0), 1, wx.EXPAND)
```

CHAPTER 15   WORKING WITH SIZERS

```
        panel.SetSizer(main_sizer)

        self.Show()

if __name__ == "__main__":
    app = wx.App(False)
    frame = MainFrame()
    app.MainLoop()
```

How It Works

Here we nest a horizontal **BoxSizer** inside our top-level vertical BoxSizer. But we surround the horizontal sizer with two faux **spacers** that happen to be tuples that have both their proportions set to 1 and the **wx.EXPAND** style flag set.

Solution #2—Using an AddStretchSpacer

wxPython's sizer's include the **AddStretchSpacer** method, which is a nice, convenient method that does basically the same thing as the previous example. Let's take a look.

```
import wx

class MainFrame(wx.Frame):
    """"""

    def __init__(self):
        """"""Constructor"""
        wx.Frame.__init__(self, None, title="Center the Button")
        panel = wx.Panel(self)

        h_sizer = wx.BoxSizer(wx.HORIZONTAL)
        main_sizer = wx.BoxSizer(wx.VERTICAL)

        btn = wx.Button(panel, label="Centered")
        h_sizer.Add(btn, 0, wx.CENTER)

        main_sizer.AddStretchSpacer(prop=1)
        main_sizer.Add(h_sizer, 0, wx.CENTER)
        main_sizer.AddStretchSpacer(prop=1)
```

```
        panel.SetSizer(main_sizer)

        self.Show()

if __name__ == "__main__":
    app = wx.App(False)
    frame = MainFrame()
    app.MainLoop()
```

How It Works

You will note that the only difference here is using the AddStretchSpacer method along with its **prop** parameter set to 1.

Solution #3—Centering Without Nested Sizers

One of my astute blog readers mentioned a third way to center the widget that does not require nesting the sizers. Let's take a look at their idea.

```
import wx

class MainFrame(wx.Frame):
    """"""

    def __init__(self):
        """Constructor"""
        wx.Frame.__init__(self, None, title="Center the Button")
        panel = wx.Panel(self)

        main_sizer = wx.BoxSizer(wx.VERTICAL)

        btn = wx.Button(panel, label="Centered")
        main_sizer.AddStretchSpacer()
        main_sizer.Add(btn, 0, wx.CENTER)
        main_sizer.AddStretchSpacer()

        panel.SetSizer(main_sizer)

        self.Show()
```

```
if __name__ == "__main__":
    app = wx.App(False)
    frame = MainFrame()
    app.MainLoop()
```

Here we just create a vertical sizer, add a stretch spacer, and then tell the button to be centered, and then we add another stretch spacer. The code is very similar to that in the previous example except that we don't use a horizontal sizer at all. Special thanks goes to a fellow named Yoriz for mentioning this to me.

Now you know several different approaches for centering widgets in your wx.Frame or wx.Panel. You will find this quite useful for buttons that need to be centered at the bottom of your windows. I have found that centering widgets is an extremely common activity and something I have needed to do in my own applications, so it's good to have different solutions for this problems.

Recipe 15-3. How to Make Widgets Wrap

Problem

Starting in the 2.9 version of wxPython, the developers introduced the world to a new type of sizer that can take widgets and automatically make them "wrap" around as you resize the frame. That sizer is known as **wx.WrapSizer**. For some reason, it is relatively unknown, so we'll spend a few minutes going over how to use it in this recipe. By the end of this recipe you will be able to use this fun sizer to wrap your widgets too!

Solution

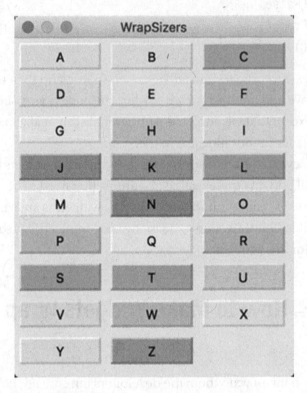

Figure 15-3. *Using a wx.WrapSizer*

The **wx.WrapSizer** widget works in much the same way as a **wx.BoxSizer**. All you need to do to use it is to instantiate it and add widgets to it. Let's take a look at a simple program.

```
import random
import wx
from wx.lib.buttons import GenButton

class MyPanel(wx.Panel):
    """"""

    def __init__(self, parent):
        """Constructor"""
        wx.Panel.__init__(self, parent)

        text = "ABCDEFGHIJKLMNOPQRSTUVWXYZ"
```

```python
        sizer = wx.WrapSizer()
        for letter in text:
            btn = GenButton(self, label=letter)
            r = random.randint(128, 255)
            g = random.randint(128, 255)
            b = random.randint(128, 255)
            btn.SetBackgroundColour(wx.Colour(r,g,b))
            btn.Refresh()
            sizer.Add(btn, 0, wx.ALL, 5)

        self.SetSizer(sizer)

class MyFrame(wx.Frame):
    """"""

    def __init__(self):
        """Constructor"""
        wx.Frame.__init__(self, None, title="WrapSizers", size=(400,500))
        panel = MyPanel(self)
        self.Show()

if __name__ == "__main__":
    app = wx.App(False)
    frame = MyFrame()
    app.MainLoop()
```

How It Works

Here we create an instance of our sizer and then loop over the letters in the alphabet, creating a button for each letter. We also change the background color of each button to add a little variety. If you haven't guessed yet, this example is based on the wxPython demo example. You will notice that as you resize the frame, the buttons will rearrange themselves as best they can. Sometimes, they may even change size a bit. Let's learn a bit more about this sizer!

The **wx.WrapSizer** can be told its orientation and you can pass it flags at instantiation. The orientation flags are **wx.HORIZONTAL** and **wx.VERTICAL**. Horizontal is the default. According to the documentation "the flags parameter can be a combination of the values **EXTEND_LAST_ON_EACH_LINE** which will cause the last item on each line to use any remaining space on that line and **REMOVE_LEADING_SPACES** which removes any spacer elements from the beginning of a row." The **WrapSizer** also has four additional methods beyond the normal wx.Sizer method: **CalcMin** (calculates minimal size), **InformFirstDirection** (appears not be used), **IsSpaceItem** (can be used to treat some normal items as spacers), and **RecalcSizes** (implements the calculation of a box sizer's dimensions and then sets the size of its children).

At this point you should know enough to start using the wx.WrapSizer in your own applications. It really is a handy sizer although there probably aren't that many applications that you will be creating that need this sort of thing. But for the cases that do, this sizer is really great!

Recipe 15-4. Adding/Removing Widgets Dynamically

Problem

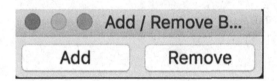

Figure 15-4. *Adding/Removing buttons*

A fairly common task that many developers end up wanting to do is to create or remove widgets at runtime. This is actually quite easy to accomplish with wxPython. I have had to do this sort of thing myself from time to time depending on what kind of user was accessing my program, so I could show slightly different options. For example, an admin might get additional controls that a normal user wouldn't be able to access. So you might want to dynamically add or remove a panel that contains admin widgets.

Solution

For this example, I decided to make this really simple. All this application will do is allow the user to add or remove buttons. The following script will create a window similar to the one at the beginning of this recipe. If you press the Add button a few times, you should see something like the screen in Figure 15-5.

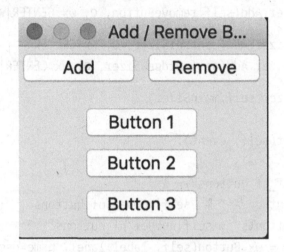

Figure 15-5. *Demonstration of adding widgets dynamically*

As you can see, you end up with more buttons! Now let's take a moment and read the code. I'll explain the code as soon as you finish reading it.

```python
import wx


class MyPanel(wx.Panel):
    """"""

    def __init__(self, parent):
        """Constructor"""
        wx.Panel.__init__(self, parent)
        self.number_of_buttons = 0
        self.frame = parent

        self.mainSizer = wx.BoxSizer(wx.VERTICAL)
        controlSizer = wx.BoxSizer(wx.HORIZONTAL)
        self.widgetSizer = wx.BoxSizer(wx.VERTICAL)
```

```python
        self.addButton = wx.Button(self, label="Add")
        self.addButton.Bind(wx.EVT_BUTTON, self.onAddWidget)
        controlSizer.Add(self.addButton, 0, wx.CENTER|wx.ALL, 5)

        self.removeButton = wx.Button(self, label="Remove")
        self.removeButton.Bind(wx.EVT_BUTTON, self.onRemoveWidget)
        controlSizer.Add(self.removeButton, 0, wx.CENTER|wx.ALL, 5)

        self.mainSizer.Add(controlSizer, 0, wx.CENTER)
        self.mainSizer.Add(self.widgetSizer, 0, wx.CENTER|wx.ALL, 10)

        self.SetSizer(self.mainSizer)

    def onAddWidget(self, event):
        """"""

        self.number_of_buttons += 1
        label = "Button %s" %  self.number_of_buttons
        name = "button%s" % self.number_of_buttons
        new_button = wx.Button(self, label=label, name=name)
        self.widgetSizer.Add(new_button, 0, wx.ALL, 5)
        self.frame.fSizer.Layout()
        self.frame.Fit()

    def onRemoveWidget(self, event):
        """"""

        if self.widgetSizer.GetChildren():
            self.widgetSizer.Hide(self.number_of_buttons-1)
            self.widgetSizer.Remove(self.number_of_buttons-1)
            self.number_of_buttons -= 1
            self.frame.fSizer.Layout()
            self.frame.Fit()

class MyFrame(wx.Frame):
    """"""

    def __init__(self):
        """Constructor"""
        wx.Frame.__init__(self, parent=None, title="Add / Remove Buttons")
```

```
        self.fSizer = wx.BoxSizer(wx.VERTICAL)
        panel = MyPanel(self)
        self.fSizer.Add(panel, 1, wx.EXPAND)
        self.SetSizer(self.fSizer)
        self.Fit()
        self.Show()

if __name__ == "__main__":
    app = wx.App(False)
    frame = MyFrame()
    app.MainLoop()
```

I think this is pretty straightforward code, so we'll just focus on the important bits. The first topic I'm going to point out is that I call the frame's **Fit()** method right before I show it. I normally avoid using Fit, but I was having trouble getting the frame to change size appropriately whenever I added or removed the buttons and Fit fixed that issue for me. I should note that Fit always tries to make the widgets fit the container and sometimes it ends up doing it in ways I don't like.

Anyway, the other bit is in the **onAddWidget** and **onRemoveWidget** methods. You normally want to call the **Layout()** method on the container object to make it update and lay out the controls whenever you add or remove a widget. Oddly enough, it seems that **Fit()** does that automatically, so those **Layout()** calls that you see in the previous code can actually be removed. I tried removing the Fit ones to see if Layout was enough, but when you do that, the frame doesn't update its size, so Fit seems to be required in this case. Now, if you happened to be adding or removing widgets in such a way that it wouldn't affect the frame's overall size, I think Layout would be enough.

Finally, as a side note, you sometimes use **Layout()** at the end of a **Freeze/Thaw** update as well.

At this point you should know the basics of adding and removing widgets in a dynamic fashion. It's actually pretty easy once you understand all the concepts. This is one of those pieces of knowledge that I think you'll find quite useful, as I have used the techniques in this chapter several times over the years.

CHAPTER 16

Threads and Timers

Recipe 16-1. How to Update a Progress Bar from a Thread

Problem

If you use GUIs (graphical user interfaces) in Python much, you know that every now and then you need to execute some long-running process. Of course, if you do that as you would with a command-line program, then you'll be in for a surprise. In most cases, you'll end up blocking your GUI's event loop and the user will see your program freeze. This is true of all the Python GUI toolkits, including Tkinter, PyQt, or wxPython. What can you do to get around such mishaps? Start the task in another thread or process, of course! In this chapter, we'll look at how to do this with wxPython and Python's threading module.

In the wxPython world, there are three related "thread-safe" methods. If you do not use one of these three when you go to update your user interface, then you may experience weird issues. Sometimes your GUI will work just fine. Other times, it will crash Python for no apparent reason, thus the need for the thread-safe methods: wx.PostEvent, wx.CallAfter, and wx.CallLater. According to Robin Dunn (creator of wxPython), wx.CallAfter uses wx.PostEvent to send an event to the application object. The application will have an event handler bound to that event and will react according to whatever the programmer has coded upon receipt of the event. It is my understanding that wx.CallLater calls wx.CallAfter with a specified time limit so that you can tell it how long to wait before sending the event.

Robin Dunn also pointed out that the Python Global Interpreter Lock (GIL) will prevent more than one thread to be executing Python bytecodes at the same time, which may limit how many CPU (central processing unit) cores are utilized by your program.

© Mike Driscoll 2018
M. Driscoll, *wxPython Recipes*, https://doi.org/10.1007/978-1-4842-3237-8_16

On the flip side, he also said that "wxPython releases the GIL while making calls to wx APIs so other threads can run at that time." In other words, your mileage may vary when using threads on multicore machines. I found this discussion to be interesting and confusing.

Anyway, what this means in regard to the three wx-methods is that **wx.CallLater** is the most abstract thread-safe method with **wx.CallAfter** next and **wx.PostEvent** being the lowest level. In the following examples, you will see how to use wx.CallAfter and wx.PostEvent to update your wxPython program.

Solution for wxPython 2.8.12 and Earlier

On the wxPython mailing list, you'll see the experts telling others to use **wx.CallAfter** along with **PubSub** to communicate with their wxPython applications from another thread. I've probably even told people to do that. So in the following example, that's exactly what we're going to do. Note that this code is using the old version of **PubSub** so it will only work with **wxPython 2.8.12** or older.

```
# wxPython 2.8.12

import time
import wx

from threading import Thread
from wx.lib.pubsub import Publisher

class TestThread(Thread):
    """Test Worker Thread Class."""

    def __init__(self):
        """Init Worker Thread Class."""
        Thread.__init__(self)
        self.daemon = True
        self.start()    # start the thread

    def run(self):
        """Run Worker Thread."""
        # This is the code executing in the new thread.
        for i in range(6):
```

```
            time.sleep(10)
            wx.CallAfter(self.postTime, i)
        time.sleep(5)
        wx.CallAfter(Publisher().sendMessage, "update", "Thread finished!")

    def postTime(self, amt):
        """

        Send time to GUI
        """

        amtOfTime = (amt + 1) * 10
        Publisher().sendMessage("update", amtOfTime)

class MyForm(wx.Frame):

    def __init__(self):
        wx.Frame.__init__(self, None, wx.ID_ANY, "Tutorial")

        # Add a panel so it looks the correct on all platforms
        panel = wx.Panel(self, wx.ID_ANY)
        self.displayLbl = wx.StaticText(panel,
            label="Amount of time since thread started goes here")
        self.btn = btn = wx.Button(panel, label="Start Thread")

        btn.Bind(wx.EVT_BUTTON, self.onButton)

        sizer = wx.BoxSizer(wx.VERTICAL)
        sizer.Add(self.displayLbl, 0, wx.ALL|wx.CENTER, 5)
        sizer.Add(btn, 0, wx.ALL|wx.CENTER, 5)
        panel.SetSizer(sizer)

        # create a pubsub receiver
        Publisher().subscribe(self.updateDisplay, "update")

    def onButton(self, event):
        """

        Runs the thread
        """

        TestThread()
        self.displayLbl.SetLabel("Thread started!")
```

```
        btn = event.GetEventObject()
        btn.Disable()

    def updateDisplay(self, msg):
        """
        Receives data from thread and updates the display
        """
        t = msg.data
        if isinstance(t, int):
            self.displayLbl.SetLabel("Time since thread started: %s
            seconds" % t)
        else:
            self.displayLbl.SetLabel("%s" % t)
            self.btn.Enable()

# Run the program
if __name__ == "__main__":
    app = wx.App(False)
    frame = MyForm().Show()
    app.MainLoop()
```

How It Works

We'll be using Python's time module to fake our long-running process. However, feel free to put something better in its place. In a real-life example, I use a thread to open Adobe Reader and send a PDF to a printer. That might not seem like anything special, but when I didn't use a thread, the print button in my application would stay stuck down while the document was sent to the printer and my GUI just hung until that was done. Even a second or two is noticeable to the user!

Anyway, let's see how this works. In our thread class (reproduced in the code that follows), we override the "run" method so it does what we want. This thread is started when we instantiate it because we have **self.start()** in its **__init__** method. In the "run" method, we loop over a range of 6, sleeping for ten seconds, in between iterations and then update our user interface using wx.CallAfter and PubSub. When the loop finishes, we send a final message to our application to let the user know what happened.

```
class TestThread(Thread):
    """Test Worker Thread Class."""

    def __init__(self):
        """Init Worker Thread Class."""
        Thread.__init__(self)
        self.daemon = True
        self.start()      # start the thread

    def run(self):
        """Run Worker Thread."""
        # This is the code executing in the new thread.
        for i in range(6):
            time.sleep(10)
            wx.CallAfter(self.postTime, i)
        time.sleep(5)
        wx.CallAfter(Publisher().sendMessage, "update", "Thread finished!")

    def postTime(self, amt):
        """

        Send time to GUI
        """

        amtOfTime = (amt + 1) * 10
        Publisher().sendMessage("update", amtOfTime)
```

Notice that in our wxPython code, we start the thread using a button event handler. We also disable the button so we don't accidentally start additional threads. That would be pretty confusing if we had a bunch of them going and the UI would randomly say that it was done when it wasn't. That is a good exercise for the reader though. You could display the PID (process ID) of the thread so you'd know which was which . . . and you might want to output this information to a scrolling text control so you can see the activity of the various threads.

The last piece of interest here is probably the PubSub receiver and its event handler.

```
def updateDisplay(self, msg):
    """

    Receives data from thread and updates the display
    """
```

```
    t = msg.data
    if isinstance(t, int):
        self.displayLbl.SetLabel("Time since thread started: %s seconds" % t)
    else:
        self.displayLbl.SetLabel("%s" % t)
        self.btn.Enable()
```

See how we extract the message from the thread and use it to update our display? We also use the type of data we receive to tell us what to show the user. Pretty cool, huh?

Solution for wxPython 3 and Newer

As you may recall from previous recipes, the PubSub module was changed in wxPython 2.9 so the code in the previous section won't work with current versions of wxPython. So let's update the code a bit to make it work for wxPython 3.0 Classic and wxPython 4.

```
# wxPython 3.0 and Newer

import time
import wx

from threading import Thread
from wx.lib.pubsub import pub

class TestThread(Thread):
    """Test Worker Thread Class."""

    def __init__(self):
        """Init Worker Thread Class."""
        Thread.__init__(self)
        self.start()    # start the thread

    def run(self):
        """Run Worker Thread."""
        # This is the code executing in the new thread.
        for i in range(6):
            time.sleep(2)
            wx.CallAfter(self.postTime, i)
```

```
        time.sleep(5)
        wx.CallAfter(pub.sendMessage, "update", msg="Thread finished!")

    def postTime(self, amt):
        """

        Send time to GUI
        """

        amtOfTime = (amt + 1) * 10
        pub.sendMessage("update", msg=amtOfTime)

class MyForm(wx.Frame):

    def __init__(self):
        wx.Frame.__init__(self, None, wx.ID_ANY, "Tutorial")

        # Add a panel so it looks the correct on all platforms
        panel = wx.Panel(self, wx.ID_ANY)
        self.displayLbl = wx.StaticText(panel,
                                        label="Amount of time since thread
                                        started goes here")
        self.btn = btn = wx.Button(panel, label="Start Thread")

        btn.Bind(wx.EVT_BUTTON, self.onButton)

        sizer = wx.BoxSizer(wx.VERTICAL)
        sizer.Add(self.displayLbl, 0, wx.ALL|wx.CENTER, 5)
        sizer.Add(btn, 0, wx.ALL|wx.CENTER, 5)
        panel.SetSizer(sizer)

        # create a pubsub receiver
        pub.subscribe(self.updateDisplay, "update")

    def onButton(self, event):
        """

        Runs the thread
        """

        TestThread()
        self.displayLbl.SetLabel("Thread started!")
        btn = event.GetEventObject()
        btn.Disable()
```

```
    def updateDisplay(self, msg):
        """
        Receives data from thread and updates the display
        """
        t = msg
        if isinstance(t, int):
            self.displayLbl.SetLabel("Time since thread started: %s
            seconds" % t)
        else:
            self.displayLbl.SetLabel("%s" % t)
            self.btn.Enable()

# Run the program
if __name__ == "__main__":
    app = wx.App(False)
    frame = MyForm().Show()
    app.MainLoop()
```

How It Works

Note that we just ended up importing pub and replacing all the references to Publisher() with pub. We also had to change the sendMessage call slightly in that we need to call it using keyword arguments that match the function that is called by the subscriber. They're all minor changes but necessary to get them to work in newer versions of wxPython. Now let's go down a level and check out how to do it with wx.PostEvent instead.

wx.PostEvent and Threads

The following code is based on an example from the wxPython wiki. It's a little bit more complicated than the wx.CallAfter code we just looked at, but I'm confident that we can figure it out.

```
import time
import wx

from threading import Thread
```

```python
# Define notification event for thread completion
EVT_RESULT_ID = wx.NewId()

def EVT_RESULT(win, func):
    """Define Result Event."""
    win.Connect(-1, -1, EVT_RESULT_ID, func)

class ResultEvent(wx.PyEvent):
    """Simple event to carry arbitrary result data."""
    def __init__(self, data):
        """Init Result Event."""
        wx.PyEvent.__init__(self)
        self.SetEventType(EVT_RESULT_ID)
        self.data = data

class TestThread(Thread):
    """Test Worker Thread Class."""

    def __init__(self, wxObject):
        """Init Worker Thread Class."""
        Thread.__init__(self)
        self.wxObject = wxObject
        self.start()    # start the thread

    def run(self):
        """Run Worker Thread."""
        # This is the code executing in the new thread.
        for i in range(6):
            time.sleep(10)
            amtOfTime = (i + 1) * 10
            wx.PostEvent(self.wxObject, ResultEvent(amtOfTime))
        time.sleep(5)
        wx.PostEvent(self.wxObject, ResultEvent("Thread finished!"))

class MyForm(wx.Frame):

    def __init__(self):
        wx.Frame.__init__(self, None, wx.ID_ANY, "Tutorial")
```

```python
        # Add a panel so it looks the correct on all platforms
        panel = wx.Panel(self, wx.ID_ANY)
        self.displayLbl = wx.StaticText(panel, label="Amount of time since
        thread started goes here")
        self.btn = btn = wx.Button(panel, label="Start Thread")

        btn.Bind(wx.EVT_BUTTON, self.onButton)

        sizer = wx.BoxSizer(wx.VERTICAL)
        sizer.Add(self.displayLbl, 0, wx.ALL|wx.CENTER, 5)
        sizer.Add(btn, 0, wx.ALL|wx.CENTER, 5)
        panel.SetSizer(sizer)

        # Set up event handler for any worker thread results
        EVT_RESULT(self, self.updateDisplay)

    def onButton(self, event):
        """

        Runs the thread
        """

        TestThread(self)
        self.displayLbl.SetLabel("Thread started!")
        btn = event.GetEventObject()
        btn.Disable()

    def updateDisplay(self, msg):
        """

        Receives data from thread and updates the display
        """

        t = msg.data
        if isinstance(t, int):
            self.displayLbl.SetLabel("Time since thread started: %s
            seconds" % t)
        else:
            self.displayLbl.SetLabel("%s" % t)
            self.btn.Enable()
```

```
# Run the program
if __name__ == "__main__":
    app = wx.App(False)
    frame = MyForm().Show()
    app.MainLoop()
```

Let's break this down a bit. For me, the most confusing stuff is the first three pieces.

```
# Define notification event for thread completion
EVT_RESULT_ID = wx.NewId()

def EVT_RESULT(win, func):
    """Define Result Event."""
    win.Connect(-1, -1, EVT_RESULT_ID, func)

class ResultEvent(wx.PyEvent):
    """Simple event to carry arbitrary result data."""
    def __init__(self, data):
        """Init Result Event."""
        wx.PyEvent.__init__(self)
        self.SetEventType(EVT_RESULT_ID)
        self.data = data
```

The **EVT_RESULT_ID** is the key here. It links the thread to the **wx.PyEvent** and that weird "EVT_RESULT" function. In the wxPython code, we bind an event handler to the EVT_RESULT function. This allows us to use **wx.PostEvent** in the thread to send an event to our custom event class, **ResultEvent**. What does this do? It sends the data on to the wxPython program by emitting that custom **EVT_RESULT** that we bound to. I hope that all makes sense.

Once you've got that figured out in your head, read on. Are you ready? Good! You'll notice that our **TestThread** class is pretty much the same as before except that we're using wx.PostEvent to send our messages to the GUI instead of PubSub. The application programming interface (API) in our GUI's display updater is unchanged. We still just use the message's data property to extract the data we want. That's all there is to it!

Ideally, you now know how to use basic threading techniques in your wxPython programs. There are several other threading methods too which we didn't have a chance to cover here, such as using **wx.Yield** or **Queues**. Fortunately, the wxPython wiki covers these topics pretty well, so be sure to check out the links below if you're interested in those methods.

Recipe 16-2. How to Update a Progress Bar from a Thread

Problem

A fairly common task is the need to update a progress bar every so often. In this recipe, we will create a frame with a button. When the button is pushed, it will launch a dialog that contains our progress bar and it will start a thread. The thread is a dummy thread in that it doesn't do anything in particular except send an update back to the dialog once a second for 20 seconds. Then the dialog is destroyed.

Solution

Let's start by looking at how we can accomplish this task using wxPython 2.8.12.1 which is still a popular version of wxPython even though it's pretty old.

```python
import time
import wx

from threading import Thread
from wx.lib.pubsub import Publisher

class TestThread(Thread):
    """Test Worker Thread Class."""

    def __init__(self):
        """Init Worker Thread Class."""
        Thread.__init__(self)
        self.daemon = True
        self.start()    # start the thread

    def run(self):
        """Run Worker Thread."""
        # This is the code executing in the new thread.
        for i in range(20):
```

```python
            time.sleep(0.25)
            wx.CallAfter(Publisher().sendMessage, "update", "")

class MyProgressDialog(wx.Dialog):
    """"""

    def __init__(self):
        """Constructor"""
        wx.Dialog.__init__(self, None, title="Progress")
        self.count = 0

        self.progress = wx.Gauge(self, range=20)

        sizer = wx.BoxSizer(wx.VERTICAL)
        sizer.Add(self.progress, 0, wx.EXPAND)
        self.SetSizer(sizer)

        # create a pubsub listener
        Publisher().subscribe(self.updateProgress, "update")

    def updateProgress(self, msg):
        """
        Update the progress bar
        """
        self.count += 1

        if self.count >= 20:
            self.EndModal(0)

        self.progress.SetValue(self.count)

class MyFrame(wx.Frame):

    def __init__(self):
        wx.Frame.__init__(self, None, title="Progress Bar Tutorial")

        # Add a panel so it looks the correct on all platforms
        panel = wx.Panel(self, wx.ID_ANY)
        self.btn = btn = wx.Button(panel, label="Start Thread")
        btn.Bind(wx.EVT_BUTTON, self.onButton)
```

```
        sizer = wx.BoxSizer(wx.VERTICAL)
        sizer.Add(btn, 0, wx.ALL|wx.CENTER, 5)
        panel.SetSizer(sizer)

    def onButton(self, event):
        """
        Runs the thread
        """
        btn = event.GetEventObject()
        btn.Disable()

        TestThread()
        dlg = MyProgressDialog()
        dlg.ShowModal()
        dlg.Destroy()

        btn.Enable()


# Run the program
if __name__ == "__main__":
    app = wx.App(False)
    frame = MyFrame()
    frame.Show()
    app.MainLoop()
```

Let's spend a few minutes breaking this down. We'll start at the bottom. The **MyFrame** class is what gets run first. When you run this script you should see something like the screen in Figure 16-1.

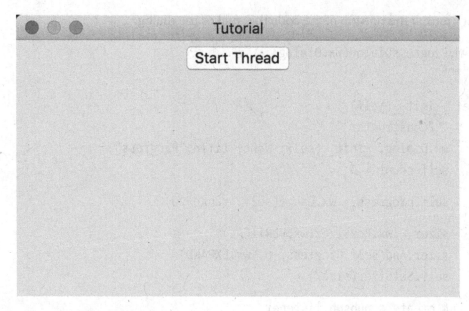

Figure 16-1. *Progress bar frame*

As you can see, all this code does is create a simple frame with a button on it. If you press the button, the following dialog will be created and a new thread will start (see Figure 16-2):

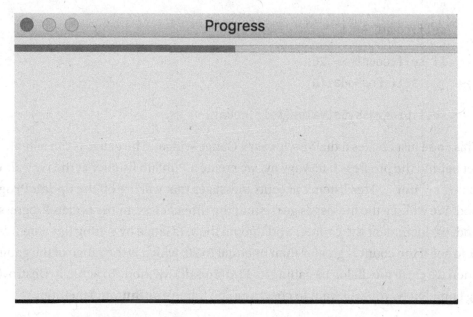

Figure 16-2. *A progress bar dialog*

Let's look at the portion of the code that makes the dialog.

```python
class MyProgressDialog(wx.Dialog):
    """"""

    def __init__(self):
        """Constructor"""
        wx.Dialog.__init__(self, None, title="Progress")
        self.count = 0

        self.progress = wx.Gauge(self, range=20)

        sizer = wx.BoxSizer(wx.VERTICAL)
        sizer.Add(self.progress, 0, wx.EXPAND)
        self.SetSizer(sizer)

        # create a pubsub listener
        Publisher().subscribe(self.updateProgress, "update")

    def updateProgress(self, msg):
        """
        Update the progress bar
        """
        self.count += 1

        if self.count >= 20:
            self.EndModal(0)

        self.progress.SetValue(self.count)
```

This code just creates a dialog with a wx.Gauge widget. The gauge is the actual widget behind the progress bar. Anyway, we create a PubSub listener at the very end of the dialog's __init__. This listener accepts messages that will fire off the **updateProgress** method. We will see the messages get sent in the thread class. In the updateProgress method, we increment the counter and update the wx.Gauge by setting its value. We also check to see if the count is greater than or equal to 20, which is the range of the gauge. If it is, then we close the dialog by calling its **EndModal()** method. To actually Destroy() the dialog completely, you will want to check out the frame's **onButton()** method.

Now we're ready to look at the threading code.

```python
class TestThread(Thread):
    """Test Worker Thread Class."""

    def __init__(self):
        """Init Worker Thread Class."""
        Thread.__init__(self)
        self.start()     # start the thread

    def run(self):
        """Run Worker Thread."""
        # This is the code executing in the new thread.
        for i in range(20):
            time.sleep(1)
            wx.CallAfter(Publisher().sendMessage, "update", "")
```

Here we created a thread and immediately started it. The thread loops over a range of 20 and uses the time module to sleep for a second in each iteration. After each sleep, it sends a message to the dialog to tell it to update the progress bar.

Updating the Code for wxPython 3.0.2.0 and Newer

The code in the previous section was written using PubSub's old API which has been tossed out the window with the advent of wxPython 2.9. So if you try to run the previous code in 2.9 or newer, you will likely run into issues. Thus for completeness, following is a version of the code that uses the new PubSub API and also works with wxPython Phoenix:

```python
import time
import wx

from threading import Thread
from wx.lib.pubsub import pub

class TestThread(Thread):
    """Test Worker Thread Class."""
```

```python
    def __init__(self):
        """Init Worker Thread Class."""
        Thread.__init__(self)
        self.daemon = True
        self.start()    # start the thread

    def run(self):
        """Run Worker Thread."""
        # This is the code executing in the new thread.
        for i in range(20):
            time.sleep(0.25)
            wx.CallAfter(pub.sendMessage, "update", msg="")

class MyProgressDialog(wx.Dialog):
    """"""

    def __init__(self):
        """Constructor"""
        wx.Dialog.__init__(self, None, title="Progress")
        self.count = 0

        self.progress = wx.Gauge(self, range=20)

        sizer = wx.BoxSizer(wx.VERTICAL)
        sizer.Add(self.progress, 0, wx.EXPAND)
        self.SetSizer(sizer)

        # create a pubsub receiver
        pub.subscribe(self.updateProgress, "update")

    def updateProgress(self, msg):
        """"""

        self.count += 1

        if self.count >= 20:
            self.EndModal(0)

        self.progress.SetValue(self.count)
```

```python
class MyForm(wx.Frame):

    def __init__(self):
        wx.Frame.__init__(self, None, wx.ID_ANY, "Tutorial")

        # Add a panel so it looks the correct on all platforms
        panel = wx.Panel(self, wx.ID_ANY)
        self.btn = btn = wx.Button(panel, label="Start Thread")
        btn.Bind(wx.EVT_BUTTON, self.onButton)

        sizer = wx.BoxSizer(wx.VERTICAL)
        sizer.Add(btn, 0, wx.ALL|wx.CENTER, 5)
        panel.SetSizer(sizer)

    def onButton(self, event):
        """
        Runs the thread
        """
        btn = event.GetEventObject()
        btn.Disable()

        TestThread()
        dlg = MyProgressDialog()
        dlg.ShowModal()
        dlg.Destroy()

        btn.Enable()

# Run the program
if __name__ == "__main__":
    app = wx.App(False)
    frame = MyForm().Show()
    app.MainLoop()
```

Note that now you import the pub module rather than the Publisher module. Also note that you have to use keyword arguments. See the PubSub documentation for additional information.

At this point, you should know how to create your own progress dialog and update it from a thread. You can use a variation of this code to create a file downloader. If you do that, you would need to check the size of the file you are downloading and download it in chunks so you can create the **wx.Gauge** with the appropriate range and update it as each chunk is downloaded. I hope this give you some ideas for how to use this widget in your own projects.

Recipe 16-3. A wx.Timer Tutorial

Problem

The wx.Timer allows the developer to execute code at specific intervals. In this chapter, I will cover several different ways to create timers. A timer object actually starts its own event loop that it controls without interfering the wxPython's main loop.

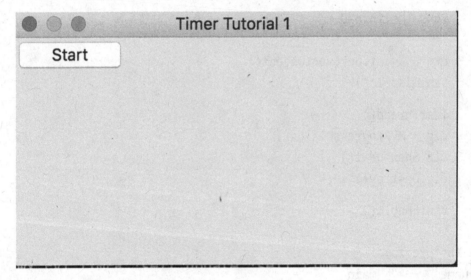

Figure 16-3. *A simple timer example*

Solution

My first example is super simple. It has only one button that starts and stops a timer. Let's take a look at the code.

```python
import time
import wx

class MyForm(wx.Frame):

    def __init__(self):
        wx.Frame.__init__(self, None, title="Timer Tutorial 1",
                          size=(500,500))

        panel = wx.Panel(self, wx.ID_ANY)

        self.timer = wx.Timer(self)
        self.Bind(wx.EVT_TIMER, self.update, self.timer)

        self.toggleBtn = wx.Button(panel, wx.ID_ANY, "Start")
        self.toggleBtn.Bind(wx.EVT_BUTTON, self.onToggle)

    def onToggle(self, event):
        btnLabel = self.toggleBtn.GetLabel()
        if btnLabel == "Start":
            print("starting timer...")
            self.timer.Start(1000)
            self.toggleBtn.SetLabel("Stop")
        else:
            print("timer stopped!")
            self.timer.Stop()
            self.toggleBtn.SetLabel("Start")

    def update(self, event):
        print("\nupdated: ", time.ctime())

# Run the program
if __name__ == "__main__":
    app = wx.App(True)
    frame = MyForm().Show()
    app.MainLoop()
```

How It Works

As you can see, I only import two modules: **wx** and **time**. I use the time module to post the time that the **wx.Timer** event fires on. The two main things to pay attention to here are how to bind the timer to an event and the event handler itself. For this example to work, you have to bind the frame to the timer event. I tried binding the timer (i.e., **self. timer.Bind**), but that didn't work. So the logical thing to do was ask Robin Dunn what was going on. He said that if the parent of the timer is the frame, then the frame is the only object that will receive the timer's events unless you derive wx.Timer and override its **Notify** method. Makes sense to me.

Regardless, let's look at my event handler. In it I grab the button's label and then use a conditional **if** statement to decide if I want to start or stop the timer as well as what to label the button. In this way, I can have just one function that toggles the button and the timer's state. The part to take note of are the methods Start and Stop. They are what control the timer.

In one of my real-life applications, I have a timer execute every so often to check my e-mail. I discovered that if I shut my program down without stopping the timer, the program would basically become a zombie process. Thus, you need to make sure that you stop all your timers when your program is closed or destroyed.

Before we get to my next example, let's take a look at refactoring this one. Robin Dunn had some suggestions that I implemented in the following code. Can you tell what's different?

```
import wx
import time

class MyForm(wx.Frame):

    def __init__(self):
        wx.Frame.__init__(self, None, title="Timer Tutorial 1",
                          size=(500,500))

        panel = wx.Panel(self, wx.ID_ANY)
```

```
        self.timer = wx.Timer(self)
        self.Bind(wx.EVT_TIMER, self.update, self.timer)

        self.toggleBtn = wx.Button(panel, wx.ID_ANY, "Start")
        self.toggleBtn.Bind(wx.EVT_BUTTON, self.onToggle)

    def onToggle(self, event):
        if self.timer.IsRunning():
            self.timer.Stop()
            self.toggleBtn.SetLabel("Start")
            print("timer stopped!")
        else:
            print("starting timer...")
            self.timer.Start(1000)
            self.toggleBtn.SetLabel("Stop")


    def update(self, event):
        print("\nupdated: ", time.ctime())

# Run the program
if __name__ == "__main__":
    app = wx.App(True)
    frame = MyForm().Show()
    app.MainLoop()
```

As you can see, I've changed the event handler to check if the timer is running or not rather than looking at the button's label. This saves us one line, but it's a little cleaner and shows how to accomplish the same thing in a slightly different way.

Using Multiple Timers

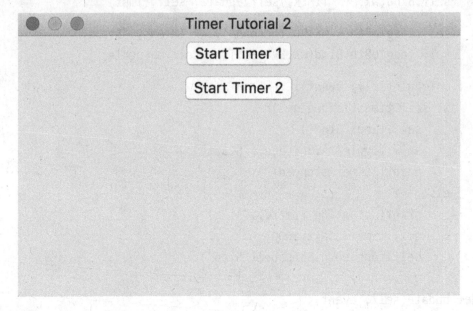

Figure 16-4. *A simple timer example*

There are many times where you will need to have multiple timers running at the same time. For example, you might need to check for updates from one or more web APIs. Here's a simple example that shows how to create a couple of timers.

```
import wx
import time

TIMER_ID1 = 2000
TIMER_ID2 = 2001

class MyForm(wx.Frame):

    def __init__(self):
        wx.Frame.__init__(self, None, title="Timer Tutorial 2")

        panel = wx.Panel(self, wx.ID_ANY)

        self.timer = wx.Timer(self, id=TIMER_ID1)
        self.Bind(wx.EVT_TIMER, self.update, self.timer)
        self.timer2 = wx.Timer(self, id=TIMER_ID2)
        self.Bind(wx.EVT_TIMER, self.update, self.timer2)
```

```python
    self.toggleBtn = wx.Button(panel, wx.ID_ANY, "Start Timer 1")
    self.toggleBtn.Bind(wx.EVT_BUTTON, self.onStartTimerOne)
    self.toggleBtn2 = wx.Button(panel, wx.ID_ANY, "Start Timer 2")
    self.toggleBtn2.Bind(wx.EVT_BUTTON, self.onStartTimerOne)

    sizer = wx.BoxSizer(wx.VERTICAL)
    sizer.Add(self.toggleBtn, 0, wx.ALL|wx.CENTER, 5)
    sizer.Add(self.toggleBtn2, 0, wx.ALL|wx.CENTER, 5)
    panel.SetSizer(sizer)

def onStartTimerOne(self, event):
    buttonObj = event.GetEventObject()
    btnLabel = buttonObj.GetLabel()
    timerNum = int(btnLabel[-1:])
    print(timerNum)

    if btnLabel == "Start Timer %s" % timerNum:
        if timerNum == 1:
            print("starting timer 1...")
            self.timer.Start(1000)
        else:
            print("starting timer 2...")
            self.timer2.Start(3000)
        buttonObj.SetLabel("Stop Timer %s" % timerNum)
    else:
        if timerNum == 1:
            self.timer.Stop()
            print("timer 1 stopped!")
        else:
            self.timer2.Stop()
            print("timer 2 stopped!")
        buttonObj.SetLabel("Start Timer %s" % timerNum)

def update(self, event):
    timerId = event.GetId()
    if timerId == TIMER_ID1:
        print("\ntimer 1 updated: ", time.ctime())
```

```
        else:
            print("\ntimer 2 updated: ", time.ctime())
# Run the program
if __name__ == "__main__":
    app = wx.App()
    frame = MyForm().Show()
    app.MainLoop()
```

To be honest, this second example is mostly the same as the first one. The main difference is that I have two buttons and two timer instances. I decided to be geeky and have both buttons bind to the same event handler. This is probably one of my better tricks. To find out which button called the event, you can use the event's **GetEventObject** method. Then you can get the label off the button. If you're a real nerd, you'll notice that I could combine lines 30 and 31 into the following one-liner:

```
btnLabel = event.GetEventObject().GetLabel()
```

I split that into two lines to make it easier to follow though. Next, I used some string slicing to grab the button's label number so I would know which timer to stop or start. Then my program enters my nested **if** statements where it checks the button label and then the timer number. Now you know how to start and stop multiple timers too.

Once again, Robin Dunn came up with a better way to do this second example, so let's see what he came up with.

```
import wx
import time

class MyForm(wx.Frame):

    def __init__(self):
        wx.Frame.__init__(self, None, title="Timer Tutorial 2")

        panel = wx.Panel(self, wx.ID_ANY)

        self.timer = wx.Timer(self, wx.ID_ANY)
        self.Bind(wx.EVT_TIMER, self.update, self.timer)
        self.timer2 = wx.Timer(self, wx.ID_ANY)
        self.Bind(wx.EVT_TIMER, self.update, self.timer2)
```

```python
        self.toggleBtn = wx.Button(panel, wx.ID_ANY, "Start Timer 1")
        self.toggleBtn.Bind(wx.EVT_BUTTON, self.onStartTimer)
        self.toggleBtn2 = wx.Button(panel, wx.ID_ANY, "Start Timer 2")
        self.toggleBtn2.Bind(wx.EVT_BUTTON, self.onStartTimer)

        sizer = wx.BoxSizer(wx.VERTICAL)
        sizer.Add(self.toggleBtn, 0, wx.ALL|wx.CENTER, 5)
        sizer.Add(self.toggleBtn2, 0, wx.ALL|wx.CENTER, 5)
        panel.SetSizer(sizer)

        # Each value in the following dict is formatted as follows:
        # (timerNum, timerObj, secs between timer events)
        self.objDict = {self.toggleBtn: (1, self.timer, 1000),
                        self.toggleBtn2: (2, self.timer2, 3000)}

    def onStartTimer(self, event):
        btn = event.GetEventObject()
        timerNum, timer, secs = self.objDict[btn]
        if timer.IsRunning():
            timer.Stop()
            btn.SetLabel("Start Timer %s" % timerNum)
            print("timer %s stopped!" % timerNum)
        else:
            print("starting timer %s..." % timerNum)
            timer.Start(secs)
            btn.SetLabel("Stop Timer %s" % timerNum)

    def update(self, event):
        timerId = event.GetId()
        if timerId == self.timer.GetId():
            print("\ntimer 1 updated: ", time.ctime())
        else:
            print ("\ntimer 2 updated: ", time.ctime())

# Run the program
if __name__ == "__main__":
    app = wx.App()
    frame = MyForm().Show()
    app.MainLoop()
```

In the **__init__** I added a dictionary that is keyed on the button objects. The values of the dictionary are the timer number, the timer object, and the number of seconds (technically milliseconds) between timer events. Next, I updated the button event handler to grab the button object from the event's **GetEventObject** method and then extract the respective values using said object for the dict's key. Then I can use the same trick I used in the refactored example I detailed previously, namely, the checking of whether or not the timer is running.

At this point you should have a pretty good handle on how you might use a **wx.Timer** in your own code base. It's a very easy way to fire an event at a specific time interval and it works pretty reliably. I have used timer objects in many projects. One good example was when I needed to check for updates in an e-mail alert program I had written. I used a timer to check my e-mail every so often to see if I had received anything new and to alert me if I did.

CHAPTER 17

Redirecting Text

Recipe 17-1. Redirect Python's Logging Module to a TextCtrl

Problem

I get a lot of interesting ideas from reading the wxPython Google group or StackOverflow. The other day I saw someone asking about how to make Python's logging module write its output to file and to a **TextCtrl**. It turns out that you need to create a custom logging handler to do it. At first, I tried just using a normal **StreamHandler** and redirecting **stdout** via the **sys** module (**sys.stdout**) to my text control, but that would only redirect my print statements, not the log messages.

Solution

Fortunately, this is not very hard to achieve in wxPython. Let's take a look at what I ended up with.

```
import logging
import logging.config
import wx

class CustomConsoleHandler(logging.StreamHandler):
    """"""

    def __init__(self, textctrl):
        """"""

        logging.StreamHandler.__init__(self)
        self.textctrl = textctrl
```

© Mike Driscoll 2018
M. Driscoll, *wxPython Recipes*, https://doi.org/10.1007/978-1-4842-3237-8_17

```python
    def emit(self, record):
        """Constructor"""
        msg = self.format(record)
        self.textctrl.WriteText(msg + "\n")
        self.flush()

class MyPanel(wx.Panel):
    """"""

    def __init__(self, parent):
        """Constructor"""
        wx.Panel.__init__(self, parent)
        self.logger = logging.getLogger("wxApp")

        self.logger.info("Test from MyPanel __init__")

        logText = wx.TextCtrl(
            self,
            style = wx.TE_MULTILINE|wx.TE_READONLY|wx.HSCROLL)

        btn = wx.Button(self, label="Press Me")
        btn.Bind(wx.EVT_BUTTON, self.onPress)

        sizer = wx.BoxSizer(wx.VERTICAL)
        sizer.Add(logText, 1, wx.EXPAND|wx.ALL, 5)
        sizer.Add(btn, 0, wx.ALL, 5)
        self.SetSizer(sizer)

        txtHandler = CustomConsoleHandler(logText)
        self.logger.addHandler(txtHandler)

    def onPress(self, event):
        """
        On the press of a button, log some messages
        """
        self.logger.error("Error Will Robinson!")
        self.logger.info("Informational message")
```

```python
class MyFrame(wx.Frame):
    """"""

    def __init__(self):
        """Constructor"""
        wx.Frame.__init__(self, None, title="Logging test")
        panel = MyPanel(self)
        self.logger = logging.getLogger("wxApp")
        self.Show()

def main():
    """

    Run the program
    """

    dictLogConfig = {
        "version":1,
        "handlers":{
                    "fileHandler":{
                        "class":"logging.FileHandler",
                        "formatter":"myFormatter",
                        "filename":"test.log"
                        },
                    "consoleHandler":{
                        "class":"logging.StreamHandler",
                        "formatter":"myFormatter"
                        }
                    },
            "loggers":{
                "wxApp":{
                    "handlers":["fileHandler", "consoleHandler"],
                    "level":"INFO",
                    }
                },
```

```
        "formatters":{
            "myFormatter":{
                "format":"%(asctime)s - %(name)s - %(levelname)s -
                %(message)s"
            }
        }
    }
    logging.config.dictConfig(dictLogConfig)
    logger = logging.getLogger("wxApp")

    logger.info("This message came from main!")

    app = wx.App(False)
    frame = MyFrame()
    app.MainLoop()

if __name__ == "__main__":
    main()
```

How It Works

Note that I ended up using Python's **logging.config** module. The **dictConfig** method was added in Python 2.7. Basically you set up your logging handler and formatters and what-not inside dictionary and then pass it to **logging.config**. If you run this code, you will notice that the first couple of messages go to stdout and the log but not to the text control. At the end of the panel class's **__init__**, we add our custom handler and that's when redirecting logging messages to the text control begins. You can press the button to see it in action!

Figure 17-1 shows what it looked like on my machine.

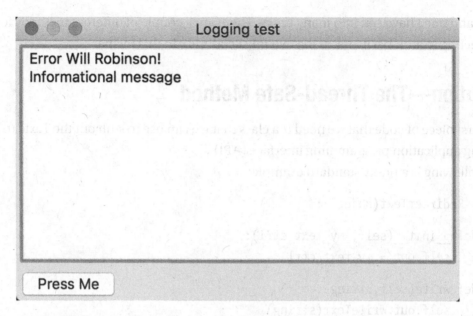

Figure 17-1. *Redirecting logging to a text control*

Note that you can see it logging to stdout and to our text control in the screenshot. You should see something like the following in your terminal and in the log file:

> 2016-11-30 14:04:35,026 - wxApp - INFO - This message came
> from main!
>
> 2016-11-30 14:04:35,026 - wxApp - INFO - Test from MyPanel __init__
>
> 2016-11-30 14:04:38,261 - wxApp - ERROR - Error Will Robinson!

At this point, you now know how to redirect Python's logging methods to a wxPython widget, specifically the **wx.TextCtrl**. This can be handy when you want to save off an application's output to file in addition to seeing it in "real time" in your application. In the next recipe, we'll look at how to redirect stdout to a wx.TextCtrl too!

Recipe 17-2. Redirecting stdout/stderr

Problem

A fairly common use case when using wxPython is the need to redirect stdout or stderr to a text control. You might find yourself launching a separate application with wxPython, but you want to capture its output in real time. This is a pretty common need and one I have run into many times. There are a couple of different methods for redirecting stdout. We'll look at the two most common in this recipe.

Solution—The Thread-Safe Method

The first piece of code that we need is a class that we can use to stub out the TextCtrl's writing application programming interface (API).

Following is a pretty standard example:

```python
class RedirectText(object):

    def __init__(self, my_text_ctrl):
        self.out = my_text_ctrl

    def write(self,string):
        self.out.WriteText(string)
```

Note that there's only one method in this class (besides the initialization method, of course). It allows us to write the text from stdout or stderr to the text control. It should be noted that the write method is not thread-safe. If you want to redirect text from threads, then change the **write** statement like the following:

```python
def write(self, string):
    wx.CallAfter(self.out.WriteText, string)
```

The **wx.CallAfter** method is thread-safe in wxPython. You could also use **wx.CallLater** or **wx.PostEvent** if you wanted to.

Now that we know what we need to write the stdout text to the TextCtrl, let's go ahead and write some code that actually demonstrates how to connect all the pieces. You will want to add the following code to the file that contains the class we just wrote. When you run the code, you will see an application that looks like the following:

```python
import sys
import wx

class RedirectText(object):

    def __init__(self, my_text_ctrl):
        self.out = my_text_ctrl
```

```python
    def write(self,string):
        wx.CallAfter(self.out.WriteText, string)

class MyForm(wx.Frame):

    def __init__(self):
        wx.Frame.__init__(self, None, title="wxPython Redirect Tutorial")

        # Add a panel so it looks the correct on all platforms
        panel = wx.Panel(self, wx.ID_ANY)
        log = wx.TextCtrl(panel, wx.ID_ANY, size=(300,100),
                          style = wx.TE_MULTILINE|wx.TE_READONLY|wx.HSCROLL)
        btn = wx.Button(panel, wx.ID_ANY, 'Push me!')
        self.Bind(wx.EVT_BUTTON, self.onButton, btn)

        # Add widgets to a sizer
        sizer = wx.BoxSizer(wx.VERTICAL)
        sizer.Add(log, 1, wx.ALL|wx.EXPAND, 5)
        sizer.Add(btn, 0, wx.ALL|wx.CENTER, 5)
        panel.SetSizer(sizer)

        # redirect text here
        redir = RedirectText(log)
        sys.stdout = redir

    def onButton(self, event):
        print("You pressed the button!")

if __name__ == "__main__":
    app = wx.App(False)
    frame = MyForm().Show()
    app.MainLoop()
```

How It Works

In the previous code, I created a read-only multiline text control and a button whose sole purpose is to print some text to stdout. I added them to a **BoxSizer** to keep the widgets from stacking on top of each other and to better handle resizing of the frame.

Next I instantiated the **RedirectText** class by passing it an instance of my text control. Finally, I set stdout to the **RediectText** instance, **redir** (i.e., **sys.stdout=redir**).

*If you want to redirect stderr as well, then just add **sys.stderr=redir** on the line following **sys.stdout=redir***

Improvements could be made to this example such as color coding (or prepending) which messages are from stdout and which are from stderr, but I'll leave that as an exercise for the reader.

Solution—The Non-Thread-Safe Method

If you don't need to worry about threads writing to your **TextCtrl**, then you can simplify your code a bit because the TextCtrl has its own **write** method. What this means is that you don't need a class that follows the TextCtrl's writing API. However, this is slightly limiting since the write method is no longer wrapped in wxPython's thread-safe method: **wx.CallAfter**. Let's go ahead and dig into the code.

```python
# wxPython Classic

import sys
import wx

class MyForm(wx.Frame):

    def __init__(self):
        wx.Frame.__init__(self, None,
                          title="wxPython Redirect Tutorial")

        # Add a panel so it looks the correct on all platforms
        panel = wx.Panel(self, wx.ID_ANY)
        style = wx.TE_MULTILINE|wx.TE_READONLY|wx.HSCROLL
        log = wx.TextCtrl(panel, wx.ID_ANY, size=(300,100),
                          style=style)
        btn = wx.Button(panel, wx.ID_ANY, 'Push me!')
        self.Bind(wx.EVT_BUTTON, self.onButton, btn)

        # Add widgets to a sizer
        sizer = wx.BoxSizer(wx.VERTICAL)
        sizer.Add(log, 1, wx.ALL|wx.EXPAND, 5)
```

```
        sizer.Add(btn, 0, wx.ALL|wx.CENTER, 5)
        panel.SetSizer(sizer)

        # redirect text here
        sys.stdout = log

    def onButton(self, event):
        print("You pressed the button!")
if __name__ == "__main__":
    app = wx.App(False)
    frame = MyForm().Show()
    app.MainLoop()
```

Note that the previous code no longer references the **RedirectText** class because we don't need it. I am pretty sure that if you want to use threads, doing it this way will not be thread-safe. You'll need to override the TextCtrl's write method in a similar manner as was previously mentioned to make it safe. Special thanks go to to one of my blog (www.blog.pythonlibrary.org/) readers, carandraug, for pointing this out to me.

This code will not work in wxPython 4 as the wx.TextCtrl no longer has a **write()** method. So let's write a version of the code that will work with Phoenix!

```
# wxPython 4

import sys
import wx

class MyCustomTextCtrl(wx.TextCtrl):

    def __init__(self, *args, **kwargs):
        """

        Initial the text control
        """

        wx.TextCtrl.__init__(self, *args, **kwargs)

    def write(self, text):
        self.WriteText(text)
```

```python
class MyForm(wx.Frame):

    def __init__(self):
        wx.Frame.__init__(self, None,
                          title="wxPython Redirect Tutorial")

        # Add a panel so it looks the correct on all platforms
        panel = wx.Panel(self, wx.ID_ANY)
        style = wx.TE_MULTILINE|wx.TE_READONLY|wx.HSCROLL
        log = MyCustomTextCtrl(panel, wx.ID_ANY, size=(300,100),
                          style=style)
        btn = wx.Button(panel, wx.ID_ANY, 'Push me!')
        self.Bind(wx.EVT_BUTTON, self.onButton, btn)

        # Add widgets to a sizer
        sizer = wx.BoxSizer(wx.VERTICAL)
        sizer.Add(log, 1, wx.ALL|wx.EXPAND, 5)
        sizer.Add(btn, 0, wx.ALL|wx.CENTER, 5)
        panel.SetSizer(sizer)

        # redirect text here
        sys.stdout = log

    def onButton(self, event):
        print("You pressed the button!")

if __name__ == "__main__":
    app = wx.App(False)
    frame = MyForm().Show()
    app.MainLoop()
```

To make a version that works with Phoenix, we need to subclass wx.TextCtrl and create our own **write()** method. The reason is that we want our custom text control to behave as a file-like object would. That way we can redirect stdout to it properly. If you followed this example, then this code should work the same way it did in the previous example for Classic.

This recipe provided some great information. Here we learned how to redirect stdout in both a thread-safe and a non-thread-safe method. I have been on several projects where I needed to redirect stdout, and the methods in this recipe have always worked well for me. You can take the information here and combine it with the previous recipe to redirect stdout to your widgets and to a log file.

Recipe 17-3. How to Use the Clipboard Problem

Everyone who uses computers regularly knows that they can copy and paste text. What they might not know is that when you copy something, it goes into a location known as the "clipboard." Most programs provide access to a clipboard of some sort, whether it be just within the program itself or to the system clipboard, which allows items to be copied to other applications. The wxPython GUI toolkit also provides clipboard access, which you can use to copy text to and from within your program and even to the system clipboard. You can also copy images to the clipboard. In this tutorial (see Figure 17-2), we'll take a look at how you can do this in your own code.

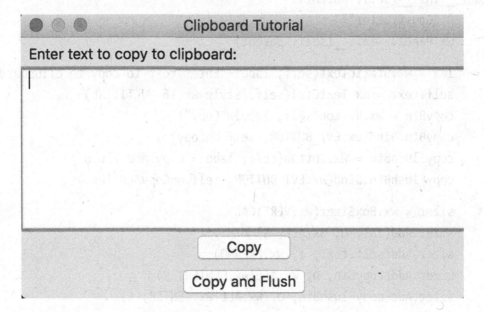

Figure 17-2. Using the clipboard

Solution

We'll learn how to use the clipboard by utilizing a really simple example. The following code contains two buttons, one that copies any text that's added to the text control and which you can then paste elsewhere, such as in the text box, in a search engine, or whatever. The other button also copies to clipboard and then closes the application after flushing the data. This is supposed to make the data available in the system clipboard even after the application is closed. Both work great on Windows, but wxGTK (i.e., the Linux version) doesn't work in the latter case. Look up the bug ticket for more information to see if it has been resolved since the time of writing.

Anyway, let's look at the code!

```python
import wx

class ClipboardPanel(wx.Panel):
    """"""

    def __init__(self, parent):
        """Constructor"""
        wx.Panel.__init__(self, parent)

        lbl = wx.StaticText(self, label="Enter text to copy to clipboard:")
        self.text = wx.TextCtrl(self, style=wx.TE_MULTILINE)
        copyBtn = wx.Button(self, label="Copy")
        copyBtn.Bind(wx.EVT_BUTTON, self.onCopy)
        copyFlushBtn = wx.Button(self, label="Copy and Flush")
        copyFlushBtn.Bind(wx.EVT_BUTTON, self.onCopyAndFlush)

        sizer = wx.BoxSizer(wx.VERTICAL)
        sizer.Add(lbl, 0, wx.ALL, 5)
        sizer.Add(self.text, 1, wx.EXPAND)
        sizer.Add(copyBtn, 0, wx.ALL|wx.CENTER, 5)
        sizer.Add(copyFlushBtn, 0, wx.ALL|wx.CENTER, 5)
        self.SetSizer(sizer)

    def onCopy(self, event):
        """"""
        self.dataObj = wx.TextDataObject()
        self.dataObj.SetText(self.text.GetValue())
```

```python
        if wx.TheClipboard.Open():
            wx.TheClipboard.SetData(self.dataObj)
            wx.TheClipboard.Close()
        else:
            wx.MessageBox("Unable to open the clipboard", "Error")

    def onCopyAndFlush(self, event):
        """
        Copy to the clipboard and close the application
        """
        self.dataObj = wx.TextDataObject()
        self.dataObj.SetText(self.text.GetValue())
        if wx.TheClipboard.Open():
            wx.TheClipboard.SetData(self.dataObj)
            wx.TheClipboard.Flush()
        else:
            wx.MessageBox("Unable to open the clipboard", "Error")

        self.GetParent().Close()

class ClipboardFrame(wx.Frame):
    """"""

    def __init__(self):
        """Constructor"""
        wx.Frame.__init__(self, None, title="Clipboard Tutorial")
        panel = ClipboardPanel(self)
        self.Show()

if __name__ == "__main__":
    app = wx.App(False)
    frame = ClipboardFrame()
    app.MainLoop()
```

How It Works

As you might have guessed, the guts of this script are in the button event handlers. The main bit is **wx.TextDataObject**, which will store the data from the text control. Next we attempt to open the clipboard. If we're successful, we add our text to the clipboard and then close it. The data is now there for the pasting. The second event handler does the same thing, but it **Flushes** to the clipboard rather than just closing it. If you wanted to copy a bitmap instead, then you'd want to use a **wx.BitmapDataObject** and pass it to a **wx.Bitmap** object. Otherwise, the rest is the same.

Note   The copy-and-flush method may not work on all operating systems. For example, it worked fine for me on Windows 7 but not on Xubuntu 14.04.

The clipboard is very handy and I know I use it almost unconsciously when I'm using the computer. So when it doesn't work it can be quite frustrating. Fortunately, making your own application work with the clipboard in wxPython is extremely easy to do. So now you know how to prevent clipboard frustration in your own users.

## CHAPTER 18

Grid Recipes

Recipe 18-1. Syncing Scrolling Between Two Grids

Problem

You will occasionally need or want to have two scrolling windows synced. You might want to have this ability when you are comparing two files, such as a diff. Or perhaps you just want to compare two sets of data or perhaps even two photos. In this recipe, we will put two grids in a **SplitterWindow** and sync them up. Note that I will only be demonstrating syncing the scrolling when you scroll using the scrollbar itself.

Solution

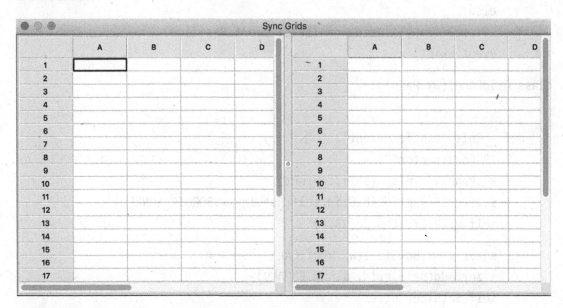

Figure 18-1. *Syncing scrolling between two grids*

M. Driscoll, *wxPython Recipes*, https://doi.org/10.1007/978-1-4842-3237-8_18

Actually syncing up two grids is not that hard. Let's write some code and find out how easy it is.

```python
import wx
import wx.grid as gridlib

class ScrollSync(object):
    def __init__(self, panel1, panel2):
        self.panel1 = panel1
        self.panel2 = panel2
        self.panel1.grid.Bind(wx.EVT_SCROLLWIN, self.onScrollWin1)
        self.panel2.grid.Bind(wx.EVT_SCROLLWIN, self.onScrollWin2)

    def onScrollWin1(self, event):
        if event.Orientation == wx.SB_HORIZONTAL:
            self.panel2.grid.Scroll(event.Position, -1)
        else:
            self.panel2.grid.Scroll(-1, event.Position)
        event.Skip()

    def onScrollWin2(self, event):
        if event.Orientation == wx.SB_HORIZONTAL:
            self.panel1.grid.Scroll(event.Position, -1)
        else:
            self.panel1.grid.Scroll(-1, event.Position)
        event.Skip()

class GridPanel(wx.Panel):
    """"""

    def __init__(self, parent):
        """Constructor"""
        wx.Panel.__init__(self, parent)
        self.grid = gridlib.Grid(self, style=wx.BORDER_SUNKEN)
        self.grid.CreateGrid(25,8)

        sizer = wx.BoxSizer(wx.VERTICAL)
        sizer.Add(self.grid, 1, wx.EXPAND)
        self.SetSizer(sizer)
```

```python
class MainPanel(wx.Panel):
    """"""

    def __init__(self, parent):
        """Constructor"""
        wx.Panel.__init__(self, parent)

        split = wx.SplitterWindow(self)

        panelOne = GridPanel(split)
        panelTwo = GridPanel(split)
        ScrollSync(panelOne, panelTwo)

        split.SplitVertically(panelOne, panelTwo)
        split.SetSashGravity(0.5)

        sizer = wx.BoxSizer(wx.VERTICAL)
        sizer.Add(split, 1, wx.EXPAND)
        self.SetSizer(sizer)

class MainFrame(wx.Frame):
    """"""

    def __init__(self):
        """Constructor"""
        wx.Frame.__init__(self, None, title="Sync Grids",
                          size=(800,400))
        panel = MainPanel(self)
        self.Show()

if __name__ == "__main__":
    app = wx.App(False)
    frame = MainFrame()
    app.MainLoop()
```

How It Works

The piece we care about most is the **ScrollSync** class. It accepts the two panels that the grids are on as arguments. We bind the grids to **wx.EVT_SCROLLWIN** and then, during that event, we change the position of the opposite grid. Now this code has several limitations. It only works when you are physically moving the scrollbars with your mouse. If you use the mouse's scroll wheel, the arrow keys, or Page up/down, the two grids no longer sync. I attempted to add mouse wheel support via the **wx.EVT_MOUSEWHEEL** event, but it doesn't provide orientation or position in the same way as **EVT_SCROLLWIN** does. In fact, its **Position** is a **wx.Point** whereas **EVT_SCROLLWIN** returns an integer. Adding those bits of functionality would be fun, but they are outside the scope of this recipe.

At this point you should have the knowledge to add the ability to synchronize the scrolling of two windows on your own. While it's not a complete solution, it's still a neat little feature that you can add that is a good way to differentiate your application from others.

Recipe 18-2. How to Get Selected Cells in a Grid Problem

In this recipe we will be looking at how to get the selected cells from a wxPython grid object. Most of the time, getting the selection is easy, but when the user selects more than one cell, getting the selection becomes more complicated. We will need to create some sample code to show how all this fits together.

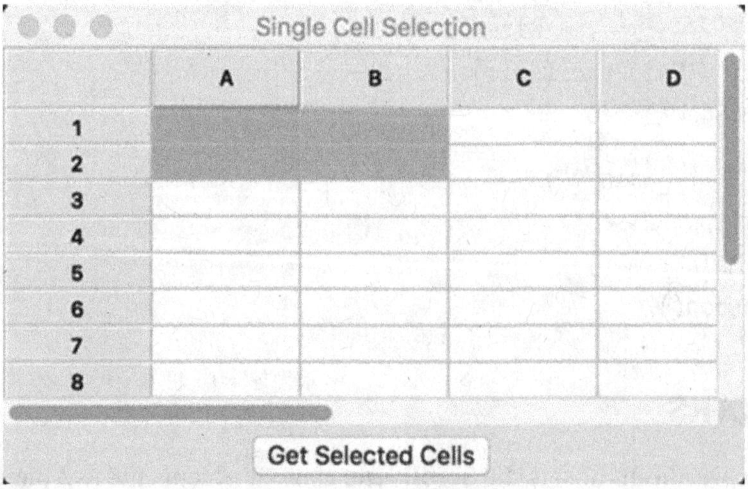

Figure 18-2. *Getting only the selected cells*

Solution

There is an interesting article on the web that covers this topic. You can read it here:
http://ginstrom.com/scribbles/2008/09/07/getting-the-selected-cells-from-a-wxpython-grid/ (or here's a shorter link: http://bit.ly/2eqafsB). However, there are several problems with the article which we will look at as well. Following is the code we'll be looking at.

```python
import wx
import wx.grid as gridlib

class MyPanel(wx.Panel):
    """"""

    def __init__(self, parent):
        """Constructor"""
        wx.Panel.__init__(self, parent)
        self.currentlySelectedCell = (0, 0)

        self.myGrid = gridlib.Grid(self)
        self.myGrid.CreateGrid(12, 8)
        self.myGrid.Bind(gridlib.EVT_GRID_SELECT_CELL, self.onSingleSelect)
        self.myGrid.Bind(gridlib.EVT_GRID_RANGE_SELECT, self.
        onDragSelection)

        selectBtn = wx.Button(self, label="Get Selected Cells")
        selectBtn.Bind(wx.EVT_BUTTON, self.onGetSelection)

        sizer = wx.BoxSizer(wx.VERTICAL)
        sizer.Add(self.myGrid, 1, wx.EXPAND)
        sizer.Add(selectBtn, 0, wx.ALL|wx.CENTER, 5)
        self.SetSizer(sizer)

    def onDragSelection(self, event):
        """
        Gets the cells that are selected by holding the left
        mouse button down and dragging
        """
```

```
        if self.myGrid.GetSelectionBlockTopLeft():
            top_left = self.myGrid.GetSelectionBlockTopLeft()[0]
            bottom_right = self.myGrid.GetSelectionBlockBottomRight()[0]
            self.printSelectedCells(top_left, bottom_right)

    def onGetSelection(self, event):
        """

        Get whatever cells are currently selected
        """

        cells = self.myGrid.GetSelectedCells()
        if not cells:
            if self.myGrid.GetSelectionBlockTopLeft():
                top_left = self.myGrid.GetSelectionBlockTopLeft()
                bottom_right = self.myGrid.GetSelectionBlockBottomRight()
                self.printSelectedCells(top_left[0], bottom_right[0])
            else:
                print(self.currentlySelectedCell)
        else:
            print(cells)

    def onSingleSelect(self, event):
        """

        Get the selection of a single cell by clicking or
        moving the selection with the arrow keys
        """

        print("You selected Row %s, Col %s" % (event.GetRow(),
                                               event.GetCol()))
        self.currentlySelectedCell = (event.GetRow(),
                                     event.GetCol())

        event.Skip()

    def printSelectedCells(self, top_left, bottom_right):
        """

        Based on code from
        http://ginstrom.com/scribbles/2008/09/07/getting-the-selected-
        cells-from-a-wxpython-grid/
```

```python
        """
        cells = []
        rows_start = top_left[0]
        rows_end = bottom_right[0]

        cols_start = top_left[1]
        cols_end = bottom_right[1]

        rows = range(rows_start, rows_end+1)
        cols = range(cols_start, cols_end+1)

        cells.extend([(row, col)
            for row in rows
            for col in cols])

        print("You selected the following cells: ", cells)

        for cell in cells:
            row, col = cell
            print(self.myGrid.GetCellValue(row, col))


class MyFrame(wx.Frame):
    """"""

    def __init__(self):
        """Constructor"""
        wx.Frame.__init__(self, parent=None, title="Single Cell Selection")
        panel = MyPanel(self)
        self.Show()

if __name__ == "__main__":
    app = wx.App(False)
    frame = MyFrame()
    app.MainLoop()
```

How It Works

Let's take a few moments to break this down. First of all, we created a grid object that we're calling **self.myGrid**. We bind to two grid-specific events, **EVT_GRID_SELECT_CELL** and **EVT_GRID_RANGE_SELECT**. This is for demonstration purposes as you usually don't need to bind to EVT_GRID_SELECT_CELL. For the single-cell selection event, we call the **onSingleSelect** handler. In it we use the event object to grab the correct row and column. If you look at the article linked to previously, you'll notice that they are using **GetGridCursorRow** and **GetGridCursorCol**. I found that these only return the previously selected cell, not the cell that is currently selected. This is the reason we are using the event object's methods instead. Also note that we are updating the value of **self.currentlySelectedCell** to equal whatever the currently selected cell is.

The other grid event is bound to **onDragSelection**. In this event handler we call the grid's **GetSelectionBlockTopLeft()** method and check to make sure it returns something. If it does not, then we do nothing else. But if it does return something, then we grab its contents as well as the contents returned from **GetSelectionBlockBottomRight()**. Then we pass these to our **printSelectedCells()** method. This code is based on the previously mentioned article, although it has been simplified a bit as I found the original's for loop was throwing an error. Basically all this method does is create two lists of values using Python's range function. Then it extends a list using a nested list comprehension. Finally it prints out the cells that were selected to stdout.

Note that the **printSelectedCells()** method doesn't work correctly in wxPython Phoenix.

The last method to look at is the button event handler: **onGetSelection**. This method calls the grid's **GetSelectedCells()** method. This will return the selected cells that single clicked. It will also work if the user drag selects some cells. If the user just selects one cell, then we will print **self.currentlySelectedCell** as it will always equal the value of the current selection.

As you can see, getting the selected cell or cells from the grid object can be a little tricky. But with a bit of work, we were able to overcome. Ideally, you will find this useful in one of your current or future projects.

CHAPTER 19

Working with Your Application

Recipe 19-1. How to Edit Your GUI Interactively Using reload( )

Problem

I came across an interesting question on StackOverflow a few years ago where the author was asking how he could write a wxPython program dynamically. In other words, he wanted to be able to edit the code and basically refresh the application without closing it and rerunning his code. The simplest way would be to use Python's built-in **reload()** functionality. If we go this route, then we'll need to build a little front end to import the code that we want to change interactively.

© Mike Driscoll 2018
M. Driscoll, *wxPython Recipes*, https://doi.org/10.1007/978-1-4842-3237-8_19

Solution

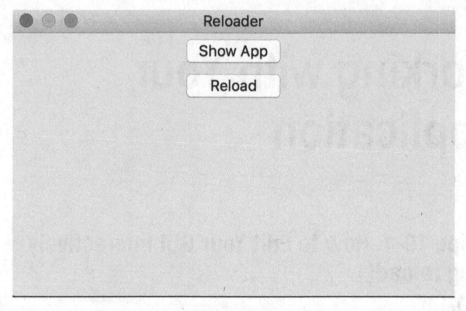

Figure 19-1. *Reloading your application live*

Creating the reloading application is very straightforward. All we need is some application code to reload dynamically. Python will do the rest. Let's look at the code for the reloading application and then we'll look at a simple application that we want to edit and reload.

```python
# main.py
import testApp
import wx

class ReloaderPanel(wx.Panel):
    """"""

    def __init__(self, parent):
        """Constructor"""
        wx.Panel.__init__(self, parent)
        self.testFrame = None

        showAppBtn = wx.Button(self, label="Show App")
        showAppBtn.Bind(wx.EVT_BUTTON, self.onShowApp)
```

```python
        reloadBtn = wx.Button(self, label="Reload")
        reloadBtn.Bind(wx.EVT_BUTTON, self.onReload)

        mainSizer = wx.BoxSizer(wx.VERTICAL)
        mainSizer.Add(showAppBtn, 0, wx.ALL|wx.CENTER, 5)
        mainSizer.Add(reloadBtn, 0, wx.ALL|wx.CENTER, 5)
        self.SetSizer(mainSizer)

    def onReload(self, event):
        """

        Reload the code!
        """

        if self.testFrame:
            self.testFrame.Close()
            try:
                reload(testApp)
            except NameError:
                # reload doesn't exist in Python 3.
                # Use importlib.reload in Python 3.4+
                # or imp.reload in Python 3.0 - 3.3
                import importlib
                importlib.reload(testApp)
            self.showApp()
        else:
            self.testFrame = None

    def onShowApp(self, event):
        """

        Call the showApp() method
        """

        self.showApp()

    def showApp(self):
        """

        Show the application we want to edit dynamically
        """

        self.testFrame = testApp.TestFrame()
```

293

```python
class ReloaderFrame(wx.Frame):
    """"""

    def __init__(self):
        """Constructor"""
        wx.Frame.__init__(self, None, title="Reloader")
        panel = ReloaderPanel(self)
        self.Show()

if __name__ == "__main__":
    app = wx.App(False)
    frame = ReloaderFrame()
    app.MainLoop()
```

How It Works

Here we import the module that we're planning to edit while this script is running. In this case, the module is called **testApp** (and the file is **testApp.py**). Next we add a couple of buttons; one to show the testApp's frame and the other to reload the testApp code and reshow it with any changes made. Yes, we should probably add some exception handling here in case we make a typo in the code and then try to reload it, but I'll leave that as an exercise for the reader.

Now we just need to create a super simple application that we can update and then reload it with our **reloader** application. Following is a little piece of code that's pretty simple:

```python
# testApp.py
import wx

class TestPanel(wx.Panel):
    """"""

    def __init__(self, parent):
        """Constructor"""
        wx.Panel.__init__(self, parent)

class TestFrame(wx.Frame):
    """"""
```

```
    def __init__(self):
        """Constructor"""
        wx.Frame.__init__(self, None, title="Test program")
        panel = TestPanel(self)
        self.Show()
if __name__ == "__main__":
    app = wx.App(False)
    frame = TestFrame()
    app.MainLoop()
```

Now all you have to do is edit this second file and reload it with the first file to see the changes. I recommend adding a button in the **TestPanel** class, saving it, and then hitting the Reload button in the other script to see the changes.

Creating a simple reloader application can help you go through iterations of your code, although it's a bit arguable whether you will actually save much time just by saving your code and rerunning it yourself. However, this is a fun way to use wxPython and learn how Python itself works. Besides, part of development is finding new and fun ways to code something. I think you should enjoy yourself when you're coding.

Recipe 19-2. Updating Your Application with Esky

Problem

The wxPython project added the ability to update your applications in a new library called **wx.lib.softwareupdate** starting in version 2.9. The software updating ability is brought to you by a mix-in class that uses the Esky package. As far as I can tell, this mix-in only allows prompted updates, not silent updates.

Solution

If you don't have Esky installed, you can do so using **pip**:

pip install esky

Depending on what platform you are on, you will also need a binary building package. For example, if you're on Windows, you'll need **py2exe** whereas on Mac, you will need **py2app**. We will be creating a simple image viewer application that we'll then add an update to. For this recipe, we will be using Windows, but it should work the same way on Mac. You can use **pip** to install py2exe and py2app.

You will also want to create a folder hierarchy that looks something like the following:

> /Releases
>
> /image_viewer0.0.1
>
> /image_viewer0.1.0

Now we just need to create an initial version of the software and save it to the **image_viewer0.0.1** folder.

Since we know we have features that we want to add to our initial release sometime in the future, we will want to add the ability for our initial application to update itself. Let's take a look at the first version of our software.

```python
import os
import wx
from wx.lib.softwareupdate import SoftwareUpdate

class PhotoCtrl(wx.App, SoftwareUpdate):
    """
    The Photo Viewer App Class
    """

    def __init__(self, redirect=False, filename=None):
        wx.App.__init__(self, redirect, filename)

        BASEURL = "http://127.0.0.1:8000"
        self.InitUpdates(BASEURL,
                         BASEURL + "/" + 'ChangeLog.txt')
        self.SetAppDisplayName('Image Viewer')
        self.CheckForUpdate()

        self.frame = wx.Frame(None, title='Photo Control')

        self.panel = wx.Panel(self.frame)

        self.PhotoMaxSize = 500

        self.createWidgets()
        self.frame.Show()
```

```python
def createWidgets(self):
    instructions = 'Browse for an image'
    img = wx.EmptyImage(240,240)
    self.imageCtrl = wx.StaticBitmap(self.panel, wx.ID_ANY,
                                     wx.BitmapFromImage(img))

    instructLbl = wx.StaticText(self.panel, label=instructions)
    self.photoTxt = wx.TextCtrl(self.panel, size=(200,-1))
    browseBtn = wx.Button(self.panel, label='Browse')
    browseBtn.Bind(wx.EVT_BUTTON, self.onBrowse)

    self.mainSizer = wx.BoxSizer(wx.VERTICAL)
    self.sizer = wx.BoxSizer(wx.HORIZONTAL)

    self.mainSizer.Add(wx.StaticLine(self.panel, wx.ID_ANY),
                       0, wx.ALL|wx.EXPAND, 5)
    self.mainSizer.Add(instructLbl, 0, wx.ALL, 5)
    self.mainSizer.Add(self.imageCtrl, 0, wx.ALL, 5)
    self.sizer.Add(self.photoTxt, 0, wx.ALL, 5)
    self.sizer.Add(browseBtn, 0, wx.ALL, 5)
    self.mainSizer.Add(self.sizer, 0, wx.ALL, 5)

    self.panel.SetSizer(self.mainSizer)
    self.mainSizer.Fit(self.frame)

    self.panel.Layout()

def onBrowse(self, event):
    """
    Browse for file
    """
    wildcard = "JPEG files (*.jpg)|*.jpg"
    dialog = wx.FileDialog(None, "Choose a file",
                           wildcard=wildcard,
                           style=wx.OPEN)
    if dialog.ShowModal() == wx.ID_OK:
        self.photoTxt.SetValue(dialog.GetPath())
```

```
        dialog.Destroy()
        self.onView()

    def onView(self):
        """
        Attempts to load the image and display it
        """
        filepath = self.photoTxt.GetValue()
        img = wx.Image(filepath, wx.BITMAP_TYPE_ANY)
        # scale the image, preserving the aspect ratio
        W = img.GetWidth()
        H = img.GetHeight()
        if W > H:
            NewW = self.PhotoMaxSize
            NewH = self.PhotoMaxSize * H / W
        else:
            NewH = self.PhotoMaxSize
            NewW = self.PhotoMaxSize * W / H
        img = img.Scale(NewW,NewH)

        self.imageCtrl.SetBitmap(wx.BitmapFromImage(img))
        self.panel.Refresh()
        self.mainSizer.Fit(self.frame)

if __name__ == '__main__':
    app = PhotoCtrl()
    app.MainLoop()
```

To enable software updating, we needed to import the **SoftwareUpdate** class from **wx.lib.softwareupdate**. Next we need to create a subclass of *both* **wx.App** and **SoftwareUpdate** because SoftwareUpdate is a mix-in class. Then in the **__init__** constructor, we need to call **InitUpdates** with a URL of our choice plus that same URL concatenated with **ChangeLog.txt**. We set the display name of the application and finally we call **CheckForUpdate**. That's it! Now we just need to package this up into an executable.

You will need to create a **setup.py** script with the following in it that you will place in the same directory as the initial release script:

```
import sys, os
from esky import bdist_esky
from setuptools import setup

import version

# platform specific settings for Windows/py2exe
if sys.platform == "win32":
    import py2exe

    FREEZER = 'py2exe'
    FREEZER_OPTIONS = dict(compressed = 0,
                           optimize = 0,
                           bundle_files = 3,
                           dll_excludes = ['MSVCP90.dll',
                                           'mswsock.dll',
                                           'powrprof.dll',
                                           'USP10.dll',],
                           )
    exeICON = 'mondrian.ico'

# platform specific settings for Mac/py2app
elif sys.platform == "darwin":
    import py2app

    FREEZER = 'py2app'
    FREEZER_OPTIONS = dict(argv_emulation = False,
                           iconfile = 'mondrian.icns',
                           )
    exeICON = None

# Common settings
NAME = "wxImageViewer"
APP = [bdist_esky.Executable("image_viewer.py",
                             gui_only=True,
```

```
                            icon=exeICON,
                            )]
DATA_FILES = [ 'mondrian.ico' ]
ESKY_OPTIONS = dict( freezer_module     = FREEZER,
                     freezer_options    = FREEZER_OPTIONS,
                     enable_appdata_dir = True,
                     bundle_msvcrt      = True,
                     )

# Build the app and the esky bundle
setup( name        = NAME,
       scripts     = APP,
       version     = version.VERSION,
       data_files  = DATA_FILES,
       options     = dict(bdist_esky=ESKY_OPTIONS),
       )
```

You'll also need a version.py file with the following:

VERSION='0.0.1'

Now you're ready to actually create the executable. Open up a terminal (**cmd.exe** on Windows) and navigate to the folder in which you put these files. I have also put a couple of icon files in my folder too, which you can find in the book's code repository (https://github.com/driscollis/wxPython_recipes_book_code; see the introduction for more details). You'll want those as the **setup.py** script expects to find them. Okay, so now we need to create the distribution. Type in the following in your terminal:

python setup.py bdist_esky

This command assumes that you have Python in your path. If you don't, then you will want to add it or just specify the full path to Python. After you run this command, you'll see a whole bunch of output. If everything goes well, you'll end up with two new subfolders: **build** and **dist**. We don't really care about the build folder. The **dist** folder should have one file in it, named something like the following:

wxImageViewer-0.0.1.win32.zip

To make things simple, you should create a **downloads** folder to copy your new zip file into. Now we just need to do the same thing to the new release. We'll be looking at that next.

How It Works

We need a reason to update our code. Fortunately, your customers love getting new features. Our first application didn't really allow us to do anything other than open a Browse button to find a photo. Let's add a couple of features to the application:

- We will add Previous and Next buttons so we can iterate over photos in a folder

- We will also add a Slideshow capability to the application

Since this will be a new release, create a new Python script with the same name as the first one and save it to the **image_viewer0.1.0** folder that you created earlier. To make things really easy, you can just copy the following code into your new script. Or you can just copy the original in and update it as you go through this code. I'll leave that up to you. The following code snippet is pretty long, so I'll break it up a bit to make it easier to digest.

```python
import glob
import os
import wx
from wx.lib.pubsub import Publisher
from wx.lib.softwareupdate import SoftwareUpdate

class ViewerPanel(wx.Panel):
    """"""

    def __init__(self, parent):
        """Constructor"""
        wx.Panel.__init__(self, parent)

        width, height = wx.DisplaySize()
        self.picPaths = []
        self.currentPicture = 0
        self.totalPictures = 0
        self.photoMaxSize = height - 200
        Publisher().subscribe(self.updateImages, ("update images"))
```

```python
        self.slideTimer = wx.Timer(None)
        self.slideTimer.Bind(wx.EVT_TIMER, self.update)

        self.layout()

    def layout(self):
        """
        Layout the widgets on the panel
        """

        self.mainSizer = wx.BoxSizer(wx.VERTICAL)
        btnSizer = wx.BoxSizer(wx.HORIZONTAL)

        img = wx.EmptyImage(self.photoMaxSize,self.photoMaxSize)
        self.imageCtrl = wx.StaticBitmap(self, wx.ID_ANY,
                                          wx.BitmapFromImage(img))
        self.mainSizer.Add(self.imageCtrl, 0, wx.ALL|wx.CENTER, 5)
        self.imageLabel = wx.StaticText(self, label="")
        self.mainSizer.Add(self.imageLabel, 0, wx.ALL|wx.CENTER, 5)

        btnData = [("Previous", btnSizer, self.onPrevious),
                   ("Slide Show", btnSizer, self.onSlideShow),
                   ("Next", btnSizer, self.onNext)]
        for data in btnData:
            label, sizer, handler = data
            self.btnBuilder(label, sizer, handler)

        self.mainSizer.Add(btnSizer, 0, wx.CENTER)
        self.SetSizer(self.mainSizer)

    def btnBuilder(self, label, sizer, handler):
        """
        Builds a button, binds it to an event handler and adds it to a sizer
        """

        btn = wx.Button(self, label=label)
        btn.Bind(wx.EVT_BUTTON, handler)
        sizer.Add(btn, 0, wx.ALL|wx.CENTER, 5)

    def loadImage(self, image):
```

```
    """
    Load the image into the application for display
    """
    image_name = os.path.basename(image)
    img = wx.Image(image, wx.BITMAP_TYPE_ANY)
    # scale the image, preserving the aspect ratio
    W = img.GetWidth()
    H = img.GetHeight()
    if W > H:
        NewW = self.photoMaxSize
        NewH = self.photoMaxSize * H / W
    else:
        NewH = self.photoMaxSize
        NewW = self.photoMaxSize * W / H
    img = img.Scale(NewW,NewH)

    self.imageCtrl.SetBitmap(wx.BitmapFromImage(img))
    self.imageLabel.SetLabel(image_name)
    self.Refresh()
    Publisher().sendMessage("resize", "")

def nextPicture(self):
    """
    Loads the next picture in the directory
    """
    if self.currentPicture == self.totalPictures-1:
        self.currentPicture = 0
    else:
        self.currentPicture += 1
    self.loadImage(self.picPaths[self.currentPicture])

def previousPicture(self):
    """
    Displays the previous picture in the directory
    """
    if self.currentPicture == 0:
        self.currentPicture = self.totalPictures - 1
```

```python
        else:
            self.currentPicture -= 1
        self.loadImage(self.picPaths[self.currentPicture])

    def update(self, event):
        """
        Called when the slideTimer's timer event fires. Loads the next
        picture from the folder by calling th nextPicture method
        """
        self.nextPicture()

    def updateImages(self, msg):
        """
        Updates the picPaths list to contain the current folder's images
        """
        self.picPaths = msg.data
        self.totalPictures = len(self.picPaths)
        self.loadImage(self.picPaths[0])

    def onNext(self, event):
        """
        Calls the nextPicture method
        """
        self.nextPicture()

    def onPrevious(self, event):
        """
        Calls the previousPicture method
        """
        self.previousPicture()

    def onSlideShow(self, event):
        """
        Starts and stops the slideshow
        """
        btn = event.GetEventObject()
        label = btn.GetLabel()
        if label == "Slide Show":
```

```
        self.slideTimer.Start(3000)
        btn.SetLabel("Stop")
    else:
        self.slideTimer.Stop()
        btn.SetLabel("Slide Show")
```

The first thing you will probably notice is that we've broken up the application into a series of classes. We now have a **ViewerPanel** that holds all our main widgets. You can see that we now have some buttons for navigating a directory full of images. We also have a slide show function that will auto-advance through the images in the folder every three seconds.

```
class ViewerFrame(wx.Frame):
    """"""

    def __init__(self):
        """Constructor"""
        wx.Frame.__init__(self, None, title="Image Viewer")
        panel = ViewerPanel(self)
        self.folderPath = ""
        Publisher().subscribe(self.resizeFrame, ("resize"))

        self.initToolbar()
        self.sizer = wx.BoxSizer(wx.VERTICAL)
        self.sizer.Add(panel, 1, wx.EXPAND)
        self.SetSizer(self.sizer)

        self.Show()
        self.sizer.Fit(self)
        self.Center()

    def initToolbar(self):
        """

        Initialize the toolbar
        """

        self.toolbar = self.CreateToolBar()
        self.toolbar.SetToolBitmapSize((16,16))
```

```
        open_ico = wx.ArtProvider.GetBitmap(
            wx.ART_FILE_OPEN, wx.ART_TOOLBAR, (16,16))
        openTool = self.toolbar.AddSimpleTool(wx.ID_ANY, open_ico,
            "Open", "Open an Image Directory")
        self.Bind(wx.EVT_MENU, self.onOpenDirectory, openTool)

        self.toolbar.Realize()

    def onOpenDirectory(self, event):
        """

        Opens a DirDialog to allow the user to open a folder with pictures
        """

        dlg = wx.DirDialog(self, "Choose a directory",
                           style=wx.DD_DEFAULT_STYLE)

        if dlg.ShowModal() == wx.ID_OK:
            self.folderPath = dlg.GetPath()
            print self.folderPath
            picPaths = glob.glob(self.folderPath + "\\*.jpg")
            print picPaths
        Publisher().sendMessage("update images", picPaths)

    def resizeFrame(self, msg):
        """"""""

        self.sizer.Fit(self)
```

Here we created a subclass of **wx.Frame**. We added a simple toolbar that allows us to open a folder of images. It also creates our panel instance. Other than that, this class really doesn't do a whole lot. However, it does simply add other functionality, such as a status bar or a menu.

```
class ImageApp(wx.App, SoftwareUpdate):
    """"""""

    def __init__(self):
        """Constructor"""
        BASEURL = "http://127.0.0.1:8000"
        self.InitUpdates(BASEURL,
                         BASEURL + 'ChangeLog.txt')
```

```
        self.CheckForUpdate()
        frame = ViewerFrame()
        self.SetTopWindow(frame)
        self.SetAppDisplayName('Image Viewer')
        return True

if __name__ == "__main__":
    app = ImageApp()
    app.MainLoop()
```

This last class is where we use the **SoftwareUpdate** mix-in with **wx.App**. It also instantiates the frame class. This is also a pretty straightforward class, so I won't elaborate upon it any further.

We now need to take a look at this version's setup.py as it is a little different.

```
import sys, os
from esky import bdist_esky
from setuptools import setup

import version

# platform specific settings for Windows/py2exe
if sys.platform == "win32":
    import py2exe
    includes = ["wx.lib.pubsub.*",
                "wx.lib.pubsub.core.*",
                "wx.lib.pubsub.core.kwargs.*"]

    FREEZER = 'py2exe'
    FREEZER_OPTIONS = dict(compressed = 0,
                           optimize = 0,
                           bundle_files = 3,
                           dll_excludes = ['MSVCP90.dll',
                                           'mswsock.dll',
                                           'powrprof.dll',
                                           'USP10.dll',],
                           includes = includes
                           )
    exeICON = 'mondrian.ico'
```

```
# platform specific settings for Mac/py2app
elif sys.platform == "darwin":
    import py2app

    FREEZER = 'py2app'
    FREEZER_OPTIONS = dict(argv_emulation = False,
                           iconfile = 'mondrian.icns',
                           )

    exeICON = None

# Common settings
NAME = "wxImageViewer"
APP = [bdist_esky.Executable("image_viewer.py",
                             gui_only=True,
                             icon=exeICON,
                             )]
DATA_FILES = [ 'mondrian.ico' ]

ESKY_OPTIONS = dict( freezer_module     = FREEZER,
                     freezer_options    = FREEZER_OPTIONS,
                     enable_appdata_dir = True,
                     bundle_msvcrt      = True,
                     )

# Build the app and the esky bundle
setup( name       = NAME,
       scripts    = APP,
       version    = version.VERSION,
       data_files = DATA_FILES,
       options    = dict(bdist_esky=ESKY_OPTIONS)
       )
```

This second script uses wxPython's **pubsub**. However, py2exe won't pick up on
that by itself, so you have to tell it explicitly to grab the PubSub parts. You do this in the
includes section, near the top of the script.

Don't forget to make sure that your version.py file has a higher release value than the
original or we won't be able to update. Here's what I put in mine.

VERSION='0.0.2'

Now do the same command-line magic as before, except this time do it in your updated release directory.

```
python setup.py bdist_esky
```

Copy the zip file to your **downloads** folder. Now we just need to serve these files on your computer's **localhost**. To do that navigate into your downloads folder via the command line and run the following command:

```
python -m SimpleHTTPServer
```

Python will now run a little HTTP server that serves those files. If you go to http://127.0.0.1:8000 in your web browser, you'll see it for yourself. Now we're ready to do the upgrading process!

At this point, we are ready to try to update our initial program to the latest version! Make sure you unzip the first version of the image viewer somewhere on your machine. Then run the file called **image_viewer.exe**. If everything goes as planned, you'll see the screen in Figure 19-2.

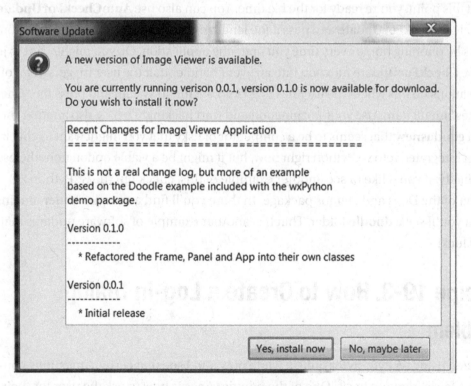

Figure 19-2. Your application prompts for an update

Go ahead and apply the update and you'll be asked the restart the application (see Figure 19-3).

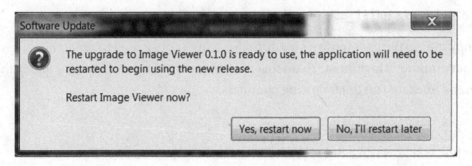

Figure 19-3. *After updating, your application prompts for a restart*

It should restart and you'll get the new image viewer interface. I noticed that when I closed the application, I received an error which turned out to be a **Deprecation Warning**. You can ignore that or if you want something to do, you can import the warnings module and suppress that.

At this point, you're ready for the big time. You can also use **AutoCheckForUpdate** instead of **CheckForUpdate** and pass it the length of days between checks so you won't always be phoning home every time you open the application. Or, you might want to just put the **CheckForUpdate** function into an event handler that the user triggers. A lot of applications do this where the user has to go into the menu system and press the "Check for updates" menu item. Use your imagination and start hacking! There's also another project called **goodasnew** that seems to be a competitor of Esky that you might want to check out. It's not integrated into wxPython right now, but it might be a viable option nonetheless.

Finally, if you'd like to see another example of this, check out the wxPython 2.9 version of the Docs and Demos package. In there you'll find a samples folder and inside of that you'll see a **doodle** folder. That has another example of software updates in it. Good luck!

Recipe 19-3. How to Create a Log-in Dialog Problem

I've been using wxPython for quite a while now and I see that certain questions come up on a fairly frequent basis. One of the popular ones is how to ask the user for their credentials before loading up the rest of the application. There are several approaches to this, but I am going to focus on two simple solutions as I believe they can be used as the basis for more complex solutions.

Basically what we want to happen is for the user to see a log-in dialog where they have to enter their username and password. If they enter it correctly, then the program will continue to load and they'll see the main interface. You see this a lot on web sites with a common use case being web e-mail clients. Desktop applications don't include this functionality as often, although you will see it for **Stamps.com**'s application and for some law enforcement software. For this recipe, we will be creating a dialog that looks as shown in Figure 19-4.

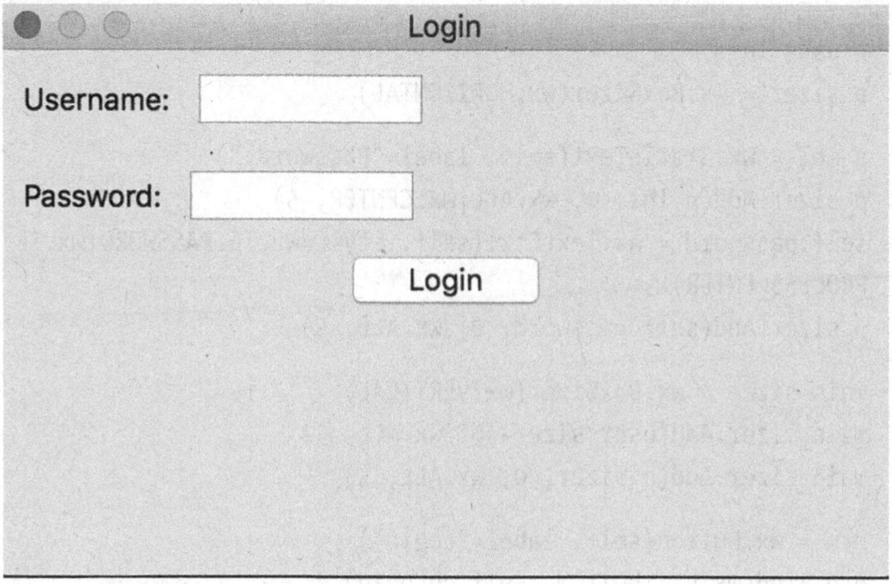

Figure 19-4. A sample log-in dialog

Solution

The first solution we will look at uses wxPython's built-in version of **pubsub**. Let's take a look at an example.

```
import wx
from wx.lib.pubsub import pub

class LoginDialog(wx.Dialog):
    """

    Class to define login dialog
    """
```

```python
    def __init__(self):
        """Constructor"""
        wx.Dialog.__init__(self, None, title="Login")

        # user info
        user_sizer = wx.BoxSizer(wx.HORIZONTAL)

        user_lbl = wx.StaticText(self, label="Username:")
        user_sizer.Add(user_lbl, 0, wx.ALL|wx.CENTER, 5)
        self.user = wx.TextCtrl(self)
        user_sizer.Add(self.user, 0, wx.ALL, 5)

        # pass info
        p_sizer = wx.BoxSizer(wx.HORIZONTAL)

        p_lbl = wx.StaticText(self, label="Password:")
        p_sizer.Add(p_lbl, 0, wx.ALL|wx.CENTER, 5)
        self.password = wx.TextCtrl(self, style=wx.TE_PASSWORD|wx.TE_
PROCESS_ENTER)
        p_sizer.Add(self.password, 0, wx.ALL, 5)

        main_sizer = wx.BoxSizer(wx.VERTICAL)
        main_sizer.Add(user_sizer, 0, wx.ALL, 5)
        main_sizer.Add(p_sizer, 0, wx.ALL, 5)

        btn = wx.Button(self, label="Login")
        btn.Bind(wx.EVT_BUTTON, self.onLogin)
        main_sizer.Add(btn, 0, wx.ALL|wx.CENTER, 5)

        self.SetSizer(main_sizer)

    def onLogin(self, event):
        """
        Check credentials and login
        """
        stupid_password = "pa$$w0rd!"
        user_password = self.password.GetValue()
        if user_password == stupid_password:
            print("You are now logged in!")
```

```python
            pub.sendMessage("frameListener", message="show")
            self.Destroy()
        else:
            print("Username or password is incorrect!")
class MyPanel(wx.Panel):
    """"""

    def __init__(self, parent):
        """Constructor"""
        wx.Panel.__init__(self, parent)

class MainFrame(wx.Frame):
    """"""

    def __init__(self):
        """Constructor"""
        wx.Frame.__init__(self, None, title="Main App")
        panel = MyPanel(self)
        pub.subscribe(self.myListener, "frameListener")

        # Ask user to login
        dlg = LoginDialog()
        dlg.ShowModal()

    def myListener(self, message, arg2=None):
        """
        Show the frame
        """
        self.Show()

if __name__ == "__main__":
    app = wx.App(False)
    frame = MainFrame()
    app.MainLoop()
```

The majority of this code is taken up by the subclass of **wx.Dialog** that we are calling **LoginDialog**. You will notice that we have set the password text control widget to use the **wx.TE_PASSWORD** style, which will hide the characters that the user types into that control. The event handler is where the real action is. Here we define a silly password that we use to compare to the one that the user enters. In the real world, you would probably take a hash of the password that is entered and compare it to one that is stored in a database. Or, you might send the credentials to your authentication server and have it tell you if the user's credentials are legitimate or not. For demonstration purposes, we opt for the simple approach and just check the password. You will notice that we completely ignore what the user enters for a username. This is not realistic, but again, this is just an example.

Anyway, if the user enters the correct password, the event handler sends a message via **pubsub** to our **MainFrame** object telling it to finish loading and then the dialog is destroyed.

Using an Instance Variable

There are other ways to tell the main frame to continue, such as using a flag in the dialog class that we can check against. Following is an implementation that demonstrates this latter method by using an instance variable as our flag:

```python
import wx

class LoginDialog(wx.Dialog):
    """
    Class to define login dialog
    """

    def __init__(self):
        """Constructor"""
        wx.Dialog.__init__(self, None, title="Login")
        self.logged_in = False

        # user info
        user_sizer = wx.BoxSizer(wx.HORIZONTAL)

        user_lbl = wx.StaticText(self, label="Username:")
        user_sizer.Add(user_lbl, 0, wx.ALL|wx.CENTER, 5)
        self.user = wx.TextCtrl(self)
        user_sizer.Add(self.user, 0, wx.ALL, 5)
```

```python
        # pass info
        p_sizer = wx.BoxSizer(wx.HORIZONTAL)

        p_lbl = wx.StaticText(self, label="Password:")
        p_sizer.Add(p_lbl, 0, wx.ALL|wx.CENTER, 5)
        self.password = wx.TextCtrl(self, style=wx.TE_PASSWORD|wx.TE_
PROCESS_ENTER)
        self.password.Bind(wx.EVT_TEXT_ENTER, self.onLogin)
        p_sizer.Add(self.password, 0, wx.ALL, 5)

        main_sizer = wx.BoxSizer(wx.VERTICAL)
        main_sizer.Add(user_sizer, 0, wx.ALL, 5)
        main_sizer.Add(p_sizer, 0, wx.ALL, 5)

        btn = wx.Button(self, label="Login")
        btn.Bind(wx.EVT_BUTTON, self.onLogin)
        main_sizer.Add(btn, 0, wx.ALL|wx.CENTER, 5)

        self.SetSizer(main_sizer)

    def onLogin(self, event):
        """
        Check credentials and login
        """
        stupid_password = "pa$$w0rd!"
        user_password = self.password.GetValue()
        if user_password == stupid_password:
            print("You are now logged in!")
            self.logged_in = True
            self.Close()
        else:
            print("Username or password is incorrect!")

class MyPanel(wx.Panel):
    """"""""

    def __init__(self, parent):
        """Constructor"""
        wx.Panel.__init__(self, parent)
```

```python
class MainFrame(wx.Frame):
    """"""

    def __init__(self):
        """Constructor"""
        wx.Frame.__init__(self, None, title="Main App")
        panel = MyPanel(self)

        # Ask user to login
        dlg = LoginDialog()
        dlg.ShowModal()
        authenticated = dlg.logged_in
        dlg.Destroy()
        if not authenticated:
            self.Close()

        self.Show()

if __name__ == "__main__":
    app = wx.App(False)
    frame = MainFrame()
    app.MainLoop()
```

In this example, we added a flag in the dialog subclass that we called **self.logged_in**. If the user enters the correct password, we tell the dialog to close. This causes wxPython to return control back to the **MainFrame** class where we check that variable to see if the user is logged in or not. If they are not, we close the application. Otherwise we load the application.

There are a few enhancements we could add, such as setting the focus to the first text control or adding a Cancel button. I'm sure you can think of a few others yourself. Overall though, this should get you started.

## CHAPTER 20

Bonus Recipes

Recipe 20-1. Catching Exceptions from Anywhere

Problem

If you use wxPython a lot, you will soon realize that some exceptions are difficult to catch. The reason it is so difficult is because wxPython is a wrapper around a C++ package called **wxWidgets**. Thus you have a mixture of C++ and Python in your application. What this means is that events bubble up from C++ to Python and back again. Where an exception occurs (the C++ side or the Python side) determines whether or not we will be able to catch it.

Solution

One solution that works in a lot of cases is using Python's **sys.excepthook**. We'll spend some time in this section digging into some code that shows how you might use this functionality.

```python
import sys
import traceback
import wx
import wx.lib.agw.genericmessagedialog as GMD

class Panel(wx.Panel):
    """"""

    def __init__(self, parent):
        """Constructor"""
        wx.Panel.__init__(self, parent)

        btn = wx.Button(self, label="Raise Exception")
        btn.Bind(wx.EVT_BUTTON, self.onExcept)
```

© Mike Driscoll 2018
M. Driscoll, *wxPython Recipes*, https://doi.org/10.1007/978-1-4842-3237-8_20

```python
    def onExcept(self, event):
        """

        Raise an error
        """

        1/0

class Frame(wx.Frame):
    """"""""

    def __init__(self):
        """Constructor"""
        wx.Frame.__init__(self, None, title="Exceptions")
        sys.excepthook = MyExceptionHook
        panel = Panel(self)
        self.Show()

class ExceptionDialog(GMD.GenericMessageDialog):
    """
    The dialog to show an exception
    """

    def __init__(self, msg):
        """Constructor"""
        GMD.GenericMessageDialog.__init__(self, None, msg, "Exception!",
                                    wx.OK|wx.ICON_ERROR)

def MyExceptionHook(etype, value, trace):
    """

    Handler for all unhandled exceptions.

    :param `etype`: the exception type (`SyntaxError`, `ZeroDivisionError`,
     etc...);
    :type `etype`: `Exception`
    :param string `value`: the exception error message;
    :param string `trace`: the traceback header, if any (otherwise, it
     prints the
    standard Python header: ``Traceback (most recent call last)``.
    """
```

```
        frame = wx.GetApp().GetTopWindow()
        tmp = traceback.format_exception(etype, value, trace)
        exception = "".join(tmp)

        dlg = ExceptionDialog(exception)
        dlg.ShowModal()
        dlg.Destroy()

if __name__ == "__main__":
    app = wx.App(False)
    frame = Frame()
    app.MainLoop()
```

How It Works

In this example, we will create a panel with a button that will deliberately cause an exception to be raised. We catch the exception by redirecting **sys.excepthook** to our **MyExceptionHook** function.

This function will use Python's traceback module to format the exception into some human-readable form and then display a dialog with the exception information.

Creating an Exception-Catching Decorator

Robin Dunn, creator of wxPython, thought it would be good if someone came up with a decorator we could use to catch exceptions, which could then be added as an example to the wxPython wiki page. My first idea for a decorator was the following:

```
import logging
import wx

class ExceptionLogging(object):

    def __init__(self, fn):
        self.fn = fn

        # create logging instance
        self.log = logging.getLogger("wxErrors")
        self.log.setLevel(logging.INFO)
```

```python
        # create a logging file handler / formatter
        log_fh = logging.FileHandler("error.log")
        formatter = logging.Formatter("%(asctime)s - %(name)s - %(message)s")
        log_fh.setFormatter(formatter)
        self.log.addHandler(log_fh)

    def __call__(self, evt):
        try:
            self.fn(self, evt)
        except Exception, e:
            self.log.exception("Exception")

class Panel(wx.Panel):
    """"""

    def __init__(self, parent):
        """Constructor"""
        wx.Panel.__init__(self, parent)

        btn = wx.Button(self, label="Raise Exception")
        btn.Bind(wx.EVT_BUTTON, self.onExcept)

    @ExceptionLogging
    def onExcept(self, event):
        """
        Raise an error
        """

        1/0

class Frame(wx.Frame):
    """"""

    def __init__(self):
        """Constructor"""
        wx.Frame.__init__(self, None, title="Exceptions")
        panel = Panel(self)
        self.Show()
```

```
if __name__ == "__main__":
    app = wx.App(False)
    frame = Frame()
    app.MainLoop()
```

In this code, we create a class that creates a logging instance. Then we override the __ **call**__ method to wrap a method call in an exception handler so we can catch exceptions. Basically what we're doing here is creating a class decorator. Next we decorate an event handler with our exception logging class. This wasn't exactly what Mr. Dunn wanted, as the decorator needed to be able to wrap other functions too. So I edited it a bit and came up with the following minor adjustment:

```
import logging
import wx

class ExceptionLogging(object):
    def __init__(self, fn, *args, **kwargs):
        self.fn = fn

        # create logging instance
        self.log = logging.getLogger("wxErrors")
        self.log.setLevel(logging.INFO)

        # create a logging file handler / formatter
        log_fh = logging.FileHandler("error.log")
        formatter = logging.Formatter("%(asctime)s - %(name)s - %(message)s")
        log_fh.setFormatter(formatter)
        self.log.addHandler(log_fh)

    def __call__(self, *args, **kwargs):
        try:
            self.fn(self, *args, **kwargs)
        except Exception as e:
            self.log.exception("Exception")

class Panel(wx.Panel):
    """"""
```

```python
    def __init__(self, parent):
        """Constructor"""
        wx.Panel.__init__(self, parent)

        btn = wx.Button(self, label="Raise Exception")
        btn.Bind(wx.EVT_BUTTON, self.onExcept)

    @ExceptionLogging
    def onExcept(self, event):
        """
        Raise an error
        """
        1/0

class Frame(wx.Frame):
    """"""

    def __init__(self):
        """Constructor"""
        wx.Frame.__init__(self, None, title="Exceptions")
        panel = Panel(self)
        self.Show()

if __name__ == "__main__":
    app = wx.App(False)
    frame = Frame()
    app.MainLoop()
```

This time the __call__ method can accept any number of arguments or keyword arguments, which gives it a bit more flexibility. This still wasn't what Robin Dunn wanted, so he wrote up the following example:

```python
from __future__ import print_function

import logging
import wx

print(wx.version())
```

```python
def exceptionLogger(func, loggerName=''):
    """
    A simple decorator that will catch and log any exceptions that may occur
    to the root logger.
    """
    assert callable(func)
    mylogger = logging.getLogger(loggerName)

    # wrap a new function around the callable
    def logger_func(*args, **kw):
        try:
            if not kw:
                return func(*args)
            return func(*args, **kw)
        except Exception:
            mylogger.exception('Exception in %s:', func.__name__)

    logger_func.__name__ = func.__name__
    logger_func.__doc__ = func.__doc__
    if hasattr(func, '__dict__'):
        logger_func.__dict__.update(func.__dict__)
    return logger_func


def exceptionLog2Logger(loggerName):
    """
    A decorator that will catch and log any exceptions that may occur
    to the named logger.
    """
    import functools
    return functools.partial(exceptionLogger, loggerName=loggerName)

class Panel(wx.Panel):
    """"""
```

```python
    def __init__(self, parent):
        """Constructor"""
        wx.Panel.__init__(self, parent)

        btn = wx.Button(self, label="Raise Exception")
        btn.Bind(wx.EVT_BUTTON, self.onExcept)

    @exceptionLog2Logger('testLogger')
    def onExcept(self, event):
        """
        Raise an error
        """
        print(self, event)
        print(isinstance(self, wx.Panel))

        # trigger an exception
        1/0

class Frame(wx.Frame):
    """"""

    def __init__(self):
        """Constructor"""
        wx.Frame.__init__(self, None, title="Exceptions")
        panel = Panel(self)
        self.Show()

if __name__ == "__main__":

    # set up the default logger
    log = logging.getLogger('testLogger')
    log.setLevel(logging.INFO)

    # create a logging file handler / formatter
    log_fh = logging.FileHandler("error.log")
    formatter = logging.Formatter("%(asctime)s - %(name)s - %(message)s")
    log_fh.setFormatter(formatter)
    log.addHandler(log_fh)
```

```
app = wx.App(False)
frame = Frame()
app.MainLoop()
```

His code shows a couple of different decorator examples. This example demonstrates the more traditional methodology of decorator construction. It has a bit more metaprogramming in it though. The first example checks to make sure what is passed to it is actually callable. Then it creates a logger and wraps the callable with an exception handler. Before it returns the wrapped function, the wrapped function is modified so that it has the same name and docstring as the original function passed to it. I believe you could drop that and use functools.wraps instead, but being explicit is probably better in a tutorial.

Note   If you run this last code example in Python 3, you can remove the **from __future__ import** as it's no longer needed. It won't hurt anything though if you happen to forget to remove it.

Now you know how you catch exceptions in a couple of different ways. I hope you will find this helpful in your own application design. Have fun!

Recipe 20-2. wxPython's Context Managers

Problem

The wxPython toolkit added context managers to its code base a few years ago, but for some reason you don't see very many examples of their use. In this chapter, we'll look at three examples of context managers in wxPython. We'll start off by rolling our own context manager and then we'll look at a couple of examples of built-in context managers in wxPython.

Solution

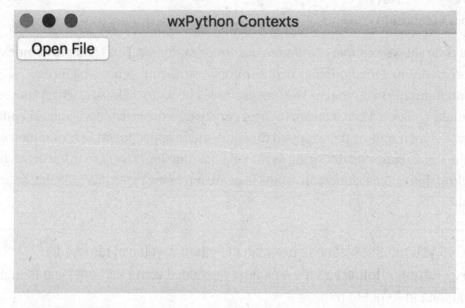

Figure 20-1. *Creating a custom context manager in wxPython*

Creating your own context manager in wxPython is pretty easy. We will use the
wx.FileDialog for our example of a context manager.

```
import os
import wx

class ContextFileDialog(wx.FileDialog):
    """"""

    def __enter__(self):
        """"""
        return self

    def __exit__(self, exc_type, exc_val, exc_tb):
        self.Destroy()
```

How It Works

In this example, we subclass **wx.FileDialog** and all we do is override the **__enter__()** and **__exit__()** methods. This will turn our **FileDialog** instance into a context manager when we call it using Python's **with** statement. Let's add some code to utilize our brand-new version of the File Dialog.

```python
class MyPanel(wx.Panel):
    """"""

    def __init__(self, parent):
        """Constructor"""
        wx.Panel.__init__(self, parent)

        btn = wx.Button(self, label='Open File')
        btn.Bind(wx.EVT_BUTTON, self.onOpenFile)

    def onOpenFile(self, event):
        """"""
        style = 0
        try:
            # wxPython 3+ syntax
            style = wx.FD_OPEN | wx.FD_MULTIPLE | wx.FD_CHANGE_DIR
        except AttributeError:
            # wxPython <= 2.8
            style = wx.OPEN | wx.MULTIPLE | wx.CHANGE_DIR

        wildcard = "Python source (*.py)|*.py|" \
            "All files (*.*)|*.*"
        kwargs = {'message':"Choose a file",
                  'defaultDir':os.path.dirname(os.path.abspath( __file__ )),
                  'defaultFile':"",
                  'wildcard':wildcard,
                  'style':style
                  }
        with ContextFileDialog(self, **kwargs) as dlg:
            if dlg.ShowModal() == wx.ID_OK:
                paths = dlg.GetPaths()
```

```
                print("You chose the following file(s):")
                for path in paths:
                    print(path)
class MyFrame(wx.Frame):
    """"""

    def __init__(self):
        """Constructor"""
        wx.Frame.__init__(self, None, title='wxPython Contexts')
        panel = MyPanel(self)
        self.Show()

if __name__ == '__main__':
    app = wx.App(False)
    frame = MyFrame()
    app.MainLoop()
```

Take a look at the code in **MyPanel**. Here you can see us using Python's **with** statement in the **onOpenFile** event handler within the **MyPanel** class. Now let's move on and look at some of wxPython's **builtin** examples!

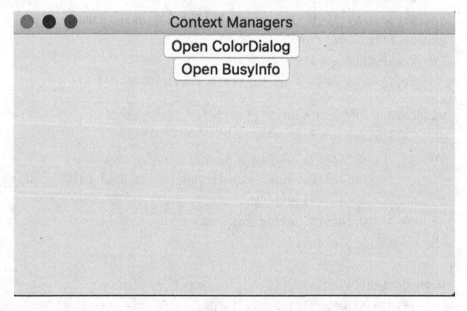

Figure 20-2. *Using wxPython's built-in context managers*

The wxPython package supports context managers in anything that subclasses wx.Dialog as well as the following widgets:

- wx.BusyInfo

- wx.BusyCursor

- wx.WindowDisabler

- wx.LogNull

- wx.DCTextColourChanger

- wx.DCPenChanger

- wx.DCBrushChanger

- wx.DCClipper

- wx.Freeze / wx.Thaw

There are probably more widgets, but this list shows the majority of the widgets with this ability. Let's look at a couple of examples.

```python
import time
import wx

class MyPanel(wx.Panel):
    """"""

    def __init__(self, parent):
        """Constructor"""
        wx.Panel.__init__(self, parent)
        self.frame = parent

        main_sizer = wx.BoxSizer(wx.VERTICAL)

        dlg_btn = wx.Button(self, label='Open ColorDialog')
        dlg_btn.Bind(wx.EVT_BUTTON, self.onOpenColorDialog)
        main_sizer.Add(dlg_btn, 0, wx.ALL|wx.CENTER)

        busy_btn = wx.Button(self, label='Open BusyInfo')
        busy_btn.Bind(wx.EVT_BUTTON, self.onOpenBusyInfo)
        main_sizer.Add(busy_btn,0, wx.ALL|wx.CENTER)
```

```python
        self.SetSizer(main_sizer)

    def onOpenColorDialog(self, event):
        """
        Creates and opens the wx.ColourDialog
        """
        with wx.ColourDialog(self) as dlg:
            if dlg.ShowModal() == wx.ID_OK:
                data = dlg.GetColourData()
                color = str(data.GetColour().Get())
                print('You selected: %s\n' % color)

    def onOpenBusyInfo(self, event):
        """
        Creates and opens an instance of BusyInfo
        """
        msg = 'This app is busy right now!'
        self.frame.Hide()
        with wx.BusyInfo(msg) as busy:
            time.sleep(5)
        self.frame.Show()

class MyFrame(wx.Frame):
    """"""

    def __init__(self):
        """Constructor"""
        wx.Frame.__init__(self, None, title='Context Managers')
        panel = MyPanel(self)

        self.Show()

if __name__ == '__main__':
    app = wx.App(False)
    frame = MyFrame()
    app.MainLoop()
```

In the foregoing code, we have two examples of wxPython's context managers. The first one is in the **onOpenColorDialog** event handler. Here we create an instance of **wx. ColourDialog** and then grab the selected color if the user presses the OK button. The second example is only a bit more complex in that it hides the frame before showing the **BusyInfo** instance. Frankly, I think this example could be improved a bit by putting the frame's hiding and showing into the context manager itself, but I'll leave that as an exercise for the reader to try out.

wxPython's context managers are quite handy and they're fun to use. I hope you'll find yourself using them in your own code sometime soon. Be sure to try out some of the other context managers in wxPython to see if they might suit your code base or just to make your code a little cleaner.

Recipe 20-3. Converting wx.DateTime to Python datetime

Problem

The wxPython GUI (graphical user interface) toolkit includes its own date/time capabilities. Most of the time, you can just use Python's **datetime** and **time** modules and you'll be fine. But occasionally you'll find yourself needing to convert from wxPython's **wx.DateTime** objects to Python's **datetime** objects. You may encounter this when you use the **wx.DatePickerCtrl** widget.

Solution

Fortunately, wxPython's calendar module has some helper functions that can help you convert **datetime** objects back and forth between wxPython and Python. Let's take a look.

```
def _pydate2wxdate(date):
    import datetime
    assert isinstance(date, (datetime.datetime, datetime.date))
    tt = date.timetuple()
    dmy = (tt[2], tt[1]-1, tt[0])
    return wx.DateTimeFromDMY(*dmy)
```

```
def _wxdate2pydate(date):
    import datetime
    assert isinstance(date, wx.DateTime)
    if date.IsValid():
        ymd = map(int, date.FormatISODate().split('-'))
        return datetime.date(*ymd)
    else:
        return None
```

How It Works

You can use these handy functions in your own code to help with your conversions.
I would probably put these into a controller or utilities script. I would also rewrite it
slightly so I wouldn't import Python's **datetime** module inside the functions. Following
is an example:

```
import datetime
import wx

def pydate2wxdate(date):
    assert isinstance(date, (datetime.datetime, datetime.date))
    tt = date.timetuple()
    dmy = (tt[2], tt[1]-1, tt[0])
    return wx.DateTimeFromDMY(*dmy)

def wxdate2pydate(date):
    assert isinstance(date, wx.DateTime)
    if date.IsValid():
        ymd = map(int, date.FormatISODate().split('-'))
        return datetime.date(*ymd)
    else:
        return None
```

This makes converting from Python **datetime** format to wxWidgets **datetime** format
extremely easy.

As I mentioned at the beginning, most of the time you won't even need to worry
about converting the date or time when using the wxPython toolkit. But if you happen

to be using one of wxPython's date- or time-related widgets, then knowing how this can be handled is quite helpful. As an aside, I should also note that databases sometimes have their own datetime format, so that can throw an additional wrench into the mix that you'll have to be cognizant of.

Recipe 20-4. Creating a URL Shortener

Problem

Back in 2009, I used to be a regular reader of Ars Technica. They would occasionally post articles about Python and I happened to see one about using **PyGTK** to shorten URLs. PyGTK was a bit of a pain to install on Windows at that time and since Windows was my primary programming environment back then, I decided to use wxPython instead. So in this chapter, we'll look at a really simple application that you can use to shorten a URL and then we'll create one that's a bit more complex.

Solution

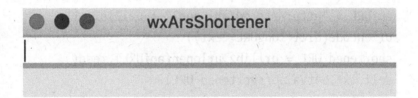

Figure 20-3. *A URL shortener based on an example from Ars Technica*

This simple shortener is loosely based on the one that the Ars writers wrote about. The code is pretty short and sweet. Let's take a look at the Python 2 version of the code.

```python
# Python 2 version

import re
import urllib
import urllib2
import wx
```

```python
class ArsShortener(wx.Frame):

    def __init__(self):
        wx.Frame.__init__(self, None, wx.ID_ANY,
                          'wxArsShortener', size=(300,70))

        # Add a panel so it looks the correct on all platforms
        panel = wx.Panel(self, wx.ID_ANY)

        self.txt = wx.TextCtrl(panel, wx.ID_ANY, "", size=(300, -1))
        self.txt.Bind(wx.EVT_TEXT, self.onTextChange)

        sizer = wx.BoxSizer(wx.VERTICAL)
        sizer.Add(self.txt, 0, wx.EXPAND, 5)
        panel.SetSizer(sizer)

    def onTextChange(self, event):
        """"""
        text = self.txt.GetValue()
        textLength = len(text)
        if re.match("^https?://[^ ]+", text) and textLength > 20:
            apiURL = "http://is.gd/api.php?" + urllib.
            urlencode(dict(longURL=text))
            shortened_URL = urllib2.urlopen(apiURL).read()
            self.txt.SetValue(shortened_URL)

if __name__ == '__main__':
    app = wx.App(False)
    frame = ArsShortener()
    frame.Show()
    app.MainLoop()
```

This is a pretty short piece of code. All you need is a frame, a panel, and a TextCtrl. The **BoxSizer** isn't required, but it's nice to have as it makes the TextCtrl stretch the entire width of the frame. The main focus should be given to our event handler, **onTextChange**. Here we grab the text that is pasted into our TextCtrl and then use a Regular Expression to determine if it's a valid URL. We also check that the text length is greater than 20. If both of these checks pass, then we shorten the URL using the https:// is.gd/ web site.

Note   This example only works on Windows out of the box. Otherwise you might receive an SSL error. If that happens to you, then you may need to upgrade and/or configure your **openSSL** package. You may also need to check your Python bindings to **openSSL** too.

In Python 3, the **urllib** libraries were consolidated into one, so the previous code needs to change accordingly. Here's the update.

```python
# Python_3

import re
import urllib.parse
import urllib.request
import wx

class ArsShortener(wx.Frame):

    def __init__(self):
        wx.Frame.__init__(self, None, wx.ID_ANY,
                          'wxArsShortener', size=(300,70))

        # Add a panel so it looks the correct on all platforms
        panel = wx.Panel(self, wx.ID_ANY)

        self.txt = wx.TextCtrl(panel, wx.ID_ANY, "", size=(300, -1))
        self.txt.Bind(wx.EVT_TEXT, self.onTextChange)

        sizer = wx.BoxSizer(wx.VERTICAL)
        sizer.Add(self.txt, 0, wx.EXPAND, 5)
        panel.SetSizer(sizer)

    def onTextChange(self, event):
        """"""

        text = self.txt.GetValue()
        textLength = len(text)
        if re.match("^https?://[^ ]+", text) and textLength > 20:
            apiURL = "http://is.gd/api.php?" + urllib.parse.\
                urlencode(dict(longURL=text))
```

```
            shortened_URL = urllib.request.urlopen(apiURL).read()
            self.txt.SetValue(shortened_URL)

if __name__ == '__main__':
    app = wx.App(False)
    frame = ArsShortener()
    frame.Show()
    app.MainLoop()
```

This is almost the same as the previous version. Just take note of how we need to import **urllib** now and that we had to change all its usages in the code to match.

Shortening URLs with Other Shorteners

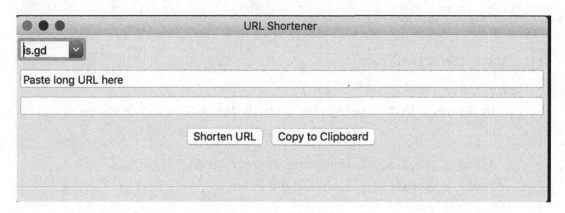

Figure 20-4. A custom URL shortener application

There are many other URL shortening services out there. For example, you might like Bit. ly or tinyURL better. There are also Python wrappers for pretty much all of these popular services. For our next example, we will use the **tinyurl** package and the **bitly** package. You can install both of these with pip.

```
pip install tinyurl bitly
```

Note that for **Bit.ly**, you will need to get an API (application programming interface) key for it to work. There is one other package I want to mention called **pyshorteners**. It actually supports a lot of these protocols in one package. So it's definitely worth a look as well.

Now let's go ahead and look at some code! Note that this code is using Python 2's urllib so if you happen to have Python 3 installed, you will want to update this example as we did in the previous section of this recipe.

```python
# Python 2

import re
import urllib
import urllib2
import wx

bitlyFlag = True
tinyURLFlag = True

try:
    import bitly
except ImportError:
    bitlyFlag = False

try:
    import tinyurl
except ImportError:
    tinyURLFlag = False

class MainPanel(wx.Panel):
    """
    """

    def __init__(self, parent):
        """Constructor"""
        wx.Panel.__init__(self, parent=parent, id=wx.ID_ANY)
        self.frame = parent

        # create the widgets
        self.createLayout()

    def createLayout(self):
        """
        Create widgets and lay them out
        """
```

```
        choices = ["is.gd"]
        if bitlyFlag:
            choices.append("bit.ly")
        if tinyURLFlag:
            choices.append("tinyURL")
        choices.sort()

        # create the widgets
        self.URLCbo = wx.ComboBox(self, wx.ID_ANY, "is.gd",
                                  choices=choices,
                                  size=wx.DefaultSize,
                                  style=wx.CB_DROPDOWN)
        self.inputURLTxt = wx.TextCtrl(self, value="Paste long URL here")
        self.inputURLTxt.Bind(wx.EVT_SET_FOCUS, self.onFocus)
        self.outputURLTxt = wx.TextCtrl(self, style=wx.TE_READONLY)

        shortenBtn = wx.Button(self, label="Shorten URL")
        shortenBtn.Bind(wx.EVT_BUTTON, self.onShorten)
        copyBtn = wx.Button(self, label="Copy to Clipboard")
        copyBtn.Bind(wx.EVT_BUTTON, self.onCopy)

        # create the sizers
        mainSizer = wx.BoxSizer(wx.VERTICAL)
        btnSizer = wx.BoxSizer(wx.HORIZONTAL)

        # layout the widgets
        mainSizer.Add(self.URLCbo, 0, wx.ALL, 5)
        mainSizer.Add(self.inputURLTxt, 0,
                      wx.ALL|wx.EXPAND, 5)
        mainSizer.Add(self.outputURLTxt, 0,
                      wx.ALL|wx.EXPAND, 5)
        btnSizer.Add(shortenBtn, 0, wx.ALL|wx.CENTER, 5)
        btnSizer.Add(copyBtn, 0, wx.ALL|wx.CENTER, 5)
        mainSizer.Add(btnSizer, 0, wx.ALL|wx.CENTER, 5)
        self.SetSizer(mainSizer)

    def onCopy(self, event):
        """
```

```
    Copies data to the clipboard or displays an error
    dialog if the clipboard is inaccessible.
    """

    text = self.outputURLTxt.GetValue()
    self.do = wx.TextDataObject()
    self.do.SetText(text)
    if wx.TheClipboard.Open():
        wx.TheClipboard.SetData(self.do)
        wx.TheClipboard.Close()
        status = "Copied %s to clipboard" % text
        self.frame.statusbar.SetStatusText(status)
    else:
        wx.MessageBox("Unable to open the clipboard", "Error")

def onFocus(self, event):
    """
    When control is given the focus, it is cleared
    """

    self.inputURLTxt.SetValue("")

def onShorten(self, event):
    """
    Shortens a URL using the service specified.
    Then sets the text control to the new URL.
    """

    text = self.inputURLTxt.GetValue()
    textLength = len(text)

    if re.match("^https?://[^ ]+", text) and textLength > 20:
        pass
    else:
        wx.MessageBox("URL is already tiny!", "Error")
        return

    URL = self.URLCbo.GetValue()
    if URL == "is.gd":
        self.shortenWithIsGd(text)
```

339

```python
            elif URL == "bit.ly":
                self.shortenWithBitly(text)
            elif URL == "tinyurl":
                self.shortenWithTinyURL(text)

    def shortenWithBitly(self, text):
        """
        Shortens the URL in the text control using bit.ly

        Requires a bit.ly account and API key
        """
        bitly.API_LOGIN = "username"
        bitly.API_KEY = "api_key"
        URL = bitly.shorten(text)
        self.outputURLTxt.SetValue(URL)

    def shortenWithIsGd(self, text):
        """
        Shortens the URL with is.gd using URLlib and URLlib2
        """

        apiURL = "http://is.gd/api.php?" + urllib.
        urlencode(dict(longURL=text))
        shortURL = urllib2.urlopen(apiURL).read()
        self.outputURLTxt.SetValue(shortURL)

    def shortenWithTinyURL(self, text):
        """
        Shortens the URL with tinyURL
        """
        print("in tinyurl")
        URL = tinyurl.create_one(text)
        self.outputURLTxt.SetValue(URL)

class URLFrame(wx.Frame):
    """

    wx.Frame class
    """
```

```
    def __init__(self):
        """Constructor"""
        title = "URL Shortener"
        wx.Frame.__init__(self, None, wx.ID_ANY,
                          title=title, size=(650, 220))
        panel = MainPanel(self)
        self.statusbar = self.CreateStatusBar()
        self.SetMinSize((650, 220))

if __name__ == "__main__":
    app = wx.App(False)
    frame = URLFrame()
    frame.Show()
    app.MainLoop()
```

This piece of code is quite a bit longer than my simple example, but it has a lot more logic built into it. Right off the bat, I have some exception handling implemented in case the programmer doesn't have one of the shortener modules installed. If they do not, then a flag is set that prevents those options from being added. You'll see this in action in the **MainPanel** class's **createLayout** method. That is where we add the options to the choices list which our **combobox** will use. Depending on what you have installed, you will see one to three options in the drop-down list.

The next interesting bit is where the input URL text control is bound to a focus event. We use this to clear the text control when we paste a URL into it. Also take note that the output text control is set to read-only mode. This prevents the user from messing up the new URL. Finally, we reach our last two widgets: the Shorten URL and the Copy to Clipboard buttons.

Let's take a quick look at what happens in the **onCopy** method since its next.

```
def onCopy(self, event):
    """

    Copies data to the clipboard or displays an error
    dialog if the clipboard is inaccessible.
    """

    text = self.outputURLTxt.GetValue()
    self.do = wx.TextDataObject()
    self.do.SetText(text)
```

```
if wx.TheClipboard.Open():
    wx.TheClipboard.SetData(self.do)
    wx.TheClipboard.Close()
    status = "Copied %s to clipboard" % text
    self.frame.statusbar.SetStatusText(status)
else:
    wx.MessageBox("Unable to open the clipboard", "Error")
```

As you can see, this grabs the current text from the input text control and creates a **TextDataObject** out of it. Then we attempt to open the clipboard and if we're successful, we put the **TextDataObject** into it using the clipboard's **SetData** method. Finally, we alert the user to what we have done by changing the frame's **statusbar** text.

In the **onShorten** method, I reuse the regular expression from the Ars program to check if the user has pasted a valid URL and we also check the length to see if the URL really needs shortening. We get the shortener URL type from the combobox and then use a conditional that passes the URL we want shortened to the appropriate shortening method. The **shortenWithIsGd** method is basically the same as the first example, so we'll skip that one. The **shortenWithBitly** method shows that we need to set the **LOGIN** and **API_KEY** properties before we can shorten the URL. Once we've done that, we just call bitly's **shorten**() method. In the **shortenWithTinyURL** method, it's even simpler: all you need to do here is call the tinyURL's **create_one**() method.

Now you know the basics for shortening your long URLs using several methods. Feel free to add your own features or try other shortening APIs to improve the application for your own use. Have fun coding!

Index

Get the eBook for only $5!

Why limit yourself?

With most of our titles available in both PDF and ePUB format, you can access your content wherever and however you wish—on your PC, phone, tablet, or reader.

Since you've purchased this print book, we are happy to offer you the eBook for just $5.

To learn more, go to http://www.apress.com/companion or contact support@apress.com.

Apress®

Printed in the United States
By Bookmasters